Feiyue Basic Chinese

汉语初级教程

Student's Book 1

主编 林柏松

编者 李蓓 于岚

华语教学出版社

SINOLINGUA

First Edition 2014

ISBN 978-7-5138-0560-5
Copyright 2014 by Sinolingua Co., Ltd
Published by Sinolingua Co., Ltd
24 Baiwanzhuang Road, Beijing 100037, China
Tel: (86)10-68320585, 68997826
Fax: (86)10-68997826, 68326333
http://www.sinolingua.com.cn
E-mail: hyjx@sinolingua.com.cn
Facebook: www.facebook.com/sinolingua
Printed by Beijing Jinghua Hucais Printing Co., Ltd

Printed in the People's Republic of China

Preface

Feiyue Basic Chinese is a set of basic level Chinese textbooks intended for English-speaking undergraduate students, high school students and adults to learn Chinese. The Chinese name Feiyue means to fly forward, which serves as a metaphor for the progression that will occur in students' Chinese proficiency levels after actively working through these meticulously designed textbooks. Upon completion, the student will have learned about 1000 frequently used Chinese words and 800 characters; as well as a proficiency level expected to reach Intermediate Mid as rated by the American Council on the Teaching of Foreign Languages (ACTFL), and Level 1 of the Interagency Language Roundtable (ILR). *Feiyue Basic Chinese* and *Feiyue Intermediate Chinese*, which has already been published, will form a two-year textbook series that meets the basic needs of teaching and learning Chinese as a foreign language outside China.

There are 22 lessons in this set of textbooks for one academic year, with the content divided evenly into two books. Each book requires about 80 class hours to complete, or one semester in the U.S. school system. Each textbook has 11 lessons and each lesson requires approximately seven 50-minute class periods. The student book is accompanied by a CD of listening materials in MP3 format and a teacher's book, which provides the keys to all the exercises and the transcripts of all listening exercises. A glossary and a character list for 22 lessons in alphabetical order are also included. In addition to the printed copy, an Internet edition is also being planned which can be used online or downloaded to computers, cell phones or iPads.

Feiyue Basic Chinese textbook is a trinity of traditional textbook, workbook, and homework book. The same format is used for each lesson in the two books:

1. Lead-in: This section aims to activate students' related memories and bring out the subject matter and the key words of the lesson with four or five pictures associated with the lesson. Practice has shown that a few minutes' lead-in is an important stage for students before they learn a new lesson.

2. The text: Starting from Lesson 4, each lesson consists of a dialog and a narrative passage, the former helping students learn spoken Chinese and the latter, written Chinese. The lesson texts mirror all aspects of American students' real life with vivid and interesting scenarios and embody the principle of "a textbook reflecting real life". Both simplified and traditional characters are used to present the texts. This agrees with the reality that both forms of writing are used in overseas Chinese communities. Tips along the margin highlight the corresponding

text's communicative functions.

3. Vocabulary: Each lesson text is followed by a vocabulary list, in which new words are arranged according to the order of their appearance in the text, with both simplified characters and traditional characters listed side by side. In addition to pinyin transcription and precise English language explanation, the parts of speech and examples of usage for each new word are also provided. This prevents students from relying on English definitions of the new words as their only guide to word usage. A glossary of all lessons is provided at the end of each book for the convenience of word searching.

4. Exercises: A considerable amount of exercises in listening, speaking, reading, writing and translation follow each lesson text. Content questions and exercises on the use of words deepen students' understanding of the contents of the texts and usages of the key words. Such understanding lays a good foundation for the comprehensive use of language skills needed in the last part of the lesson, "Using the Language". Reflecting the principle to attach more importance in listening and speaking in foreign language teaching, this set of textbooks provides a significant amount of listening exercises, ensuring language input in large quantity and with high quality.

5. Phonetics: A special section of "Phonetics" is added to Lessons 1-7 in the attempt to help build a solid foundation on Chinese phonetics. Chinese initials, finals, tones, neutral tones, tone sandhi, retroflex ending "-r", and pinyin spelling rules are systematically introduced in this section with a great amount of practices and exercises, including the pronunciation and transcription of single syllables, multi-syllables, phrases, and sentences. One thing worth mentioning is this book's new teaching approach on the Chinese third tone, which is based on current research findings and successful teaching experience. The third tone is treated as a low falling tone when it is first introduced to students, thus effectively avoiding problems that foreign students often have in pronouncing the so called "half-third tone".

6. Chinese characters: Learning Chinese characters is a difficult yet important task for foreign learners of Chinese. Following the principle of "recognizing long form, writing in short form, and typing with pinyin," which is accepted by many overseas Chinese teachers, this set of textbooks introduces characters with the innovative character-component teaching approach. Each new character is introduced with an analysis of its components, which helps students learn the formation of Chinese characters. Students are required to hand-write all the one-component characters, which are considered the basic characters, so that they will gain a better understanding of the stroke order and character components to avoid producing "stroke-missing" characters. Since radicals are the most important components, we have selected 44

high frequency radicals from the texts of Book 2 to explain their origin and meaning. In order to stimulate students' enthusiasm for learning characters, we have designed many fun exercises such as character formation games. Chinese composition used to be the bottleneck in teaching Chinese as a foreign language due to difficulties in writing and recognizing Chinese characters. Taking full advantage of computer technology, this set of textbooks provides a large amount of exercises for typing characters on the computer, in addition to writing characters by hand, to enhance students' skill in recognizing, reading and typing characters.

7. Language Points: This set of textbooks explains grammar in a simple, precise and practical way without trying to present a complete grammar system using complicated grammar terminology. The language points are selected with an eye on the special difficulties that English-speaking students often have in learning Chinese, and exercises are designed accordingly. Easy language points are introduced before more difficult ones and important language points are recycled with progression in spirals.

8. Using the Language: This is the teaching focus of the entire lesson. The aim is to develop students' abilities to use Chinese in the real world. Authentic materials related to each lesson's topic are used, such as store names, street signs, advertisements, handwritten notices and letters etc. The words and sentence structures in these materials are not confined to those taught in the texts. Therefore, this section not only helps students review what they have learned but also expands upon the lesson contents. The exercises in this section take a variety of forms that feature an integration of listening, speaking, reading and writing. The formats that American students often encounter in major tests such as the AP Exam and OPI Test are adopted in the designing of the exercises, such as multiple choice questions, situational role plays and writing essays based on pictures. The "Cultural Tips" of this section familiarizes students with the cultural knowledge and is thus of considerable reference value.

This set of textbooks is an attempt at applying new approaches to Chinese teaching and is by no means complete. We welcome feedback from fellow teachers and experts in the field so that we may further improve the textbooks. Thank you in advance for your help and support.

Patrick Lin
October 2013

目录

词类简称
Abbreviations for Parts of Speech

adj.	adjective 形容词
adv.	adverb 副词
a.v.	auxiliary verb 助动词
conj.	conjunction 连词
intj.	interjection 叹词
m.	measure word 量词
n.	noun 名词
nc.	numeral-classifier 数量词
num.	numeral 数词
ono.	onomatopoeia 拟声词
part.	particle 助词
pn.	proper noun 专有名词
pron.	pronoun 代词
pref.	prefix 前缀
prep.	preposition 介词
suff.	suffix 后缀
v.	verb 动词

第一课
Lesson One
问候
Greetings

一、导入 Lead-in

Exercise 1

Look at the pictures below and say any relevant greetings that you know in Chinese.

After learning this lesson, you will be able to:

1. Understand common Chinese greetings and greet Chinese people appropriately.

2. Understand Chinese syllables, the four basic Chinese tones, 3rd tone changes, and spelling rules.

3. Recognize traditional and simplified characters, recognize the basic characters presented in this lesson.

4. Use an adjective as a predicate, and use the particles 吗 , 呢 and the suffix 们 correctly.

二、课文 Texts

课文（一）Text (1)

你好

简体版

Xiao Wang meets Xiao Zhang on campus for the first time.

小王：你好！

小张：你好！

Tips: the most common Chinese greeting

你好

繁体版

Xiao Wang meets Xiao Zhang on campus for the first time.

小王：你好！

小張：你好！

Kèwén (yī)　*Text (1)*

Nǐ Hǎo!

拼音版

Xiao Wang meets Xiao Zhang on campus for the first time.

Xiǎo Wáng:　Nǐ hǎo!

Xiǎo Zhāng: Nǐ hǎo!

飞跃——汉语初级教程学生用书　上册

2

生词（一） New Words (1)

	简体（繁體）	拼音	词性	解释
1	你	nǐ	*pron.*	you 你好！/ 你早！
2	好	hǎo	*adj.*	good 你好！/ 你好吗？

课文（二） Text (2)

你早

简体版

Miss Jiang meets Mr. Wang in the morning.

江小姐：王先生，你早！

王先生：早，江小姐。

Tips: a common greeting in the morning

江小姐：再见！

王先生：再见！

你早

繁体版

Miss Jiang meets Mr. Wang in the morning.

江小姐：王先生，你早！

王先生：早，江小姐。

江小姐：再見！

王先生：再見！

Nǐ Zǎo

拼音版

Miss Jiang meets Mr. Wang in the morning.

Jiāng xiǎojiě: Wáng xiānsheng, nǐ zǎo!

Wáng xiānsheng: Zǎo, Jiāng xiǎojiě.

Jiāng xiǎojiě: Zàijiàn!

Wáng xiānsheng: Zàijiàn!

生词（二）*New Words (2)*

	简体（繁體）	拼音	词性	解释
1	先生	xiānsheng	*n.*	Mr., gentleman 王先生 / 先生，你好！
2	早	zǎo	*adj.*	early; morning 你早！/ 老师早！
3	小姐	xiǎojiě	*n.*	Miss; young lady 江小姐 / 小姐，你早！
4	再见（見）	zàijiàn	*v.*	goodbye 老师，再见！/ 王先生，再见！
专有名词 Proper Nouns				
1	江	Jiāng	*pn.*	a Chinese surname, Jiang
2	王	Wáng	*pn.*	a Chinese surname, Wang

Exercise 1 👂 🗣✳

Listen to Texts (1) and (2). Repeat after the recording until you can pronounce the words correctly.

Exercise 2 👂 ✎

Listen to the two short dialogs and fill in the missing words with pinyin and tone marks.

Dialog 1

A: Zhāng _____, nǐ hǎo!

B: Wáng _____, nǐ hǎo!

Dialog 2

A: _____ xiǎojiě, zàijiàn!

B: _____ wáng, zàijiàn!

Exercise 3

Match the Chinese words in Column I with the appropriate English equivalents in Column II.

Column I	Column II
（　）1. 早上好	a. Thank you
（　）2. 先生	b. Good morning
（　）3. 小姐	c. Miss
（　）4. 谢谢	d. goodbye
（　）5. 再见	e. Mr.

课文（三）Text (3)

你好吗？

简体版

In the classroom, Xiao Wang meets Xiao Zhang again.

小王：小张，你好吗？

小张：我很好。你呢？

Tips: greetings between friends

小王：我也很好，谢谢！

(Instructor Jiang comes in.)

同学们：老师，您好！

江老师：同学们，你们好！

Tips: a polite way to greet a senior

你好嗎？

繁体版

In the classroom, Xiao Wang meets Xiao Zhang again.

小王：小張，你好嗎？

小張：我很好。你呢？

小王：我也很好，謝謝！

(Instructor Jiang comes in.)

5

同學們：老師，您好！
江老師：同學們，你們好！

Kèwén (sān)　*Text (3)*

Nǐ Hǎo ma?

In the classroom, Xiao Wang meets Xiao Zhang again.

Xiǎo Wáng: Xiǎo Zhāng, nǐ hǎo ma?

Xiǎo Zhāng: Wǒ hěn hǎo. Nǐ ne?

Xiǎo Wáng: Wǒ yě hěn hǎo. Xièxie!

(Instructor Jiang comes in.)

Tóngxuémen: Lǎoshī, nín hǎo!

Jiāng lǎoshī: Tóngxuémen, nǐmen hǎo!

生词（三）　*New Words (3)*

	简体（繁體）	拼音	词性	解释
1	吗（嗎）	ma	*part.*	(question marker) 你好吗？/老师好吗？
2	我	wǒ	*pron.*	I, me 我是老师。/我很好！
3	很	hěn	*adv.*	very 他很好。/我也很好。
4	呢	ne	*part.*	(question marker) 我很好，你呢？/我是学生，你呢？
5	也	yě	*adv.*	also 我也很好。/我也是学生。
6	谢谢（謝）	xièxie	*v.*	thank, thanks 谢谢你。/谢谢小王！
7	们（們）	men	*suff.*	(plural marker for people) 先生们/小姐们/你们好！
8	老师（師）	lǎoshī	*n.*	teacher 谢谢老师。/他是王老师。
9	您	nín	*pron.*	you (polite form) 您好！/您早！/王老师，您好吗？

| 10 | 同学（學） | tóngxué | *n.* | schoolmate 同学们好！/ 王同学，你好！ |
| 11 | 你们（們） | nǐmen | *pron.* | you 你们好！/ 你们早！/ 谢谢你们！ |

Exercise 4 👂 🗣

Listen to Text (3) and answer the following questions.

1. How is Xiao Zhang?

2. How is Xiao Wang?

3. How does the instructor address students?

Exercise 5 👂 ✍

Listen to Text (3) and fill in the missing words with pinyin and tone marks.

小王：小张，＿＿＿＿＿＿＿ 吗？

小张：我很好。＿＿＿＿＿＿＿ ？

小王：我也很好，＿＿＿＿＿＿＿ ！

同学们：＿＿＿＿＿＿＿，您好！

江老师：＿＿＿＿＿＿＿，你们好！

Exercise 6 🗣

Translate the following sentences into Chinese orally.

1. Hello!

2. How are you?

3. I am fine, thank you.

4. We are also fine.

5. How are you, teacher!

6. Goodbye, students!

三、语音 Phonetics

1. Chinese syllables

A syllable in Mandarin Chinese usually consists of three parts: initial, final, and tone. An initial, as its name indicates, is a consonant that begins the syllable; while a final is the rest of the syllable in spelling. A tone is a sound pitch of the syllable used to distinguish meaning. For example, in the syllable "jiàn" (见), "j" is the initial and "ian" is the final. The tone of the syllable is indicated by the tone mark " ` ", which is put above the main vowel "a". In Mandarin Chinese, there are 21 initials, 36 finals, and 4 basic tones.

2. Four tones

In Mandarin Chinese, tones are distinguished by their pitch range and shape. The following tone diagram describes the characteristics of the four basic tones, in which "5" represents the highest pitch in a person's speech, and "1" the lowest.

	1st tone	2nd tone	3rd tone	4th tone
5 4 3 2 1				
	55	35	214	51

3. Third tone sandhi

The third tone is a unique tone that is worth mentioning. The third tone is pronounced low falling in most cases. That is why the third tone is shown as low falling (21) in the above tone diagram. When it is in an end position and for emphasis purpose, the 3rd tone may start low, dip to the bottom, and then rise toward the top (shown as 214 in the tone diagram).

A 3rd tone will change to a 2nd tone when the 3rd tone precedes another 3rd tone, but the tone mark "ˇ" remains unchanged. For example:

> Nǐ + hǎo → Ní hǎo (but spelling remains "Nǐ hǎo" 你好！)
> Nǐ + zǎo → Ní zǎo (but spelling remains "Nǐ zǎo" 你早！)

4. Neutral tone

In addition to four basic tones, there is a special form of tone called the neutral tone in Mandarin Chinese. The neutral tone is normally pronounced short and light. And it is usually unmarked. For example: wǒmen 我们，Nǐ hǎo ma? 你好吗?

5. Spelling rules (1)

a. When "i", "u", or "ü" serves as a syllable by itself, it will be preceded by "y", "w", and

"y" respectively as follows:

i → yi ;　　　　　　　u → wu ;　　　　　　　ü → yu

b. When "i", "u", or "ü" is at the beginning of a syllable, it will be written as "y", "w", and "y" respectively as follows:

ian → yan　　　　　uang → wang　　　　　ün → yun

c. When j, q, or x combines with ü group, the two dots above ü will be omitted:

j + ü → ju　　　　　q + ü → qu　　　　　x + üe → xue

Exercise 1 📖

Read aloud the following classroom expressions.

Gēn wǒ niàn. 跟我念。	Read after me.
Duì le! 对了！	Correct!
Hěn hǎo! 很好！	Very good!

Exercise 2 📖

Read aloud the following tones.

mā	má	mǎ	mà	ma
nē	né	ně	nè	ne
mēn	mén	měn	mèn	men
xiē	xié	xiě	xiè	xie

Exercise 3 📖

Read aloud the following words and phrases paying attention to the neutral tones.

nǐmen 你们 you (plural)	wǒmen 我们 we / us	tóngxuémen 同学们 students/ classmates
hǎo ma 好吗？ Is it OK ?	Nǐ ne 你呢？ And you?	xièxie 谢谢 Thanks!

Exercise 4 📖

Read aloud the following syllables.

nǐ 你 – nín 您 you – you (respectful)	xué 学 – xiè 谢 study – thanks	xiǎo 小 – xué 学 small – school
xiè 谢 – yě 也 thanks – also	hǎo 好 – zǎo 早 good – early	Jiāng 江 – Zhāng 张 Jiang – Zhang

hěn 很 – men 们 very – plural ending	Yīng 英 – tóng 同 English – same	Yīng 英 – wáng 王 English – king
wǒmen 我们 – nǐmen 你们 we / us – you	zàijiàn 再见 – zàixiàn 在线 goodbye – online	tóngxué 同学 – hóngsè 红色 classmate – red color

Exercise 5 📖

Read aloud the following expressions paying attention to the 3rd tone sandhi.

hěn hǎo 很好 Very good.	Nǐ zǎo. 你早。 Good morning!	Nǐ hǎo. 你好。 Hi!	qǐzǎo 起早 get up early
xǐzǎo 洗澡 to bathe	Wǒ hěn hǎo. 我很好。 I am very well.	wǒ yě hěn hǎo. 我也很好。 I am also very well.	Xiǎo Hǎo mǎile yì zhī xiǎoniǎo. 小郝买了一只小鸟。 Xiao Hao bought a small bird.

Exercise 6 👂 ✍

Write down what you hear with correct pinyin and tone marks.

1	2	3
4	5	6
7	8	9
10	11	12

四、汉字 Chinese Characters

1. New characters in this lesson

序号	拼音	简/繁	部件	构词
1	hǎo	好	女＋子	你好 / 你们好 / 你好吗
2	hěn	很	彳＋艮	很好 / 很早 / 我也很好
3	jiàn	见 / 見	见	再见 / 老师，再见
4	Jiāng	江	氵＋工	江小姐 / 江小华 / 小江
5	jiě	姐	女＋且	小姐 / 王小姐 / 姐姐
6	lǎo	老	耂＋匕	老师 / 张老师 / 老张

7	ma	吗 / 嗎	口 + 马	你好吗 / 老师好吗
8	men	们 / 們	亻 + 门	你们 / 我们 / 同学们
9	ne	呢	口 + 尼	你呢 / 你们呢 / 我呢
10	nǐ	你	亻 + 尔	你好 / 你们 / 你好吗
11	nín	您	亻 + 尔 + 心	您好 / 您早 / 您好吗
12	shēng	生	生	先生 / 王先生 / 学生
13	shī	师 / 師	刂 + 帀	老师 / 张老师 / 老师早
14	tóng	同	冂 + 一 + 口	同学 / 同学们 / 王同学
15	wáng	王	王	王先生 / 老王 / 王老师
16	wǒ	我	我	我们 / 我很好 / 我也很好
17	xiān	先	生 + 儿	先生 / 王先生 / 张先生
18	xiǎo	小	小	小王 / 小姐 / 小张
19	xiè	谢 / 謝	讠 + 身 + 寸	谢谢 / 谢谢你 / 谢谢您
20	xué	学 / 學	𭕄 + 冖 + 子	同学 / 学生 / 小学生
21	yě	也	也	也好 / 也很好 / 我也很好
22	zài	再	再	再见 / 再谢谢你
23	zǎo	早	日 + 十	你早 / 您早 / 老师早
24	Zhāng	张 / 張	弓 + 长	小张 / 张先生 / 张老师

Exercise 1 📖

Read aloud the new characters in this lesson with correct pronunciation.

2. A brief introduction of Chinese characters

Chinese characters were derived from pictographs created several thousand years ago, and have undergone many stages of evolution of forms since then. The following shows the evolution of the characters "人" (man), and "目" (eye).

The majority of characters in use today are not pictographs, but rather pictophonetic characters, which are formed by the meaning component and the sound component. The meaning part usually indicates the category the character belongs to, while the sound part gives a hint of the character's sound. Take 们 (men, plural suffix for people) as an example, the meaning part, 亻, indicates that the character's meaning is related to people; while the sound part, 门 (mén, door), indicates the character's sound, which has nothing to do with its meaning, "door".

3. The number of Chinese characters

Chinese characters have a history of 4000 years. There are over 56,000 Chinese characters recorded in Chinese dictionaries, but most of them are seldom used today. According to the "List of Frequently Used Characters in Modern Chinese" which was published in China in 1987, there are approximately 3500 frequently used characters today.

4. The traditional and simplified characters

Because Chinese characters are so numerous and hard to learn, the Chinese government inaugurated a writing system reform in the 1950s, and simplified Chinese characters by choosing or creating characters that have fewer strokes. For example, 學 (xué, study) was simplified to 学, and 麗 (lì, beautiful) to 丽. In 1964, the Chinese government released an official list of 2238 simplified characters to be used in China's mainland. However, traditional characters are still used in Taiwan, Hong Kong, Macao, and overseas Chinese communities.

Exercise 2

Decide whether the following statements are true (T) or false (F) based on the above texts.

1. There are 3500 frequently used Chinese characters in daily life.	( )
2. Every Chinese character has traditional and simplified forms.	( )
3. Traditional characters are still used in Chinese communities in the U. S.	( )
4. Most Chinese characters in use today are pictophonetic characters.	( )
5. The meaning component in a pictophonetic character indicates the character's exact meaning.	( )

五、语言点 Language Points

1. Grammatical characteristics of the Chinese language

The Chinese language doesn't possess changes in words to denote certain grammatical features, such as tense, case, etc. Instead, different grammatical relations are indicated by the use of function words and the word order in a sentence. The important function words include particles, such as 吗, 呢, 的, 了, etc. The typical word order in Chinese is as follows:

> **Subject (Noun, Pronoun, etc.) + Predicate (Verb, Adjective, Noun, etc.)**

> 同学们 + 再见!
> 老师 + 早!
> 我 + 很好。
> 小王 + 十八岁。

2. The Chinese greetings 你好 and 你早

The Chinese greeting 你好 is usually used when two people meet for the first time or just for the day. It is the same as "Hi!" and is not a question. The proper response is 你好. While 你好 can be used anytime of the day, 你早 is used in the morning meaning "Good morning!" The proper response is 你早 or 早.

3. Raise a question with the particle 吗

The modal particle 吗 is used to add to the end of a sentence to turn it into a question. For example, adding 吗 to the greeting 你好 will form a question "你好吗?" meaning "How are you?" The proper response to this greeting would be 我很好, which means "I am fine".

4. An adjective used as a predicate

An adjective in Chinese can function as a stative verb to serve as a predicate without a linking verb "to be". For example, 你早! means "Good morning!" (Literally "You early!") Adjectives can be modified by placing an adverb immediately before them. For example:

(1) 我很好。(I am pretty good.)

(2) 江小姐也很好。(Miss Jiang is also pretty good.)

5. Raise a question with the particle 呢

呢 is also a modal particle which can function as a question marker. 你呢? means "How about you?" or "And you?" It usually follows a preceding statement. Here is an example:

A：你好吗 ? (How are you?)

B：我很好。你呢? (I am pretty good. How about you?)

6. The suffix 们

In Chinese, 们 is a suffix used after a personal pronoun or a noun to indicate the plural for people, such as 同学们 (students), 老师们 (teachers), 你们 (you), and 我们 (we).

Exercise 1

Match the following greetings in Column I with the appropriate responses in Column II.

Column I	Column II
( ) 1. 小王，你早！	a. 我很好，谢谢！你呢?
( ) 2. 小江，你好吗?	b. 江小姐，再见！
( ) 3. 老师，您好！	c. 同学们，你们好！
( ) 4. 王先生，再见！	d. 你早，小张。

Exercise 2 📖

Read the following greetings and choose the proper response for each of them.

1. A: 你好！

B: _____

    a. 我好   b. 你好！   c. 你也好！

2. A: 江小姐，你早！

B: _____

    a. 我早！   b. 你早，王先生！   c. 你也早！

3. A: 小谢，你好吗?

B: _____

    a. 你好！   b. 我好！   c. 我很好。你呢?

4. A: 老师，您好！

    B: _____

       a. 你好！   b. 谢谢！   c. 我好，你好吗？

5. A: 我很好，谢谢！你呢？

    B: _____

       a. 我也很好。   b. 谢谢你！   c. 我好。

6. A: 老师，再见！

    B: _____

       a. 你们好！   b. 谢谢你们！   c. 同学们，再见！

六、语言运用 Using the Language

Activity 1

Listen to the greetings and orally respond to each of them.

Activity 2

What do you say in Chinese in the following situations?

1. In the morning, you see a Chinese person on the street who notices you.

2. In the afternoon, you see a Chinese student who is walking next to you on campus.

3. In the classroom, you see your classmate Xiao Wang, whom you have not seen for a couple of days.

4. In the early morning, you meet your Chinese instructor Mr. Wang.

5. Chinese class has just ended. You want to say something to your instructor before you leave the classroom.

Activity 3

Read the following dialogs and translate them into English.

1. A: 你好！王先生！

    B: 你好！江小姐！

2. A: 小王，你早！

    B: 老张，你早！

3. A: 张老师早！

    B: 你早！

4. A: 张先生，再见！

    B: 江小姐，再见！

5. A: 同学们早！

B: 老师早！

6. A: 王老师，您好！

B: 小张，你好！

7. A: 同学们，你们好！

B: 老师好！

8. A: 江老师，你好吗？

B: 我很好，谢谢！你呢？

A: 我也很好。

B: 再见！

A: 再见！

Activity 4

Write an appropriate expression in pinyin or Chinese characters for the following four pictures.

Cultural Tip

Chinese characters evolved from ancient carvings on pottery, cliffs, bones and tortoise shells. Many were images of what they represented. Gradually, the characters became more abstract, yet the original pictures can still be seen in some characters today, such as 山 mountain, 水 water, 火 fire, 木 wood. One notable fact about the Chinese writing system is that the characters are not based on pronunciation. Still, a large portion of the characters are called "pictophonetic" characters, in which the sound components roughly indicate the pronunciation of these characters.

姓名

Names

一、导入 Lead-in

Exercise 1

Look at the pictures below and learn the key words in Chinese.

After learning this lesson, you will be able to:

1. Ask someone's full name in a polite way and introduce yourself by name.

2. Pronounce Chinese initials and finals correctly, and use the spelling rules properly.

3. Understand Chinese character components and basic strokes of Chinese characters.

4. Form affirmative-negative questions, using a 是 sentence and the negative adverb 不.

飞跃——汉语初级教程学生用书 上册

二、课文 Texts

课文（一）Text (1)

您贵姓？

简体版

Jiang Xiaohua meets Instructor Zhang in the classroom.

江小华：老师好！

张老师：你好！

Tips: a polite way to ask a senior's surname

江小华：老师，您贵姓？

张老师：我姓张。你叫什么名字？

Tips: how to ask a junior's name

江小华：我叫江小华。

您貴姓？

繁体版

Jiang Xiaohua meets Instructor Zhang in the classroom.

江小華：老師好！

張老師：你好！

江小華：老師，您貴姓？

張老師：我姓張。你叫什麼名字？

江小華：我叫江小華。

Kèwén (yī) Text (1)

Nín Guìxìng?

拼音版

Jiang Xiaohua meets Instructor Zhang in the classroom.

Jiāng Xiǎohuá: Lǎoshī hǎo!

Zhāng lǎoshī: Nǐ hǎo!

Jiāng Xiǎohuá: Lǎoshī, nín guìxìng?

Zhāng lǎoshī: Wǒ xìng Zhāng. Nǐ jiào shénme míngzi?

Jiāng Xiǎohuá: Wǒ jiào Jiāng Xiǎohuá.

生词（一） New Words (1)

	简体（繁體）	拼音	词性	解释
1	贵（貴）姓	guìxìng	*n.*	What is your (honorable) name? 您贵姓？ / 先生，您贵姓？
2	姓	xìng	*v.*	have …as surname 你姓什么？ / 我姓张。
3	叫	jiào	*v.*	be named 你叫什么名字？ / 我叫小文。
4	什么（甚麼）	shénme	*pron.*	what 你姓什么？ / 你叫什么？
5	名字	míngzì	*n.*	name 我的名字 / 你叫什么名字？
专有名词 Proper Noun				
	江小华（華）	Jiāng Xiǎohuá	*pn.*	Jiang Xiaohua, a Chinese name

Exercise 1 👂 ✍

Listen to Text (1) and fill in the table below with correct pinyin and tone marks.

	Surname	Given name
Teacher		
Student		

Exercise 2 📖 ✍

Read Text (1) and fill in the missing words with pinyin and tone marks.

A：老师 _____ ！

B：_____ ！

A：老师，_____ ？

B：我姓 _____。你叫什么 _____ ？

A：我叫 _____。

课文〔二〕 *Text (2)*

您工作忙吗？

简体版

Chen Yu chats with her neighbor Mrs. Wang in the morning.

陈　雨：王太太，早上好！

王太太：你好，小陈。

陈　雨：王太太，您工作忙吗？

王太太：很忙。你呢？

陈　雨：我不太忙。

> **Tips:** adding the prefix 小 (young) to show intimacy

> **Tips:** a common way to start a chat

您工作忙嗎？

繁体版

Chen Yu chats with her neighbor Mrs. Wang in the morning.

陳　雨：王太太，早上好！

王太太：你好，小陳。

陳　雨：王太太，您工作忙嗎？

王太太：很忙。你呢？

陳　雨：我不太忙。

Kèwén (èr)　*Text (2)*

Nín Gōngzuò Máng ma?

拼音版

Chen Yu chats with her neighbor Mrs. Wang in the morning.

Chén Yǔ: Wáng tàitai, zǎoshang hǎo!

Wáng tàitai: Nǐ hǎo, Xiǎo Chén.

Chén Yǔ: Wáng tàitai, nín gōngzuò máng ma?

Wáng tàitai: Hěn máng. Nǐ ne?

Chén Yǔ: Wǒ bú tài máng.

生词（二）New Words (2)

	简体（繁體）	拼音	词性	解释
1	太太	tàitai	*n.*	Mrs. 江太太 / 王太太
2	早上	zǎoshang	*n.*	morning 早上好 / 我早上工作。
3	工作	gōngzuò	*n.*	job, work 什么工作？ / 你工作忙吗？
4	忙	máng	*adj.*	busy 你忙吗？ / 你学习忙吗？
5	不	bù	*adv.*	not 我不忙。 / 我不是老师。
6	太	tài	*adv.*	very, extremely 老师太忙。 / 我工作不太忙。
专有名词 Proper Noun				
	陈（陳）雨	Chén Yǔ	*pn.*	Chen Yu, a Chinese name

Exercise 3 👂 ✍

Listen to Text 2 and fill in the missing words with correct pinyin and tone marks.

A: Wáng tàitai, _____ hǎo!

B: Nǐ hǎo, _____.

A: Wáng tàitai, nín _____ ma?

B: Hěn máng. _____?

A: Wǒ _____ máng.

Exercise 4 🗣

Translate the following sentences into Chinese orally.

1. What is your surname? My surname is Zhang.

2. Are you busy? I am very busy.

3. His surname is Jiang. He is not busy with his work.

课文（三）Text (3)

我们都是学生

简体版

On campus, Li Wen meets two new students John Lee and Mary.

李文：你们好！

约翰、玛丽：你好！

李文：我姓李，叫李文。　　　**Tips:** a self-introduction

约翰：我也姓李，叫约翰。她叫玛丽。

玛丽：你好，李文！你是不是学生？

李文：是，我是学生。你呢？

玛丽：我也是学生。

约翰：我们都是学生。

我们都是學生

繁体版

　　On campus, Li Wen meets two new students John Lee and Mary.

李文：你們好！

約翰、瑪麗：你好！

李文：我姓李，叫李文。

約翰：我也姓李，叫約翰。她叫瑪麗。

瑪麗：你好，李文！你是不是學生？

李文：是，我是學生。你呢？

瑪麗：我也是學生。

約翰：我們都是學生。

Kèwén (sān)　*Text (3)*

Wǒmen Dōu Shì Xuésheng

拼音版

　　On campus, Li Wen meets two new students John Lee and Mary.

Lǐ Wén: Nǐmen hǎo!

Yuēhàn, Mǎlì: Nǐ hǎo!

Lǐ Wén: Wǒ xìng Lǐ, jiào Lǐ Wén.

Yuēhàn: Wǒ yě xìng Lǐ, jiào Yuēhàn. Tā jiào Mǎlì.

Mǎlì: Nǐ hǎo, Lǐ Wén! Nǐ shì bu shì xuésheng?

Lǐ Wén: Shì, wǒ shì xuésheng. Nǐ ne?

Mǎlì: Wǒ yě shì xuésheng.

Yuēhàn: Wǒmen dōu shì xuésheng.

生词（三） *New Words (3)*

	简体（繁體）	拼音	词性	解释
1	她	tā	*pron.*	she, her 她是王太太。/ 她叫玛丽。
2	是	shì	*v.*	is, are, am 你是王小文吗？
3	学（學）生	xuésheng	*n.*	student 我是学生。
4	都	dōu	*adv.*	all 我们都是学生。
专有名词 Proper Nouns				
1	李文	Lǐ Wén	*pn.*	Li Wen, a Chinese name
2	玛丽（瑪麗）	Mǎlì	*pn.*	Mary
3	约（約）翰	Yuēhàn	*pn.*	John

Exercise 5 🎧🗣

Listen to Text (3) and answer the questions.

1. How did they greet each other?

2. How did Li Wen introduce himself?

3. What did Mary find about Li Wen?

4. What do these people have in common?

Exercise 6 ✎

Fill in the blanks with the given words.

a. 我们 b. 是 c. 姓 d. 学生 e. 叫 f. 也

1. 李文：我姓李，_____ 李文。

2. 约翰：我也 _____ 李，叫约翰。

3. 玛丽：我叫玛丽。李文，你 _____ 学生吗？

4. 李文：是，我是 _____。你呢？

5. 玛丽：我 _____ 是学生。

6. 约翰：_____ 都是学生。

Exercise 7

Make sentences by matching the Chinese words in Column I with the appropriate words in Column II.

Column I	Column II
(　　) 1. 她姓	a. 学生
(　　) 2. 他是不是	b. 很忙
(　　) 3. 你叫	c. 什么名字
(　　) 4. 我工作	d. 陈

三、语音 Phonetics

1. List of initials

There are six groups of 21 initials in Mandarin Chinese:

	Un-aspirated	Aspirated	Nasal	Fricative	Voiced	Lateral
Labial	b	p	m	f		
Blade-alveolar	d	t	n			l
Velar	g	k		h		
Palatal	j	q		x		
Dental	z	c		s		
Blade-palatal	zh	ch		sh	r	

Pronunciation tips

p, m, f, t, n, l, k, h are similar to their counterparts in English.

b, d, g are pronounced unaspirated and voiceless: *b* like "p" in "spoil" ; *d* like "t" in "store" ; and *g* like "k" in "sky".

To produce the sound *j*, first raise the front of the tongue to the hard palate and press the tip of the tongue against the back of the lower teeth, and then loosen the tongue

第二课　姓名

and let the air squeeze out through the channel thus made.

q It is produced in the same manner as "j", but it is aspirated.

x To produce this sound, first raise the front of the tongue toward but not touching the hard palate and then let the air squeeze out.

z like "ds" in "beds".

c like "ts" in "cats".

s like "s" in "see".

zh like "j" in "jerk" with the tip of the tongue curled farther back.

ch like "ch" in "church" with the tip of the tongue curled farther back.

sh like "sh" in "sheep" with the tip of the tongue curled farther back.

r With lips unrounded, the tip of the tongue curled farther back, let the air squeeze it out.

2. Simple finals and compound finals

Altogether there are 36 finals in Mandarin Chinese, including six simple finals and 30 compound finals.

A simple final has only a vowel standing by itself while a compound final consists of one main vowel and another vowel or consonant(s). The six simple finals are: *a, o, e, i, u, ü*. The vowels *i, u, ü* can also serve as a medial between an initial and the main vowel.

A typical compound final consists of a medial, vowel, and ending. For example, the compound final "ian" has a medial "i", a main vowel "a", and an ending "n". The final "uang" has a medial "u", a main vowel "a", and an ending "ng".

3. List of Finals

	i	u	ü
a	ia	ua	
o		uo	
e	ie		üe
ai		uai	
ei		uei (-ui)	
ao	iao		
ou	iou (-iu)		
an	ian	uan	üan
en	in	uen (-un)	üen(-ün)

ang	iang	uang	
eng	ing	ueng	
ong	iong		
er			

Pronunciation tips

a   It is pronounced like "a" in "jar" when it stands alone. However, "a" is pronounced differently in some compound finals. "ian" is pronounced like "Yen" in "Japanese Yen", and "*üan*" similar to "ian" except the lips are rounded.

o   It is pronounced like "a" in "wall" when it stands alone. "ou" is pronounced like the letter "o" in English.

e   It is pronounced like "e" in "her" when it stands alone. However, "e" is pronounced differently in some compound finals. "ie" is pronounced like "ye" in "yes".

i   It is pronounced like "ee" in English when it stands alone. However, "i" is pronounced differently when it follows initials z, c, s, zh, ch, sh, and r.

u   It is pronounced like "oo" in English when it stands alone. When "u" serves as a medial in some compound finals, it is pronounced like "w" in "wind".

ü   English doesn't have similar sound, but French does. To pronounce this sound, just pretend to pronounce "i", but quickly round your lips.

4. Spelling rules (2)

When preceded by initials, the final *uei* is shortened as *ui*. For example:

$$g + uei \rightarrow gui (贵)$$

Exercise 1

Read aloud the following classroom expressions.

Dǎkāi shū. 打开书。	Open your books.
Fāndào dì-wǔ yè. 翻到第 5 页。	Turn to page 5.
Dǒng le mā? 懂了吗?	Do you understand?
Dǒng le. 懂了。	Yes, I understand.
Méi dǒng. 没懂。	No, I do not understand.
Qǐng lǎoshī zài shuō yí biàn. 请老师再说一遍。	Teacher, please say it again.

Exercise 2 📖

Read aloud the following initials.

b – p – m – f	d – t – n – l	g – k – h	z – c – s
zh – ch – sh – r	zh – z – ch – c	m – n – l	j – z – zh
q – c – ch	x – s – sh	b – p	d – t
g – k	j – q	sh – s	s – x

Exercise 3 📖

Read aloud the following finals.

a – o – e	i – u – ü	a – ia – ua	ai – uai
an – uan	ang – uang	ian – üan	o – uo
ou – iu	ong – iong	e – er	en – un
eng – ueng	ie – üe	i – ai – ei	in – ing
ang – ong – eng – ing	u – ou – ua	ui – un	ü – u – i
üe – üan – ün			

Exercise 4 📖

Read aloud the following syllables paying attention to the tones.

zhāng – zháng – zhǎng – zhàng	jiāng – jiáng – jiǎng – jiàng
guī – guí – guǐ – guì	kuī – kuí – kuǐ – kuì
xuē – xué – xuě – xuè	shī – shí – shǐ – shì
shēng – shéng – shěng – shèng	xīng – xíng – xǐng – xìng

Exercise 5 📖

Read aloud the following expressions paying attention to tone sandhi and neutral tones.

1. hěn hǎo—wǒ hěn hǎo—wǒ yě hěn hǎo
（很好—我很好—我也很好）

2. shénme—xìng shénme—nǐ xìng shénme
（什么—姓什么—你姓什么）

3. máng ma—gōngzuò máng ma—nín gōngzuò máng ma
（忙吗—工作忙吗—您工作忙吗）

4. máng—bù máng—wǒ bù máng—wǒ bú tài máng

（忙—不忙—我不忙—我不太忙）

Exercise 6 👂 ✍️

Write down what you hear with correct pinyin and tone marks.

1.　　　2.　　　3.　　　4.　　　5.

6.　　　7.　　　8.　　　9.　　　10.

Exercise 7 📖

Read the following pairs of words paying attention to their differences.

dàmā—dàmǎ	大妈—大马	(aunt – big horse)
wèn nǐ—wěn nǐ	问你—吻你	(ask you – kiss you)
qǐng zuò—qǐng zǒu	请坐—请走	(please take a seat – please go away)
kètǐ—kètí	客体—课题	(objective entities – research subject)
xuéxí—xuèxǐ	学习—血洗	(to study – bring bloodshed to)
luòtǐ—luǒtǐ	落体—裸体	(falling object – naked body)
qìguān—qìguǎn	器官—气管	(body organ – trachea)
kèběn—kèwén	课本—课文	(text book – text)
guìxìng—kuíxīng	贵姓—魁星	(respected surname – Chinese god of scholars)
lǎoshī—lǎoshi	老师—老实	(teacher – honest)
xiǎoshí— xiāoshī	小时—消失	(hour – to disappear)
yōuxiān— yǒuxiàn	优先—有限	(priority – limited)

四、汉字 Chinese Characters

1. New characters in this lesson

序号	拼音	简 / 繁	部件	构词
1	bù	不	不	不忙 / 不是 / 不好
2	Chén	陈 / 陳	阝+东	陈雨 / 小陈 / 陈小姐
3	dōu	都	者+阝	都好 / 都很好 / 都是学生
4	gōng	工	工	工作 / 不工作 / 工作忙吗
5	guì	贵 / 貴	中+一+贝	贵姓 / 您贵姓 / 太贵

6	hàn	翰	十＋曰＋十＋人＋习＋习	约翰 / 李约翰 / 我叫约翰
7	huá	华 / 華	化＋十	小华 / 江小华 / 江小华小姐
8	jiào	叫	口＋丩	叫什么名字 / 我叫李文
9	Lǐ	李	木＋子	李文 / 小李 / 李老师
10	lì	丽 / 麗	一＋冂＋冂	玛丽 / 玛丽小姐 / 她叫玛丽
11	mǎ	玛 / 瑪	王＋马	玛丽 / 你是玛丽吗
12	máng	忙	忄＋亡	你忙吗 / 不忙 / 工作很忙
13	me	么 / 麼	丿＋厶	姓什么 / 叫什么 / 什么名字
14	míng	名	夕＋口	姓名 / 名字 / 你叫什么名字
15	shàng	上	上	早上 / 早上好 / 上学
16	shén	什 / 甚	亻＋十	什么 / 什么名字 / 什么工作
17	shì	是	日＋疋	不是 / 是不是 / 是不是学生
18	tā	她	女＋也	她们 / 她是江小姐
19	tài	太	大＋丶	王太太 / 太忙 / 不太忙
20	wén	文	文	李文 / 李文同学 / 李文先生
21	xìng	姓	女＋生	贵姓 / 姓名 / 我姓王
22	yǔ	雨	雨	陈雨 / 小雨 / 我姓陈，叫陈雨
23	yuē	约 / 約	纟＋勺	纽约 / 约翰 / 约见
24	zì	字	宀＋子	名字 / 汉字 / 文字 / 写字
25	zuò	作	亻＋乍	工作 / 不工作 / 工作不忙

Exercise 1 📖

Read aloud the new characters in this lesson with correct pronunciation.

2. Character components

Chinese characters are formed by one or more character components. For example, the character 们 is formed by two components, 亻 and 门. The character 谢 is formed by three components: 讠, 身 and 寸. Some characters, like 王 and 生, only have one component. According to the Chinese Character Component Standards published by the Chinese government on December 1st, 1997, there are 514 Chinese character components. Learning how character components are used to form characters will help with the recognition and memorization of Chinese characters. That is why the text contains a character formation analysis for each new character.

3. Basic strokes of Chinese characters

If we take a close look at the character components, we will find that every character component consists of one or more strokes. There are six basic strokes in character formation. The following table shows the names, examples, and directions of writing these five basic strokes:

Stroke	一	｜	ノ	乀	丶	⸝
Name	横 héng horizontal	竖 shù vertical	撇 piě down left	捺 nà down right	点 diǎn dot	提 tí upward slant
Writing direction	→	↓	↙	↘	↘	↗
Example	一	中	力	八	门	我

4. Variations and combinations of basic strokes

As shown in the following table, there are dozens of strokes that are actually variations or combinations of the six basic strokes.

Stroke	Direction	Name	Examples	Stroke	Direction	Name	Example
⁻	→	横钩	你 买	⁊	→	横折	口 五
⅃	→	横折钩	的 也	↳	→	横折提	请 说
乙	→	横折弯钩	九 几	⺈	→	横撇弯钩	那 都
⋟	→	横折折撇	建 延	⼷	→	横折折折钩	乃 仍
亅	↓	竖钩	小 东	↓	↓	竖提	很 跟
㇗	↓	短竖折	山 出	㇄	↓	竖折	区 母
㇟	↓	竖折折钩	马 与	⟩	↓	弯钩	狗 猪
＇	↙	左点	小 点	丶	↘	长点	不 只
⸌	↙	平撇	千 毛	⌣	↙	卧钩	心 您
＜	↙	撇折	女 好	∠	↙	撇平折	么 东
⌇	→	平捺	这 还	⺄	→	横撇	又 友
乀	↘	斜钩	找 我	㇄	↓	竖弯钩	儿 先

Exercise 2 ✍

Put the following Chinese characters in the table according to the number of their components. Some examples are provided for you.

你 们 您 好 吗 呢 忙 谢 也 很 王 小 文 早 姓 作

One component	Two components	Three components
也	你	您

Exercise 3 ✍

Write each of the six basic strokes ten times with the correct directions of writing.

Stroke	一	丨	丿	乀	丶	㇀
Name	横 héng	竖 shù	撇 piě	捺 nà	点 diǎn	提 tí
Writing direction	→	↓	↙	↘	↘	↗
Copy here	一	丨	丿	乀	丶	㇀

Exercise 4 📖

Count the stroke number of the following characters.

Character	我	你	他	她	们	好	忙	吗	谢
Strokes									

五、语言点 Language Points

1. Addressing Chinese people

Chinese people have first and last names like everyone else. However, Chinese last name always comes before the first name. For example, in the Chinese name 江小华, 江 (Jiang) is the last name. In China, first names are only used by close friends or family members. Chinese people often add the prefix "Lao" (old) or "Xiao" (young) before a friend's last name to show familiarity and intimacy, such as, 老张 (Old Zhang) and 小陈 (Young Chen).

In China, it is common to address a person by his or her last name with a title or even an occupation. Note that common titles or occupations should be placed after the person's last name. Here are some examples:

> (1) 张先生 (Mr. Zhang)
>
> (2) 王小姐 (Miss Wang)
>
> (3) 张老师 (Teacher Zhang)
>
> (4) 江同学 (Student Jiang/Classmate Jiang)

2. The 是 sentence

A sentence with the verb 是 as its predicate is called a 是 sentence. The pattern is:

> **A (Nominal) + 是 + B (Nominal)**

> (1) 我是学生。I am a student.
>
> (2) 她也是学生。She is a student, too.
>
> (3) 你是学生吗? Are you a student?
>
> (4) 我们都是学生。We are all students.

3. The negation adverb 不

In Chinese, the negation adverb is placed before the verb or adjective.

> (1) 我是学生。→ 我不是学生。
>
> (I am a student. → I am not a student.)
>
> (2) 您工作忙。→ 您工作不忙。
>
> (You are busy at work. → You are not busy at work.)

(3) 我姓李。→ 我<u>不</u>姓李。

(I am surnamed Li. → I am not surnamed Li.)

4. The affirmative-negative question (1)

To form an affirmative-negative question, just place the affirmative verb or adjective and its negative counterpart together.

(1) 你是学生。→ 你是<u>不</u>是学生?

(You are a student. → Are you a student?)

(2) 您工作忙。→ 您工作<u>忙不忙</u>?

(You are busy at work. → Are you busy at work?)

5. The position of adverbs 也, 太 and 都

As a simple rule, an adverb always precedes the verb, adjective or adverb it modifies. For example:

(1) 我<u>也</u>是学生。

I am also a student.

(2) 我们<u>都</u>是学生。

We are all students.

(3) 我不<u>太</u>忙。

I am not very busy.

(4) 我<u>也</u>很好。

I am also pretty well.

Exercise 1 👂 ✍️

Listen to four Chinese names twice. Write down the last names in Column I and first names in Column II in pinyin with tone marks.

Column I	Column II

Exercise 2 📖

Match the Chinese sentences in Column I with the English translations in Column II.

Column I	Column II
（　）1. 我姓王，叫王红。	a. May I ask, what is your honorable surname?
（　）2. 请问，您贵姓？	b. I am not very busy.
（　）3. 你也是学生吗？	c. Are you also a student?
（　）4. 我工作很忙。你呢？	d. My last name is Wang. My (full) name is Wang Hong.
（　）5. 他们都不是老师。	e. I am fine. He is fine, too.
（　）6. 我很好，他也很好。	f. None of them are teachers.
（　）7. 我不太忙。	g. I am very busy with my work. How about you?

Exercise 3 📖 ✍

Read the following sentences and fill in the blanks with 姓 or 叫.

1. 请问，您贵 _____？

2. 我 _____ 张，我 _____ 张林。

3. 我 _____ 小文。你 _____ 什么名字？

4. 你的老师 _____ 什么？他 _____ 江吗？

5. 你哥哥也 _____ 王文吗？

6. 我们两个都 _____ 李，都 _____ 李红。

Exercise 4 ✍

Change the following sentences into questions with the word 吗 and 是不是. Then give them negative answers.

Example:　他是老师。

　　　　　他是老师吗？　　　他是不是老师？　　　他不是老师。

1. 他们是学生。

_____？　　_____？　　_____。

2. 张老师工作很忙。

_____？　　_____？　　_____。

3. 他叫李文。

_____？　　_____？　　_____。

第二课　姓名

4. 她姓江。

_____ ? _____ ? _____ 。

Exercise 5 📖🖋

Choose the right word to complete each of the following sentences.

1. 你是张老师 _____ ?

　　a. 呢　　　　　　　　b. 吗　　　　　　　　c. 不

2. 你工作忙，我 _____ 忙。

　　a. 也　　　　　　　　b. 是　　　　　　　　c. 也是

3. 请问，您贵姓？我 _____ 。

　　a. 叫小方　　　　　　b. 贵姓李　　　　　　c. 姓林

4. 他是学生，我 _____ 学生。

　　a. 不　　　　　　　　b. 也是　　　　　　　c. 也

5. 他们两个 _____ 老师，都是学生。

　　a. 是不　　　　　　　b. 都不是　　　　　　c. 都不

6. 我姓张，_____ 张小明。

　　a. 叫　　　　　　　　b. 是　　　　　　　　c. 是叫

7. 我们不是学生，你 _____ 学生吗？

　　a. 也不　　　　　　　b. 不也是　　　　　　c. 也不是

8. 你好！你 _____ 什么名字？

　　a. 姓　　　　　　　　b. 叫　　　　　　　　c. 是

Exercise 6 🖋📖

Translate the following dialogs into English. Then read the Chinese dialogs aloud with your partner.

Dialog 1

A: 你好！

B: 你好！你叫什么名字？

A: 我叫王大卫。你呢？

B: 我姓李，叫李红。

A: 我是学生。你也是学生吗？

B: 是，我也是学生。

A: 我们都是学生。

Dialog 2

A: 大卫，早上好！

B: 你好，李红。

A: 大卫，你学习忙吗？
B: 很忙。你呢？
A: 我也很忙。
B: 我们学习都很忙。

六、语言运用 Using the Language

Activity 1

Listen to the following conversations and answer the questions.

Dialog 1

1. Who is the man?

Dialog 2

1. Who is the woman looking for?

2. Who is the man? Is he a teacher?

3. What is the surname of the man?

4. What is the full name of the teacher?

Activity 2

Work in pairs. Read the following name list and say what the five people do.

Name	Age	Title
江小华	19	学生
陈雨	27	老师
李文	21	学生
王太太	45	老师
玛丽	30	老师

Activity 3

What do you say?

1. At a party, you meet a Chinese lady and want to know her surname.

2. When a Chinese person asks you: "What is your honorable surname?"

3. In class, you meet a classmate and want to know his/her name.

4. On campus, you meet a young Chinese person and want to know whether he/she is a student.

5. After greeting each other, you want to start a casual chat with a Chinese person.

6. You are a teacher and you meet a new student and want to know his/her surname.

Cultural Tip

The way Chinese people address each other is interesting. Firstly, there is a difference between a respectful greeting and a casual greeting. To ask what someone's surname is, the respectful way is 请问您贵姓？ and the casual way is 你姓什么？ Chinese kinship terms can also be used to address non-kin by putting them after the surname, such as 王叔叔 Uncle Wang, 李姐 Sister Li, 王婶 Aunt Wang. Some job titles can also be used after the surnames for addressing people, such as 张老师 Teacher Zhang, 王工 Engineer Wang, and 张总 CEO Zhang.

第三课
Lesson Three
家乡
Hometown

一、导入 Lead-in

Exercise 1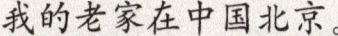

Look at the pictures below and say the names of the cities or countries in Chinese.

我的老家在中国北京。

台北是我的老家。

我是在英国伦敦出生的。

我是美国纽约人。

After learning this lesson, you will be able to:

1. Tell and ask about one's nationality, birthplace and hometown.

2. Know the tone sandhi of 不, the neutral tone, and all the spelling rules.

3. Recognize the new characters in this lesson, and the stroke order of characters.

4. Use the structural particle 的, the 是 … 的 construction; and the question words 哪, 哪儿.

二、课文 Texts

课文〔一〕 Text (1)

你是哪国人？

简体版

John and his teacher are talking about their nationalities.

张老师：约翰，你是哪国人？

Tips: how to ask about nationality

约　翰：我是美国人。

张老师：你的同学玛丽也是美国人吗？

约　翰：不是，她是英国人。张老师，我们的老师都是中国人吗？

张老师：不都是。我是中国人。李老师是美国人。

你是哪國人？

繁体版

John and his teacher are talking about their nationalities.

張老師：約翰，你是哪國人？

約　翰：我是美國人。

張老師：你的同學瑪麗也是美國人嗎？

約　翰：不是，她是英國人。張老師，我們的老師都是中國人嗎？

張老師：不都是。我是中國人。李老師是美國人。

Kèwén (yī)　Text (1)

Nǐ Shì Nǎ Guó Rén?

拼音版

John and his teacher are talking about their nationalities.

Zhāng lǎoshī: Yuēhàn, nǐ shì nǎ guó rén?

Yuēhàn: Wǒ shì Měiguórén.

飞跃——汉语初级教程学生用书　上册

Zhāng lǎoshī: Nǐ de tóngxué Mǎlì yě shì Měiguórén ma?

Yuēhàn: Bú shì, tā shì Yīngguórén. Zhāng lǎoshī, wǒmen de lǎoshī dōu shì Zhōngguórén ma?

Zhāng lǎoshī: Bù dōu shì. Wǒ shì Zhōngguórén. Lǐ lǎoshī shì Měiguórén.

生词（一）New Words (1)

简体（繁體）	拼音	词性	解释
1 哪	nǎ	*pron.*	which 哪个人 / 哪国人 / 哪个是老师？
2 国（國）	guó	*n.*	country 美国很大。/ 你是哪国人？
3 的	de	*part.*	(structural particle) 我的 / 你的 / 他是在中国出生的。
专有名词 Proper Nouns			
1 美国（國）	Měiguó	*pn.*	the United States of America
2 英国（國）	Yīngguó	*pn.*	the United Kingdom
3 中国（國）	Zhōngguó	*pn.*	China

Exercise 1 👂 ✍

Listen to Text (1) and write down the information about the people mentioned.

	Last name or name	Nationality
Teacher 1		
The male student		
Mary		
Teacher 2		

Exercise 2 📖

Read Text (1) and decide whether the following statements are true or false.

1. 张老师是中国人。（　　）	2. 李老师也是中国人。（　　）
3. 约翰是学生，他是美国人。（　　）	4. 玛丽是约翰的同学。（　　）
5. 玛丽和约翰都是美国人。（　　）	6. 玛丽是英国人，不是美国人。（　　）

Exercise 3 📖 ✎

Read the following sentences and fill in the blanks with the correct characters according to the pinyin.

1. 他是老师。他 _____ (xìng) 张， _____ (jiào) 大卫。

2. 玛丽是 _____ (Měiguórén)。

3. 玛丽的同学 _____ (yě shì) 美国人。

4. 小王是 _____ (nǎ guó rén) ？

Exercise 4 🗣✎

Translate the following sentences into Chinese orally.

1. David is a teacher. He is from the U.S.

2. Mary is not American. She is British.

3. Are your classmates all American? No, not all of them are American.

4. We are also Chinese.

课文（二）Text (2)

你的老家在哪儿？

简体版

David, Mary, Xiao Lin, and Xiaohong are talking about their hometowns.

Tips: how to ask about one's hometown

大卫：玛丽，你的老家在哪儿？

玛丽：我的老家在伦敦，我是在英国出生的。你呢？

大卫：我是在美国出生的，我的老家在纽约。

玛丽：小林和小红，你们也是在美国出生的吗？

小林：我不是。我是在台湾生的，我的老家在台北。

小红：我是在北京生的，我是北京人。

你的老家在哪儿？

繁体版

David, Mary, Xiao Lin, and Xiaohong are talking about their hometowns.

大衛：瑪麗，你的老家在哪兒？

瑪麗：我的老家在倫敦，我是在英國出生的。你呢？

大衛：我是在美國出生的，我的老家在紐約。

瑪麗：小林和小紅，你們也是在美國出生的嗎？

小林：我不是。我是在臺灣生的，我的老家在臺北。

小紅：我是在北京生的，我是北京人。

Kèwén (èr) Text (2)

Nǐ de Lǎojiā Zài Nǎr?

拼音版

David, Mary, Xiao Lin, and Xiaohong are talking about their hometowns.

Dàwèi: Mǎlì, Nǐ de lǎojiā zài nǎr?

Mǎlì: Wǒ de lǎojiā zài Lúndūn, wǒ shì zài Yīngguó chūshēng de. Nǐ ne?

Dàwèi: Wǒ shì zài Měiguó chūshēng de, wǒ de lǎojiā zài Niǔyuē.

Mǎlì: Xiǎo Lín hé Xiǎohóng, Nǐmen yě shì zài Měiguó chūshēng de ma?

Xiǎo Lín: Wǒ bú shì. Wǒ shì zài Táiwān shēng de, wǒ de lǎojiā zài Táiběi.

Xiǎohóng: Wǒ shì zài Běijīng shēng de, wǒ shì Běijīngrén.

生词（二） *New Words (2)*

简体（繁體）	拼音	词性	解释
1 老家	lǎojiā	*n.*	native place; hometown 我的老家在北京。/ 你老家在哪儿？
2 在	zài	*v.*	be in 我在北京。/ 你在哪儿？
3 哪儿（兒）	nǎr	*pron.*	where; what place 你是哪儿的人？
4 在	zài	*prep.*	at, in 我是在美国出生的。
5 （出）生	(chū)shēng	*v.*	be born 我是在中国出生的。/ 我是在北京生的。
6 和	hé	*conj.*	and 小林和小红 / 你和我 / 爸爸和妈妈
7 人	rén	*n.*	person, people 我是美国人，你呢？

专有名词 Proper Nouns

简体（繁體）	拼音	词性	解释
1 北京	Běijīng	*pn.*	Beijing, capital of China
2 伦（倫）敦	Lúndūn	*pn.*	London, capital of the United Kingdom
3 纽约（紐約）	Niǔyuē	*pn.*	New York
4 台湾（臺灣）	Táiwān	*pn.*	Taiwan
5 台（臺）北	Táiběi	*pn.*	Taipei, capital city of Taiwan Province
6 大卫（衛）	Dàwèi	*pn.*	David
7 林	Lín	*pn.*	Lin, a surname
8 小红（紅）	Xiǎohóng	*pn.*	Xiaohong, a Chinese name

Exercise 5 👂 ✍

Listen to Text (2) and fill in the missing words in pinyin with tone marks.

大卫：玛丽，你的 _____ 在哪儿？

玛丽：我的老家在伦敦，我是在英国 _____ 的。你呢？

大卫：我是在美国出生的，我的老家在 _____。

玛丽：小林和小红，你们 _____ 是在美国出生的吗？

小林：我不是。我是在 _____ 生的，我的老家在 _____。

小红：我是在北京生的，我是 _____。

飞跃——汉语初级教程学生用书　上册

Exercise 6

Select the correct words to complete the following statements based on the information provided in Text (2).

1. 玛丽的老家在 _____ 。
   a. 纽约   b. 北京   c. 伦敦   d. 台北
2. 大卫是在 _____ 出生的。
   a. 英国   b. 美国   c. 中国   d. 中国台湾
3. 小林和小红 _____ 是在美国出生的。
   a. 也   b. 都   c. 不都   d. 都不
4. 小红是 _____ 人。
   a. 纽约   b. 伦敦   c. 北京   d. 台北

Exercise 7

Answer the following questions orally in Chinese based on your background.

1. What is your name?

2. Where are you from?

3. Where were you born?

4. Are you a student or a teacher?

5. Are you busy?

三、语音 Phonetics

1. Tone sandhi of 不

不 (bù) is pronounced as the 4th tone when by itself and combining with 1st, 2nd, and 3rd tones:

> bù + gāo → bù gāo (不高)   bù + máng → bù máng (不忙)
>
> bù + hǎo → bù hǎo (不好)

When 不 (bù) is followed by another 4th tone, it changes to 2nd tone. Its tone mark will change accordingly. For example:

> bù + shì → bú shì (不是)   bù + tài máng → bú tài máng (不太忙)

2. Neutral tone

In Lesson 1 we learned the neutral tone, which is pronounced short and light. Particles in Mandarin Chinese are usually pronounced in neutral tone, such as *ma* (吗) and *ne* (呢) in Lesson 1, and *de* (的) in this lesson.

3. Spelling rules (3)

When preceded by an initial, the final *uen* is shortened as *un*, and *iou* is shortened as *iu*. For example:

> d + *uen* → d*un* (as in Lúndūn 伦敦)
>
> n + *iou* → n*iu* (as in Niǔyuē 纽约)

Exercise 1 📖

Read aloud the following classroom expressions.

Lǎoshī hǎo! 老师好！	Hello, teacher!
Tóngxuémen hǎo! 同学们好！	Hello, boys and girls!
Wǒmen shàngkè. 我们上课。	Let's begin class.
Qǐng dǎkāi shū. 请打开书。	Please open your books.
Qǐng fāndào dì … yè. 请翻到第……页。	Please turn to page….
Qǐng gēn wǒ dú kèwén. 请跟我读课文。	Please read the text after me.
Xiàkè. 下课。	Class is dismissed.
Xièxie lǎoshī. 谢谢老师。	Thank you, teacher.
Bú kèqi. Zàijiàn! 不客气。再见！	You're welcome. Bye!
Yòng Zhōngwén zěnme shuō "teacher"? 用中文怎么说"teacher"？	How do you say "teacher" in Chinese?

Exercise 2 📖

Read aloud the following syllables paying attention to their tone marks.

zhōng		zhǒng	zhòng
guō	guó	guǒ	guò
	méi	měi	mèi

tōng	tóng	tǒng	tòng
xuē	xué	xuě	xuè
	ná	nǎ	nà
lāo	láo	lǎo	lào
jiā	jiá	jiǎ	jià
bēi		běi	bèi
jīng		jǐng	jìng
tāi	tái		tài
wān	wán	wǎn	wàn

Exercise 3 📖

Read aloud the following words, paying attention to the tone sandhi.

chūshēng 出生 be born	kāixué 开学 begin school	shāngchǎng 商场 department store	gāoxìng 高兴 happy
Lúndūn 伦敦 London	tóngxué 同学 classmate	Táiběi 台北 Taipei	xuéxiào 学校 school
lǎoshī 老师 teacher	Xiǎowén 小文 Xiaowen	lǎoshǔ 老鼠 mouse	Mǎlì 玛丽 Mary
guàngjiē 逛街 go window shopping	dàxué 大学 university	diànyǐng 电影 movie	zàijiàn 再见 goodbye

Exercise 4 📖

Read aloud the following expressions paying attention to tone sandhi and neutral tones.

1. nǎr—zài nǎr 哪儿—在哪儿
2. nǎ—nǎ gúo—nǎ guó rén 哪—哪国—哪国人
3. wǒ de—nǐ de—nǐmen de—tā de—tāmen de 我的—你的—你们的—他的—他们的
4. bù—bú shì—shì bu shì—wǒ bú shì 不—不是—是不是—我不是

Exercise 5 👂 ✎

Write down what you hear with the correct pinyin and tone marks.

1.　　　　2.　　　　3.　　　　4.

5.　　　　6.　　　　7.　　　　8.

Read aloud the following Chinese poem "Quiet Night Thoughts".

Jìng Yè Sī Lǐ Bái Chuáng qián míng yuèguāng, Yí shì dìshang shuāng. Jǔ tóu wàng míng yuè, Dī tóu sī gùxiāng.	《静夜思》 李白 床前明月光， 疑是地上霜。 举头望明月， 低头思故乡。
Quiet Night Thoughts By Li Bai The bright moonlight shines in front of my bed, I suspect it is frost on the ground. Looking up I see a bright moon, Looking down I think of my hometown.	Li Bai (701-762), one of the most famous Chinese poets in the Tang Dynasty.

四、汉字 Chinese Characters

1.New characters in this lesson

序号	拼音	简/繁	部件	构词
1	běi	北	扌+匕	北京 / 台北 / 北京人
2	chū	出	出	出生 / 在美国出生
3	dà	大	大	大卫 / 大学生 / 大国
4	de	的	白+勺	你的 / 我的 / 在中国出生的
5	dūn	敦	享+攵	伦敦 / 英国伦敦 / 伦敦人
6	ér	儿 / 兒	儿	哪儿 / 老家在哪儿 / 哪儿人
7	guó	国 / 國	口+玉	中国 / 美国 / 英国 / 国家
8	hé	和	禾+口	你和我 / 我和老师
9	hóng	红 / 紅	纟+工	小红 / 小红是北京人
10	jiā	家	宀+豕	我家 / 你家 / 老家 / 大家

11	jīng	京	亠 + 口 + 小	北京 / 北京人 / 老家在北京
12	lín	林	木 + 木	小林 / 林老师 / 林先生
13	lún	伦 / 倫	亻 + 仑	伦敦 / 伦敦人 / 老家在伦敦
14	měi	美	羊 + 大	美国 / 美人 / 美丽
15	nǎ	哪	口 + 那	哪儿 / 哪国人 / 老家在哪儿
16	niǔ	纽 / 紐	纟 + 丑	纽约 / 美国纽约 / 纽约人
17	rén	人	人	中国人 / 好人 / 忙人
18	tái	台 / 臺	厶 + 口	台湾 / 台北 / 在台湾生的
19	wān	湾 / 灣	氵 + 弯	台湾 / 台湾人 / 在台湾出生
20	wèi	卫 / 衛	卫	大卫 / 卫生 / 大卫是美国人
21	yīng	英	艹 + 央	英国 / 英国人 / 美国和英国
22	zài	在	𠂇 + 土	在宿舍 / 在家 / 在学校
23	zhōng	中	中	中国 / 中文 / 中学生

Exercise 1 📖

Read aloud the above new characters and their combinations in the right column.

2. The stroke order of characters

When writing a character, Chinese people usually follow certain rules for the order of the strokes. For foreign learners, following the correct order of strokes not only makes the calligraphy look better, but also makes the character easier to memorize. Here are the basic rules of stroke order:

a) From top to bottom
    Example 三: 一 二 三

b) From left to right
    Example 人: 丿 人

c) Horizontal precedes vertical
    Example 十: 一 十

d) From outside to inside

Example 回: 丨 冂 冂 冋 回 回

e) Sealing stroke goes last

Example 四: 丨 冂 冂 四 四

f) Middle precedes the two sides

Example 小: 亅 小 小

3. Applying the stroke order in writing

When writing a character, we need to combine all the rules above systematically. For example, when writing the character 吗, we need to apply the rule "From left to right" and first write the left part 口, before the right component 马. When writing 口, we need to apply the rule "From left to right" and "Sealing stroke goes last." When writing the right component 马, we need to follow the rule "From top to bottom" again. The entire writing procedure can be illustrated as follows:

吗: 丨 冂 口 叮 吗 吗

Exercise 2 ✎

Study the following single-component characters in Lessons 1-3. Copy each of them four times with the correct stroke order as illustrated.

xiǎo	小	亅 小 小			
yě	也	ㄱ 九 也			
wáng	王	一 二 干 王			
jiàn	见	丨 冂 贝 见			
shēng	生	丿 ㇒ 牛 生			

拼音	字	笔顺	练习
zài	再	一 フ 丙 更 再 再	
bù	不	一 ブ 不 不	
gōng	工	一 丁 工	
lì	丽	一 丆 丙 面 丽 丽 丽	
me	么	ノ 乙 么	
tài	太	一 ナ 大 太	
wén	文	、 亠 ナ 文	
yǔ	雨	一 丆 币 币 雨 雨 雨 雨	
shàng	上	丨 卜 上	
chū	出	乚 屮 屮 出 出	
dà	大	一 ナ 大	
ér	儿	ノ 儿	
rén	人	ノ 人	
wèi	卫	乛 ㄋ 卫	
zhōng	中	丨 𠃌 口 中	

4. Single component characters and compound characters

In terms of composition, all Chinese characters fall into two categories:

a) Single component characters

Some characters, like 五, 八, 女, 王, 生, have only a single component; they are thus called "single component characters." According to the statistics collected by the State Langauge and Character Committee of China, there are 256 commonly-used single component characters in modern Chinese. It is helpful to master those single-component characters since they are basic characters in the Chinese writing system. Starting from Lesson 3, we will introduce those single-component characters that appear in each lesson and illustrate the correct stroke order.

b) Compound characters

Most of the modern Chinese characters are made up of two or more components, like 爸 (父 + 巴), 什 (亻 + 十), 好 (女 + 子), 很 (彳 + 艮), 语 (讠 + 五 + 口), 谢 (讠 + 身 + 寸). They are called "compound characters". When learning a compound character, it is helpful to know how components are put together to form this character. Starting from this lesson, we will analyze each compound character as they appear in each lesson.

Exercise 3

Put the following characters into two categories: single component characters and compound characters.

人 你 好 也 爸 妈 王 生 国 学 不 英 上 中 谢 小 工 您 很 女

Single component characters	
Compound characters	

飞跃——汉语初级教程学生用书 上册

五、语言点 Language Points

1. *Raise a question with question words* 哪 *and* 哪儿

The question words 哪 and 哪儿 are different: 哪 means "which" while 哪儿 refers to "where".

> (1) 你是哪国人？ Which country are you from?
> (2) 哪个学生是你的同学？ Which student is your classmate?
> (3) 你的老家在哪儿？ Where is your hometown?
> (4) 你是在哪儿出生的？ Where were you born?

2. 在 *as a verb and a preposition*

在 can be used as a main verb or a preposition. When used as a main verb, 在 means "to be in, on, at" and requires a noun or a place word as its object. For example:

> (1) 你老家在哪儿？ Where is your hometown?
> 我的老家在北京。 My hometown is in Beijing.

As a preposition, 在 means "in, on, at" and indicates a location where an action takes place.

> (2) 我是在英国出生的。I was born in England. (出生 is the main verb here.)
> (3) 她在台北工作。She works in Taipei. (工作 is the main verb here.)

3. *The* 是 … 的 *construction (1)*

The 是 … 的 construction is used to stress various circumstances (when, where, how, who, and why) connected with the action of the verb. The pattern is:

> **Subject + 是 + Emphasized Part + Verb + 的**

> (1) 我是在英国出生的。
> It was in England where I was born.
> (2) 你们也是在美国出生的吗？
> Were you also born in America?

To negate the 是 … 的 construction, add the negation adverb 不 right before 是. The pattern is:

Subject + 不 + 是 + Emphasized Part + Verb + 的

(3) 我不是在英国出生的。我是在中国出生的。
I was not born in England. I was born in China.

4. The structural particle 的

The principal function of the structural particle 的 is to link attributive words (modifiers) with their heading words (the words being modified). The structural particle 的 can also be used to form the 是 … 的 construction and some other constructions.

(1) 你的同学玛丽也是美国人吗?
(2) 我们的老师都是中国人吗?
(3) 我的老家在伦敦。
(4) 我是在美国生的。

5. The conjunction 和

Like "and" in English, the conjunction 和 is used to join nouns and noun phrases. However, unlike "and", 和 cannot be used to join clauses and sentences.

(1) 小林和小红,你们也是在美国出生的吗?
(2) 李老师和张老师都是我们的中文老师。

Exercise 1 🗩 😗

Listen to two short self-introductions and answer the questions orally in Chinese.

Self-introduction 1:
Questions:
1. What is her name?
2. Where was she born?
3. How is her study?

Self-introduction 2:

Questions:

1. What is his last name and first name?

2. Where is he from?

3. Is he a teacher or a student?

Exercise 2 📖 ✍

Read the following sentences first. Then create questions using 哪 and 哪儿.

1. 江先生是美国人，他的老家在纽约。

Questions: _____ ?

_____ ?

2. 王小姐是中国人，她是在北京出生的。

Questions: _____ ?

_____ ?

3. 玛丽的老家在伦敦，她是在英国出生的。

Questions: _____ ?

_____ ?

Exercise 3 ✍

Fill in the blanks with 是 where necessary.

1. 我姓 _____ 李，叫 _____ 李文，我 _____ 学生。

2. 我 _____ 张老师，你们 _____ 好吗？

3. 我们都 _____ 很好，谢谢！

4. "小陈，你学习 _____ 忙不忙？" "不 _____ 忙。"

5. 老师，您 _____ 贵姓？ 您 _____ 哪国人？

6. 我们都 _____ 在美国出生的，你呢？——我也 _____。

7. "您工作 _____ 忙吗？" "我工作 _____ 不太忙。"

8. "你是不 _____ 玛丽？" "我不 _____。"

Exercise 4 📖 ✍

Complete the following questions by choosing the correct answer for each of them.

1. 请问，你是 _____ 人？ 是英国人吗？

a. 谁国   b. 哪国   c. 什么国

2. 你的老家 _____ 美国哪儿？

a. 是   b. 叫   c. 在

3. 你的爸爸妈妈 _____ 中国出生的吗？

a. 是在   b. 是   c. 在哪儿

4. 小林和小红 _____ 在美国出生的吗？

　　a. 都不是 　　　　　　 b. 是不都 　　　　　　 c. 都是不

5. 你们是哪国人？ _____ 法国人吗？

　　a. 是在 　　　　　　　 b. 在 　　　　　　　　 c. 是

6. 你是在纽约出生 _____ 吗？

　　a. 是 　　　　　　　　 b. 的 　　　　　　　　 c. 也

7. 你的同学 _____ 美国人吗？

　　a. 不是都 　　　　　　 b. 不都是 　　　　　　 c. 是不都

Exercise 5

Translate the following sentences into Chinese orally.

1. I was not born in America. I was born in China.

2. Where do Xiao Zhang and Xiao Wang work?

3. Where is your hometown? Is it London?

4. Both Xiao Lin and Xiaohong were not born in America.

5. Is your classmate Mary an American?

6. Not all of our teachers are from China.

Exercise 6

Translate the two dialogs into English. Then read the Chinese dialogs aloud with your partner.

Dialog 1

学生：请问，您贵姓？

老师：我姓林。

学生：您是我们的中文老师吗？

老师：是的，我是你们的中文老师。

学生：您是美国人吗？

老师：是的，我是美国人。不过，我的老家不在美国，
　　　在中国。

_____

_____

_____

_____

_____

Dialog 2

老师：你是中文系的学生吗?

学生：是的，我是中文系的学生。

老师：你的老家在哪儿?

学生：在美国的加州 (California)。我是在旧金山 (San Francisco) 出生的。

老师：你叫什么名字?

学生：我的中文名字叫王学文。

老师：很好的中文名字。

学生：谢谢!

_____

_____

_____

_____

_____

_____

六、语言运用 Using the Language

Activity 1

Listen to the following conversations and answer the questions.

Conversation One

1. Where is the woman from?

2. Where was the man born?

Conversation Two

1. Where is the woman's hometown?

2. Was the man born in New York?

Activity 2 📖 🗣✱

Work in pairs. Each person reads one residence card to find out as much personal information as possible. Tell your partner about the person on your card.

姓　名：林学文
性　别：男
出生地：台北
职　业：学生

姓　名：王丽红
性　别：女
出生地：北京
职　业：教师

Activity 3 📖 🗣✱

Read the following passage and answer the questions.

　　大卫在北京学中文。他的同学玛丽是英国人。玛丽的男朋友是在台北出生的。大卫和玛丽的老师叫张京生，是北京人。张老师的太太不是北京人，也不是中国人，她是美国人，是在纽约出生的。张老师工作很忙。大卫和玛丽也很忙。

1. Where is Mary from?
2. Where was Mary's boyfriend born?
3. Is Mr. Zhang's wife Chinese?
4. Where was Zhang's wife born?
5. What is Mr. Zhang's name?
6. Where is Mr. Zhang from?
7. What do Mr. Zhang, David and Mary all have in common?

飞跃——汉语初级教程学生用书　上册

Activity 4

What do you say?

1. You meet a Chinese person in a theater. You want to ask what his/her last name is politely.

2. You want to ask this person's first name.

3. You want to ask a person about their nationality.

4. You want to ask this person where their hometown is.

5. You want to know this person's birthplace.

Cultural Tip

The Chinese value their family roots very much. Therefore, you may often find people asking you 你是哪儿的人？ (Where are you from?) 你老家在哪儿？ (Where is your old home?) Sharing the same hometown implies a natural bond that might even extend to social obligations such as assistance in difficult times.

第四课 Lesson Four 家人 Family Members

一、导入 Lead-in

Exercise 1

Look at the pictures below and guess the meanings of the Chinese captions.

我家有四口人。

爸爸、妈妈、姐姐和我。

我和姐姐都是在中国出生的。

我姐姐有一个男朋友。

After learning this lesson, you will be able to:

1. Tell and ask about one's family members, their ages and occupations.

2. Know the tone sandhi of 一, and pronounce the neutral tones correctly.

3. Understand different kinds of character components and radicals.

4. Use a 有 sentence, and understand the use of 几 and 多, and the Chinese numeral system.

二、课文 Texts

课文（一）Text (1)

你家有几口人？

简体版

Li Wen and Lisa are talking about their family members.

李文：丽莎，你家有几口人？　　**Tips:** how to ask about the number of family members

丽莎：我家有四口人，爸爸、妈妈、哥哥和我。你呢？

李文：我家有七口人，爷爷、奶奶、爸爸、妈妈、我、妹妹、还有一个小弟弟。　**Tips:** how to ask a senior's age

丽莎：你的爷爷和奶奶多大年纪？

李文：我爷爷七十二岁，奶奶六十八岁。

丽莎：你的小弟弟多大了？

李文：他今年十二岁。　**Tips:** how to ask a junior's age

你家有幾口人？

繁体版

Li Wen and Lisa are talking about their family members.

李文：麗莎，你家有幾口人？

麗莎：我家有四口人，爸爸、媽媽、哥哥和我。你呢？

李文：我家有七口人，爺爺、奶奶、爸爸、媽媽、我、妹妹、還有一個小弟弟。

麗莎：你的爺爺和奶奶多大年紀？

李文：我爺爺七十二歲，奶奶六十八歲。

麗莎：你的小弟弟多大了？

李文：他今年十二歲。

第四课　家人

Kèwén (yī) *Text (1)*

Nǐ Jiā Yǒu Jǐ Kǒu Rén?

拼音版

Li Wen and Lisa are talking about their family members.

Lǐ Wén: Lìshā, nǐ jiā yǒu jǐ kǒu rén?

Lìshā: Wǒ jiā yǒu sì kǒu rén, bàba, māma, gēge hé wǒ. Nǐ ne?

Lǐ Wén: Wǒ jiā yǒu qī kǒu rén, yéye, nǎinai, bàba, māma, wǒ, mèimei, hái yǒu yí gè xiǎodìdi.

Lìshā: Nǐ de yéye hé nǎinai duō dà niánjì?

Lǐ Wén: Wǒ yéye qīshíèr suì, nǎinai liùshíbā suì.

Lìshā: Nǐ de xiǎodìdi duō dà le?

Lǐ Wén: Tā jīnnián shí'èr suì.

生词（一） *New Words (1)*

	简体（繁體）	拼音	词性	解释
1	家	jiā	*n.*	home, family 你家在哪儿？
2	有	yǒu	*v.*	have; there be 她有一个弟弟。/ 我家有五口人。
3	几（幾）	jǐ	*pron.*	how many 你家有几口人？
4	口	kǒu	*m.*	(measure word for individual person when referring to family population) 几口人 / 三口人
5	爸爸	bàba	*n.*	father 我有爸爸和妈妈。
6	妈妈（媽媽）	māma	*n.*	mother 妈妈好吗？
7	哥哥	gēge	*n.*	elder brother 我哥哥叫王文。
8	爷爷（爺爺）	yéye	*n.*	father's father 我爷爷很好，你爷爷呢？
9	奶奶	nǎinai	*n.*	father's mother 你奶奶多大年纪？
10	妹妹	mèimei	*n.*	younger sister 小红是我妹妹。
11	还（還）	hái	*adv.*	still, yet 我还有一个妹妹。
12	个（個）	gè	*m.*	(measure word for people or certain objects) 四个人 / 三个同学

简体（繁體）	拼音	词性	解释
13　小	xiǎo	*adj.*	small, little, young 小妹妹 / 小弟弟 / 小同学
14　弟弟	dìdi	*n.*	younger brother 我有弟弟，没有哥哥。
15　多	duō	*pron.*	how much 你弟弟多大了？
16　大	dà	*adj.*	big, old 我弟弟很大了。
17　年纪（紀）	niánjì	*n.*	age 你爷爷的年纪有多大？
18　岁（歲）	suì	*m.*	year, age 我 18 岁了，你呢？
19　了	le	*part.*	(particle indicating a completed action) 我妹妹十三岁了。
20　他	tā	*pron.*	he, him 他叫王平。
21　今年	jīnnián	*n.*	this year 今年我 20 岁。
22　年	nián	*n.*	year 今年 / 明年 / 今年多大了？
专有名词 Proper Noun			
1　丽（麗）莎	Lìshā	*pn.*	Lisa, a female student

Chinese numbers

简体（繁體）	拼音	词性	解释
1　一	yī	*num.*	1
2　二	èr	*num.*	2
3　三	sān	*num.*	3
4　四	sì	*num.*	4
5　五	wǔ	*num.*	5
6　六	liù	*num.*	6
7　七	qī	*num.*	7
8　八	bā	*num.*	8
9　九	jiǔ	*num.*	9
10　十	shí	*num.*	10
11　十一	shíyī	*num.*	11

简体（繁體）	拼音	词性	解释
12 二十	èrshí	*num.*	20
13 二十一	èrshíyī	*num.*	21
14 三十	sānshí	*num.*	30
15 三十一	sānshíyī	*num.*	31

Exercise 1 🦻

Listen to Text (1) and decide whether the following statements are true or false.

1. There are six people in Lisa's home.	(	)
2. Li Wen's grandparents live with his parents.	(	)
3. Lisa has a younger brother.	(	)
4. Li Wen's grandparents are both less than 65 years old.	(	)

Exercise 2 📖 🗣

Read Text (1) and answer the following questions.

1. Who is in Lisa's family?

2. How many generations are alive in Li Wen's family?

3. What are the similarities between the two families?

4. What are the differences between the two families?

Exercise 3 ✍

Fill in each blank with the right word from the list below to complete the following sentences. Then translate them into English.

a. 年纪   b. 岁   c. 和   d. 口

1. 你家有几 _____ 人？

2. 我家有爸爸，妈妈，哥哥，弟弟 _____ 我。

3. 你爸爸多大 _____ ？

4. 我爸爸五十二 _____ 了。

Exercise 4 🗣

Translate the following sentences into Chinese orally.

1. There are three people in Lisa's family.

2. My grandpa has an elder brother.

3. How old is your little sister?

4. Li Wen's grandma is 68 years old.

课文〔二〕*Text (2)*

我的一家

简体版

A self-introduction written by Jiang Xiaohua

　　我叫江小华，今年十八岁。我家有六口人，外公、外婆、爸爸、妈妈、姐姐和我。

　　我外公外婆都没有工作。我爸爸是医生，妈妈是小学老师。我姐姐在银行工作，她有一个男朋友。我是大学生。我的外公外婆和父母都是在中国出生的，我和姐姐是在美国出生的。

Tips: how to state one's birthplace

我的一家

繁体版

A self-introduction written by Jiang Xiaohua

　　我叫江小華，今年十八歲。我家有六口人，外公、外婆、爸爸、媽媽、姐姐和我。

　　我外公外婆都沒有工作。我爸爸是醫生，媽媽是小學老師。我姐姐在銀行工作，她有一個男朋友。我是大學生。我的外公外婆和父母都是在中國出生的，我和姐姐是在美國出生的。

Kèwén (èr) *Text (2)*

Wǒ de Yì Jiā

A self-introduction written by Jiang Xiaohua

Wǒ jiào Jiāng Xiǎohuá, jīnnián shíbā suì. Wǒ jiā yǒu liù kǒu rén, wàigōng, wàipó, bàba, māma, jiějie hé wǒ. Wǒ wàigōng wàipó dōu méiyǒu gōngzuò. Wǒ bàba shì yīshēng, māma shì xiǎoxué lǎoshī. Wǒ jiějie zài yínháng gōngzuò, tā yǒu yí gè nán péngyǒu. Wǒ shì dàxuéshēng. Wǒ de wàigōng wàipó hé fùmǔ dōu shì zài Zhōngguó chūshēng de, Wǒ hé jiějie shì zài Měiguó chūshēng de.

生词（二）*New Words (2)*

	简体（繁體）	拼音	词性	解释
1	外公	wàigōng	*n.*	mother's father 外公是妈妈的爸爸。/ 她外公71岁。
2	外婆	wàipó	*n.*	mother's mother 外婆是妈妈的妈妈。/ 她外婆69岁。
3	姐姐	jiějie	*n.*	elder sister 我姐姐是学生。
4	医（醫）生	yīshēng	*n.*	doctor, physician 我爸爸是医生。
5	小学（學）	xiǎoxué	*n.*	primary school 我妈妈是小学老师。
6	银（銀）行	yínháng	*n.*	bank 我哥哥在银行工作。
7	男	nán	*adj.*	male 男学生 / 我姐姐有一个男朋友。
8	朋友	péngyou	*n.*	friend 我们的朋友都很好。
9	大学（學）生	dàxuéshēng	*n.*	college student; university student 大学生学习很忙。

Exercise 5

Listen to Text (2) and match the people in Column I with their professions in Column II.

Column I	Column II
( ) 1. Father	a. school teacher
( ) 2. Mother	b. college student
( ) 3. Sister's boyfriend	c. bank clerk
( ) 4. Elder sister	d. doctor
( ) 5. Jiang Xiaohua	e. unknown
( ) 6. Grandparents	f. don't work

Exercise 6

Read Text (2) and decide whether the following statements are true or false.

1. 江小华今年十六岁。	( )
2. 江小华的妈妈在小学工作。	( )
3. 江小华是大学生。	( )
4. 江小华的外婆在银行工作。	( )
5. 江小华的姐姐是在中国出生的。	( )
6. 江小华的爸爸是医生。	( )

Exercise 7

Fill in the blanks according to Text (2) with characters.

1. 江小华家里有 _____ 人。

2. 江小华 _____ 姐姐。

3. 江小华的爸爸是 _____。

4. 江小华的妈妈在 _____ 工作。

5. 江小华是 _____。

Exercise 8

Translate the following phrases into Chinese orally.

1. the family of Lisa

2. born in the United States

3. university teacher

4. the age of grandpa

5. the name of the doctor

6. have an elder sister in addition

7. both are 74 years old

8. elder sister's boyfriend

三、语音 Phonetics

1. Tone sandhi of 一

一 (yī) is pronounced in the 1st tone when standing alone, or as an ordinal number, or at the end position of a word:

> yībǎ yīshíyī（一百一十一，111）;　　　　　tǒngyī（统一，to unify）

When it is followed by a 4th tone, 一 (yī) changes to the 2nd tone:

> yī + dìng → yídìng（一定，certainly);　　　yī + gè → yí gè（一个，one)
>
> yī + gòng → yígòng（一共，altogether);　　yī + bàn → yíbàn（一半，half)

When it is followed by the other tones (1st, 2nd, or 3rd tone), 一 (yī) changes to the 4th tone:

> yī + jiā → yì jiā（一家，a family);　　　yī + tiān → yì tiān（一天，one day)
>
> yī + tóng → yìtóng（一同，together);　　yī + rén → yì rén（一人，one person)
>
> yī + zǎo → yìzǎo（一早，early morning);　yī + qǐ → yìqǐ（一起，together)

2. Tone pitch of the neutral tone

In Lesson 1 we learned that the neutral tone is pronounced short and light. However, the pitch contour of the neutral tone is entirely determined by the preceding syllable:

> 1st tone + neutral tone: 哥哥 (elder brother) gē + gē → gēge
>
> 2nd tone + neutral tone: 爷爷 (grandfather) yé + yé → yéye
>
> 3rd tone + neutral tone: 姐姐 (elder sister) jiě + jiě → jiějie
>
> 4th tone + neutral tone: 弟弟 (younger brother) dì + dì → dìdi

From the above illustration we can see that a neutral tone following a 3rd tone is pronounced almost as high as a first tone, but very short. A neutral tone following a 4th tone is pronounced the lowest and very short.

Exercise 1 📖

Read aloud the following classroom expressions.

Qǐng nǐmen bǎ zuòyè zài zuò yí biàn. 请你们把作业再做一遍。	Please do your homework again.
Jiāo kǎojuàn yǐqián, qǐng zǐxì jiǎnchá yí biàn. 交考卷以前，请仔细检查一遍。	Please check your test paper once again before handing in.
Qǐng dàjiā yì rén niàn yí jù. 请大家一人念一句。	Please read one sentence each.
Míngtiān kǎo kǒuyǔ, wǒmen zhǔnshí kāishǐ. 明天考口语，我们准时开始。	Tomorrow we will test speaking. We'll start on time.

Exercise 2 📖

Read aloud the following sounds with the correct tones.

bā	bá	bǎ	bà	ba
mā	má	mǎ	mà	ma
gē	gé	gě	gè	ge
dī	dí	dǐ	dì	di
jiē	jié	jiě	jiè	jie
	méi	měi	mèi	mei
jiā	jiá	jiǎ	jià	
jī	jí	jǐ	jì	
chēng	chéng	chěng	chèng	
pēng	péng	pěng	pèng	
yī	yí	yǐ	yì	
jī	jí	jǐ	jì	

Exercise 3 🗣✳📖

Read aloud the following combination of tones.

yīshēng 医生 doctor	jīnnián 今年 this year	sānjiě 三姐 third sister	gōngzuò 工作 work
Táiwān 台湾 Taiwan	tóngxué 同学 classmate	píngguǒ 苹果 apple	niánjì 年纪 age
lǎojiā 老家 hometown	xiǎoxué 小学 primary school	wǔ kǒu 五口 five family members	Mǎlì 玛丽 Mary
shàngbān 上班 go to work	xiàoyuán 校园 campus	fùmǔ 父母 parents	àihào 爱好 hobby

Exercise 4 📖

Read aloud the following words paying attention to the neutral tones.

māma（妈妈）	gēge（哥哥）	tāmen（他们）
yéye（爷爷）	háizi（孩子）	érzi（儿子）
nǎinai（奶奶）	jiějie（姐姐）	wǒmen（我们）
bàba（爸爸）	mèimei（妹妹）	dìdi（弟弟）

Exercise 5 📖

Read aloud the following three-syllable words or phrases.

gōngchéngshī 工程师 engineer	nǚpéngyou 女朋友 girlfriend	dàxuéshēng 大学生 college student	Jiāng Xiǎohuá 江小华 Jiang Xiaohua
Jiùjīnshān 旧金山 San Francisco	Zhōngwénxì 中文系 Chinese Department	kàn diànyǐng 看电影 watch a movie	jǐ kǒu rén 几口人 how many people
sì kǒu rén 四口人 four people	wǔ kǒu rén 五口人 five people	liù kǒu rén 六口人 six people	qī kǒu rén 七口人 seven people

四、汉字 Chinese Characters

1. New characters in this lesson

序号	拼音	简/繁	部件	构词
1	bā	八	八	八个 / 十八岁 / 八月
2	bà	爸	父 + 巴	爸爸 / 老爸 / 爸妈
3	dì	弟	弟	弟弟 / 弟妹 / 一个弟弟
4	duō	多	夕 + 夕	多大 / 多少 / 很多
5	èr	二	二	二十 / 十二岁 / 十二口人
6	fù	父	父	父母 / 生父 / 她的生父
7	gē	哥	可 + 可	哥哥 / 大哥 / 我哥
8	gè	个 / 個	个	一个 / 四个人 / 一个男朋友
9	gōng	公	八 + 厶	外公 / 公公 / 老公公
10	hái	还 / 還	不 + 辶	还有 / 还是 / 还没有工作
11	háng	行	彳 + 亍	银行 / 中国银行 / 美国银行
12	jǐ	几 / 幾	几	几口人 / 几个 / 几样
13	jì	纪 / 紀	纟 + 己	年纪 / 世纪
14	jīn	今	今	今年 / 今天
15	jiǔ	九	九	九个 / 九天 / 九十九
16	kǒu	口	口	几口人 / 人口 / 开口
17	le	了	了	多大了 / 十八岁了
18	liù	六	六	六岁 / 六个 / 六口人
19	mā	妈 / 媽	女 + 马	妈妈 / 老妈 / 大妈
20	méi	没	氵 + 殳 (几 + 又)	没有 / 没有哥哥 / 没有工作
21	mèi	妹	女 + 未	妹妹 / 姐妹 / 小妹
22	mǔ	母	母	父母 / 生母 / 我父母
23	nǎi	奶	女 + 乃	奶奶 / 奶妈 / 我奶奶
24	nán	男	田 + 力	男朋友 / 男人 / 男老师
25	nián	年	年	年纪 / 今年 / 三年

26	péng	朋	月+月	朋友/男朋友/女朋友
27	pó	婆	波（氵+皮）+女	外婆/婆婆
28	qī	七	七	七岁/七天/七口人
29	sān	三	三	三岁/三年/三个同学
30	shā	莎	艹+沙（氵+少）	丽莎
31	shí	十	十	十八岁/八十岁/几十人
32	sì	四	四	四口人/四个/四岁
33	suì	岁/歲	山+夕	几岁/年岁/岁月
34	tā	他	亻+也	他们/他的/他走了
35	wài	外	夕+卜	外公/外婆/室外/门外
36	wǔ	五	五	五口人/星期五
37	yé	爷/爺	父+卩	爷爷/老爷
38	yī	一	一	一个/一年/一家人
39	yī	医/醫	匸+矢	医生/医院/医学院
40	yín	银/銀	钅+艮	银行/银子
41	yǒu	友	𠂇+又	朋友/友好/友爱
42	yǒu	有	𠂇+月	有人/没有/有没有
43	zài	在	𠂇+土	在宿舍/在家/在学校

Exercise 1 ✎

Copy the following single component characters with the correct stroke order in the spaces provided.

yī	一	一	
èr	二	一 二	
sān	三	一 二 三	
sì	四	丨 冂 冈 四 四	

wǔ	五	一 丁 五 五				
liù	六	、 亠 六 六				
qī	七	一 七				
bā	八	ノ 八				
jiǔ	九	ノ 九				
shí	十	一 十				
dì	弟	、 ` ` 丷 当 当 弟 弟				
fù	父	、 丷 少 父				
gè	个	ノ 人 个				
jǐ	几	ノ 几				
jīn	今	ノ 人 亼 今				
kǒu	口	丨 口 口				
le	了	⁊ 了				
mǔ	母	乚 𠃊 母 母 母				
nián	年	ノ 𠂉 𠂊 午 午 年				

2. Character components and non-character components

Character components are characters themselves while non-character components are not. For example, the component 也 in 他 is a character component, and the component 亻 is a non-character component.

3. The radicals

A radical is a character component that classifies the character for placement in most dictionaries. For instance, all characters containing the component 女, such as 姐, 妹, 妈, 她, 婆, 娶, are classed together in a character dictionary under 女. Thus 女 is called the "radical" or "indexing component". More often than not, a radical also suggests the character's category in meaning. Going back to the above examples, since 女 means "female", characters containing 女 usually have something to do with "female" in meaning, such as 妈 (mother), 姐妹 (sisters), 她 (she), 娶 (marry a lady), etc. We will introduce the most common radicals in later lessons.

Exercise 2 ✎

Fill in the following chart with help of a Chinese-English dictionary.

Character	妈	他	姓	哪	家	您
Pinyin						
Radical						

五、语言点 Language Points

1. The use of 几

几 can be used as a question word in questions to ask a number from 1 to 9. 几 can also be used as a numeral in statements indicating a number from 1 to 9. Here are some examples.

(1) 你家有几口人?
How many people are there in your family?

(2) 你的小弟弟几岁?
How many years old is your younger brother? / How old is your younger brother?

(3) 你们班 (bān, class) 有几个学生?

> How many students are there in your class?
>
> (4) 我们班有<u>几个</u>十几岁的学生。
>
> There are several teenagers in our class.

Note: When asking about a number over ten, 多少 ("how many") should be used.

2. The question word 多

The question word 多 is often used before an adjective to indicate "how" or "to what extent", such as: 多大 (how old), 多早 (how early), 多忙 (how busy), and 多好 (how well). Here are two examples from this lesson:

> (1) 你的小弟弟<u>多</u>大了？
>
> How old is your younger brother?
>
> (2) 你的爷爷和奶奶<u>多</u>大年纪？
>
> How old are your grandparents?

3. The measure words 口 and 个

Unlike in English where a number is usually directly placed before countable nouns, Chinese usually requires a measure word to be added between the numeral and the noun. For example:

> (1) 你家有几<u>口</u>人？
>
> How many people are there in your family?
>
> (2) 我们家有四<u>口</u>人。
>
> There are four people in our family.
>
> (3) 我有一<u>个</u>小弟弟。
>
> I have a younger brother.
>
> (4) 我姐姐有一<u>个</u>男朋友。
>
> My elder sister has a boyfriend.

4. The 有 sentence

The Chinese verb 有 can indicate both possession ("to have") and existence ("there be"). It requires a noun as its object. If a number is involved, a measure word is usually needed.

> **Subject (person, place, etc.) + 有 + (Number + Measure Word) + Noun**

(1) 我<u>有</u>一个小弟弟。
I have a younger brother.
(2) 我姐姐<u>有</u>一个男朋友。
My elder sister has a boyfriend.
(3) 我家<u>有</u>七口人。
There are seven people in my family.

The negative form of the verb 有 is 没（有）, meaning "do not have" or "there is/are not". Sometimes the 有 after 没 can be dropped.

> **Subject (person, place, etc.) ＋没（有）＋(Number＋Measure Word) ＋ Noun**

(4) 我<u>没（有）</u>弟弟。我<u>有</u>一个哥哥。
I don't have a younger brother. I have an elder brother.
(5) 我家<u>有</u>四口人，<u>没有</u>七口人。
There are four people in my family, not seven.
(6) 我外公外婆都<u>没有</u>工作。
Both of my grandparents do not work.

There are three ways to form a question with the verb 有 : with a question marker 吗, or an affirmative-negative form 有没有, or a question word 几 or 多少:

> **Subject (person, place, etc.) ＋有＋(Number＋Measure Word) ＋ Noun＋吗?**

or

> **Subject (person, place, etc.) ＋有没有＋(Number ＋ Measure Word) ＋ Noun?**

or

> **Subject (person, place, etc.) ＋有＋几 or 多少＋Measure Word ＋ Noun?**

(7) 她<u>有</u>男朋友吗? / 她<u>有</u>没有男朋友?
Does she have a boyfriend?

(8) 你们家<u>有</u>七口人<u>吗</u>? / 你们家<u>有没有</u>七口人?

Are there seven people in your family?

(9) 你家<u>有</u><u>几</u>口人?

How many people are there in your family?

(10) 你们班 (bān, class) <u>有</u><u>多少</u>个学生?

How many students are there in your class?

5. Noun used as predicate

In Chinese, a noun or a numeral phrase may directly serve as the predicate when it refers to age, money, or time. Unlike in English, such sentences do not need 是 as the verb. For example:

(1) 你的爷爷和奶奶多大<u>年纪</u>?

What are your grandparents' ages?

(2) 我爷爷<u>六十三岁</u>, 奶奶<u>五十九岁</u>。

My grandpa is 63 and my grandma is 59.

(3) 他今年<u>十二岁</u>。

He is 12 this year.

6. Numbers in Chinese

The Chinese language still uses characters for its numerical system, while also adopting Arabic numerals.

0~10:

0	1	2	3	4	5	6	7	8	9	10
零	一	二	三	四	五	六	七	八	九	十
líng	yī	èr	sān	sì	wǔ	liù	qī	bā	jiǔ	shí

11~19: 十一, 十二, 十三, 十四, 十五, 十六, 十七, 十八, 十九

20~90: 二十, 三十, 四十, 五十, 六十, 七十, 八十, 九十

Exercise 1

The whole class forms a circle for a number counting game 数数游戏. The teacher starts with a number and the next student will say the next number as soon as possible according to the criteria below. The student who makes a mistake will be asked to do a performance (singing a song, telling a joke, etc.)

a. Count by 5 (5, 10, 15 ···)

b. Count by 2 (2, 4, 6 ···)

c. Count by 3 (3, 6, 9 ···)

Exercise 2 👂 ✍ 🗣

Listen to the introduction of John's family. For each member, fill in the age, job status, and other information in the chart below. Then orally introduce John's family in Chinese.

Family Member	Age	Other Information

Exercise 3 📖

Match the Chinese sentences in Column I with the English translations in Column II.

Column I	Column II
(　　) 1. 我家有六口人。	a. I'm a college student.
(　　) 2. 我爸爸在银行工作。	b. My grandparents are 70 years old.
(　　) 3. 我妈妈是老师，工作很忙。	c. My father works at a bank.
(　　) 4. 我是一个大学生。	d. My mother is a teacher. She is very busy with her work.
(　　) 5. 我的爷爷奶奶都七十岁了。	e. There are six people in my family.
(　　) 6. 我妹妹今年十三岁。	f. Both my younger sister and I were born in America.
(　　) 7. 我和妹妹都是在美国出生的。	g. My younger sister is 13 years old.

Exercise 4 ✍

Change the following 有 sentences into three types of questions.

Example: 江小姐有两个孩子。

　　　　　A. 江小姐有两个孩子吗?

　　　　　B. 江小姐有没有两个孩子?

　　　　　C. 江小姐有几个孩子?

1. 他们班有两个英国学生。

A. _____ ?

B. _____ ?

C. _____ ?

2. 大卫有两个弟弟。

A. _____ ?

B. _____ ?

C. _____ ?

3. 丽莎家有四口人。

A. _____ ?

B. _____ ?

C. _____ ?

Exercise 5

Read the sentences first. Then write questions regarding the underlined characters.

1. 小文家有<u>三口人</u>，爸爸、妈妈和他。

Question: _____ ?

2. 小文今年<u>十八岁</u>，是一个大学生。

Question: _____ ?

3. 他爸爸在<u>银行</u>工作。

Question: _____ ?

4. 他妈妈是一个<u>老师</u>。

Question: _____ ?

5. 小文有<u>三个</u>好朋友。

Question: _____ ?

6. 丽莎的班有<u>二十一个</u>学生。

Question: _____ ?

Exercise 6

Choose the right answer for each of the following sentences.

1. 你们家 _____ 人？

a. 是几口　　　　　b. 有几口　　　　　c. 是多大

2. 我们家有爸爸、妈妈、弟弟 _____ 我。

a. 也　　　　　b. 还　　　　　c. 和

3. 我爸爸 _____ 学校工作，他很忙。

    a. 是   b. 在   c. 不是

4. 他的外公和外婆是在中国北京出生 _____ 。

    a. 了   b. 呢   c. 的

5. 王老师，您的儿子 _____ 了?

    a. 多大   b. 多少   c. 几年

6. 陈雨有 _____ 哥哥?

    a. 几个   b. 几口   c. 多大

7. 我的爷爷今年 _____ 。

    a. 六十八年   b. 六十八年纪   c. 六十八岁

8. 玛丽有一个哥哥和一个弟弟，_____ 姐姐。

    a. 不有   b. 没有   c. 有不

9. 大卫有两个姐姐，_____ 一个小弟弟。

    a. 也   b. 还有   c. 不有

10. 玛丽和大卫 _____ 弟弟吗?

    a. 不有   b. 有没有   c. 都有

Exercise 7 📖 ✎

Read the following dialogs aloud and translate them into English.

Dialog 1

A: 你有姐妹吗?

B: 我没有姐妹，我有一个弟弟。

A: 你弟弟在哪儿工作?

B: 他在银行工作。

A: 他今年多大了?

B: 他二十二岁了。

_____

_____

_____

_____

_____

_____

Dialog 2

A: 小雨，你们家有几口人?

B: 我们家有四口人，爸爸、妈妈、姐姐和我。

A: 你爸爸和妈妈在哪儿工作?

B: 我爸爸在大学工作,是老师。我妈妈没有工作。

A: 你姐姐呢?

B: 我姐姐是一个大学生。

_____

_____

_____

_____

_____

_____

六、语言运用 Using the Language

Activity 1 📖 🗣

Look at the following picture and read the description. Then answer the questions orally in Chinese.

这是一张全家福。这里面有姥姥(lǎolao 妈妈的妈妈)、爸爸、妈妈、儿子和女儿。

What family members are there in this photo?

Activity 2 🗣

Work in pairs. Look at the following family tree and talk about the relationship between the family members. The triangles represent males and the circles represent females.

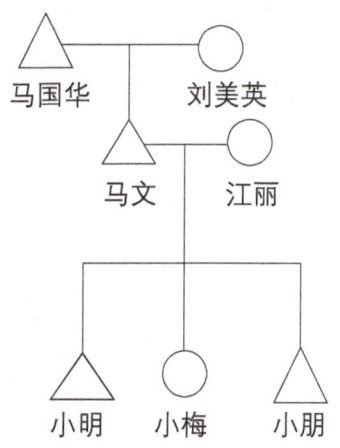

Names from top to bottom, from left to right:

马国华 Mǎ Guóhuá; 刘美英 Liú Měiyīng
马文 Mǎ Wén; 江丽 Jiāng Lì
小明 Xiǎomíng; 小梅 Xiǎoméi; 小朋 Xiǎopéng

Example: 马国华是刘美英的先生（xiānsheng, husband）。

Activity 3 📖 🗣*

Work in pairs. Read the following form about Mr. Wang's personal information and answer the questions below. Based on the context, guess the meaning of the characters that are new to you.

姓名	王文同	出生年月	1985. 12. 23
性别	男	出生地	北京
学历	大学	参加工作时间	2007. 10. 1

家庭成员

姓名	关系	职业
王成	爷爷	没有工作
刘丽华	奶奶	没有工作
王京生	爸爸	老师
李梅	妈妈	医生
王文学	弟弟	银行职员
王文美	妹妹	学生

Questions:

1. When was Wang Wentong born?

2. Where was he born?

3. What is his highest level of education?

4. How many people are there in his family? Who are they?

5. What do his parents do?

6. What do his siblings do?

Activity 4 👂 📖

You overheard a conversation at a speed dating event between a man and a woman. Determine whether the following statements are true or false.

1. 王伟是北京人。	(	)
2. 王伟的弟弟不在北京。	(	)
3. 王伟没有爷爷奶奶。	(	)
4. 李小月的妹妹是老师。	(	)
5. 李小月的爷爷奶奶不在北京。	(	)

| 6. 李小月的爸爸是老师。 | ( ) |
| 7. 李小月有两个妹妹。 | ( ) |

Activity 5

Work in pairs. Look at the following pictures and talk about the family of Wang Jingsheng. Each person will then give a monologue about the family.

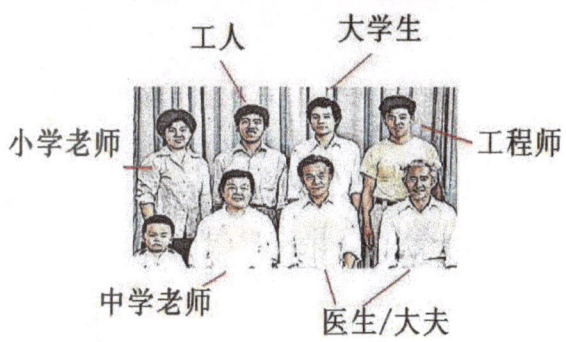

In the picture, from left to right:
First row:
Wang Jingsheng's younger sister's son, Wang Jingsheng's parents, Wang 's uncle
Second row:
Wang's younger sister, sister's husband, Wang's younger brother, Wang Jingsheng

Your conversation should include the size of the family, the members of the family and their professions.

New words: 工程师：gōngchéngshī, engineer   工人：gōngrén, worker
医生：yīsheng, doctor   大夫：dàifu, doctor

| Cultural Tip |

The Chinese word for "country, state" is 国家, actually a combination of two characters meaning "country/state" and "family" respectively. This shows the importance of family within Chinese society. Traditionally, the Chinese value extended family very much. As society changes, however, nuclear families have become more common. Still, the Chinese prefer that family members should not live too far away from one another so that they can meet easily for social events and assist one another.

第五课
Lesson Five

介绍
Introduction

一、导入 Lead-in

Exercise 1 📖 🗣✳

Look at the pictures below and talk about what you see in Chinese.

我和约翰每天一起上中文课。

早上我们一起去跑步。

晚上一起去食堂吃饭。

我们常常在学校图书馆做作业。

After learning this lesson, you will be able to:

1. Introduce someone by name, occupation, hometown, and relationship with you.
2. Understand the combination of Chinese initials and finals, and apply it to pinyin spelling.
3. Recognize the new characters in this lesson, and know how to input characters into a computer.
4. Use the words 来, 去, 谁, 常常, 一起, 一下, and the time expressions and verbs in series.

飞跃——汉语初级教程学生用书 上册

二、课文 Texts

课文（一）*Text (1)*

这是我女朋友

简体版

Chen Yu and her brother meet John and his girlfriend Mary in front of a theater.

陈雨：约翰，你是来看电影的吗？

约翰：是的。你呢？

陈雨：我也是。这位女孩是谁？

Tips: how to introduce a friend.

约翰：来来来，我来介绍一下吧，这是我女朋友玛丽。玛丽，这是我中文系的同学陈雨。

陈雨：玛丽，你好！认识你很高兴！

玛丽：你好，陈雨！我也很高兴认识你。

Tips: how to greet a newly introduced friend

约翰：陈雨，那位男孩是你的男朋友吗？

Tips: same as "What are you talking about!"

陈雨：什么呀，不是！他是我哥！

这是我女朋友

繁体版

Chen Yu and her brother meet John and his girlfriend Mary in front of a theater.

陳雨：約翰，你是來看電影的嗎？

約翰：是的。你呢？

陳雨：我也是。這位女孩是誰？

約翰：來來來，我來介紹一下吧，這是我女朋友瑪麗。
　　　瑪麗，這是我中文系的同學陳雨。

陳雨：瑪麗，你好！認識你很高興！

瑪麗：你好，陳雨！我也很高興認識你。

約翰：陳雨，那位男孩是你的男朋友嗎？

陳雨：什麼呀，不是！他是我哥！

Kèwén (yī)　*Text (1)*

Zhè Shì Wǒ Nǚpéngyou

拼音版

Chen Yu and her brother meet John and his girlfriend Mary in front of a theater.

Chén Yǔ: Yuēhàn, nǐ shì lái kàn diànyǐng de ma?

Yuēhàn: Shì de. Nǐ ne?

Chén Yǔ: Wǒ yě shì. Zhè wèi nǚhái shì shéi?

Yuēhàn: Lái lái lái, Wǒ lái jièshào yíxià ba, zhè shì wǒ nǚpéngyou
　　　　Mǎlì. Mǎlì, zhè shì wǒ Zhōngwénxì de tóngxué Chén Yǔ.

Chén Yǔ: Mǎlì, nǐ hǎo! Rènshi nǐ hěn gāoxìng!

Mǎlì: Nǐ hǎo, Chén Yǔ! Wǒ yě hěn gāoxìng rènshi nǐ.

Yuēhàn: Chén Yǔ, nà wèi nánhái shì nǐ de nánpéngyou ma?

Chén Yǔ: Shénme ya, bú shì! Tā shì wǒ gē!

生词（一）　*New Words (1)*

	简体（繁體）	拼音	词性	解释
1	来（來）	lái	v.	come 他来了吗？/ 来我家看电影。/ 我来介绍一下。

左侧竖排

飞跃——汉语初级教程学生用书　上册

footer
86

简体（繁體）	拼音	词性	解释
2 看	kàn	v.	see; look at; visit 看电影 / 看医生 / 看同学 / 你看！
3 电（電）影	diànyǐng	n.	movie, film 看电影 / 电影很好看。
4 这（這）	zhè	pron.	this 这本书 / 这是我朋友。/ 这是什么？
5 位	wèi	m.	(measure word for people when referred to by their titles) 这位老师叫什么？ / 这位同学叫陈雨。
6 女孩	nǚhái	n.	girl 我家有一个女孩，两个男孩。
7 谁（誰）	shéi	pron.	who 他是谁？ / 谁叫约翰？
8 介绍（紹）	jièshào	v.	introduce 我来介绍一个朋友。/ 这是谁呀？请你介绍介绍。
9 一下	yíxià	nc.	(numeral-classifier for a short duration of an action) 看一下 / 我来介绍一下。
10 吧	ba	part.	(particle at the end of a suggestion) 我来介绍一下吧！
11 中文	Zhōngwén	n.	the Chinese language 学中文 / 中文学校
12 系	xì	n.	department 我们是中文系的学生。
13 认识（認識）	rènshi	v.	know, recognize 你认识他吗？ / 你认识这个汉字吗？
14 高兴（興）	gāoxìng	adj.	happy, glad 认识你很高兴。
15 那	nà	pron.	that 那个人 / 那是我的老师。
16 男孩	nánhái	n.	boy 那位男孩是你男朋友吗？
17 呀	ya	part.	(particle showing a certain mood) 你看什么呀？

Exercise 1

Listen to Text (1) and answer the questions orally in Chinese.

1. Where do they meet?
2. Who is with John?
3. What does Chen Yu say to the person?
4. Whom is Chen Yu with?

Exercise 2 📖 🗣

Read the following sentences and rearrange them to form a proper dialog.

1. 你好，约翰！

2. 陈雨，你好！我也很高兴认识你。

3. 他是我哥哥。

4. 陈雨，那位男孩是谁？

5. 你好，玛丽！认识你很高兴。

6. 你好，陈雨！我来介绍一下。这是我女朋友玛丽。

Exercise 3 🗣

Translate the following sentences into Chinese orally.

1. Let me introduce my friend. This is Xiao Zhang.

2. Is that girl his girlfriend?

3. It is a pleasure to meet you.

4. Are you here for the movie?

Exercise 4 👂 📖

You will hear four statements followed by three responses. Select the response that best corresponds to each statement.

1. a. 我叫文中。

　　b. 是我哥哥。

　　c. 是你朋友吗？

2. a. 不是，我来看陈雨。

　　b. 我很高兴认识你。

　　c. 那两个美国朋友是谁？

3. a. 你高兴什么？

　　b. 小文很高兴。

　　c. 我也很高兴认识你。

4. a. 你的同学是谁？

　　b. 陈雨，你好。

　　c. 陈雨看电影。

課文〔二〕*Text (2)*

我的好朋友

简体版

A brief introduction of two good friends.

这是约翰，这是林华，他们都是我的好朋友。

约翰是我的室友。我们每天一起上中文课。早上我们一起去跑步，晚上一起去食堂吃晚饭。约翰是在旧金山出生的，他常常回家看他的父母。

林华是从台湾来的，她的家人都在台湾。林华是英文系的学生。约翰、林华和我常常一起在图书馆做作业。

我的好朋友

繁体版

A brief introduction of two good friends.

這是約翰，這是林華，他們都是我的好朋友。

約翰是我的室友。我們每天一起上中文課。早上我們一起去跑步，晚上一起去食堂吃晚飯。約翰是在舊金山出生的，他常常回家看他的父母。

林華是從臺灣來的，她的家人都在臺灣。林華是英文系的學生。約翰、林華和我常常一起在圖書館做作業。

Wǒ de Hǎopéngyou

拼音版

A brief introduction of two good friends.

Zhè shì Yuēhàn, zhè shì Lín Huá, tāmen dōu shì wǒ de hǎopéngyou.

Yuēhàn shì wǒ de shìyǒu. Wǒmen měi tiān yìqǐ shàng Zhōngwénkè. Zǎoshang wǒmen yìqǐ qù pǎobù, wǎnshang yìqǐ qù shítáng chī wǎnfàn. Yuēhàn shì zài Jiùjīnshān chūshēng de, tā chángcháng huí jiā kàn tā de fùmǔ.

Lín Huá shì cóng Táiwān lái de, tā de jiārén dōu zài Táiwān. Lín Huá shì Yīngwénxì de xuéshēng. Yuēhàn, Lín Huá hé wǒ chángcháng yìqǐ zài túshūguǎn zuò zuòyè.

生词（二） *New Words (2)*

	简体（繁體）	拼音	词性	解释
1	他们（們）	tāmen	*pron.*	they, them 他们是我的朋友。/ 我喜欢他们。
2	室友	shìyǒu	*n.*	roommate 我的室友是美国人。
3	每	měi	*pron.*	each, every 每个人 / 每个学校 / 每个学生
4	天	tiān	*n.*	day 每天 / 天天 / 我天天都学中文。
5	一起	yìqǐ	*adv.*	together 我们一起学中文。
6	上	shàng	*v.*	go to (class, work); attend (class) 上课 / 我们一起去上课。
7	课（課）	kè	*n.*	class, lesson 中文课 / 下课了。
8	去	qù	*v.*	go 我去中国。/ 我去学校。/ 早上我们一起去跑步。
9	跑步	pǎobù	*v.*	run 每天我都跑步。
10	晚上	wǎnshang	*n.*	evening 晚上你有课吗？
11	食堂	shítáng	*n.*	dining hall 去食堂 / 约翰常常去食堂吃饭。

飞跃——汉语初级教程学生用书　上册

简体（繁體）		拼音	词性	解释
12	吃	chī	*v.*	eat 吃早饭
13	晚饭（飯）	wǎnfàn	*n.*	dinner; evening meal; supper 吃晚饭 / 做晚饭 / 晚饭很好吃。
14	常常	chángcháng	*adv.*	frequently, often 我常常去图书馆。
15	回家	huí jiā		go home; come back home 你常常回家看父母吗？
16	从（從）	cóng	*prep.*	from 林华是从台湾来的。
17	英文	Yīngwén	*n.*	the English language 我学英文。/ 他是我的英文老师。
18	图书馆（圖書館）	túshūguǎn	*n.*	library 图书馆在哪儿？
19	做	zuò	*v.*	do, make 做功课 / 做练习
20	作业（業）	zuòyè	*n.*	school assignment; homework 做作业 / 留作业 / 改作业
专有名词 Proper Nouns				
1	旧（舊）金山	Jiùjīnshān	*pn.*	San Francisco
2	林华（華）	Lín Huā	*pn.*	Lin Hua, a Chinese name

Exercise 5 👂

Listen to Text (2) and decide whether the following statements are true or false.

1. John is my teacher.	(	)
2. John and I often do things together.	(	)
3. Lin Hua is John's girlfriend.	(	)
4. Lin Hua is busy and seldom sees John.	(	)
5. John's father and mother do not live with him.	(	)
6. Lin Hua's siblings are in the U.S.	(	)
7. John was born in San Francisco.	(	)

Exercise 6 📖 🗣

Read Text (2) and answer the questions orally in Chinese.

1. How did John and the author become good friends?

2. Is John a good son? How do you know?

3. Does Lin Hua see her family everyday? How do you know?

4. What do the three of them often do together?

Exercise 7 📖 ✍

Read the following Chinese phrases and translate them into English.

Chinese	English
我的好朋友	
约翰的室友	
一起上中文课	
去跑步	
去食堂吃晚饭	
常常回家看父母	
从台湾来的	
英文系的学生	
在图书馆做作业	
家人都在美国	

Exercise 8 👂 📖

You will hear four statements followed by four responses. Select the response that best responds to each statement.

1. a. 请问您叫什么名字？

b. 认识你很高兴。

c. 我是老师。

d. 谁是玛丽？

2. a. 我妈妈是医生。

b. 认识你很高兴。

c. 我爸爸是在美国出生的。

d. 你有兄弟姐妹吗？

3. a. 小华也是在北京出生的吗？

b. 我来介绍一下我的美国朋友。

c. 玛丽是约翰的女朋友。

d. 他是在旧金山出生的吗？

4. a. 小华是在北京出生的。

b. 认识你很高兴。

c. 谢谢，我姓张，叫大明。

d. 约翰是我的室友。

三、语音 Phonetics

1. Combination of initials and finals

The following sound chart indicates all possible combinations of initials and finals.

Combination of Initials and Finals

	b	p	m	f	d	t	n	l	g	k	h	j	q	x	z	c	s	zh	ch	sh	r
a	ba	pa	ma	fa	da	ta	na	la	ga	ka	ha				za	ca	sa	zha	cha	sha	
o	bo	po	mo	fo																	
e			me		de	te	ne	le	ge	ke	he				ze	ce	se	zhe	che	she	re
ai	bai	pai	mai		dai	tai	nai	lai	gai	kai	hai				zai	cai	sai	zhai	chai	shai	
ei	bei	pei	mei	fei	dei		nei	lei	gei	kei	hei				zei			zhei		shei	
ao	bao	pao	mao		dao	tao	nao	lao	gao	kao	hao				zao	cao	sao	zhao	chao	shao	rao
ou		pou	mou	fou	dou	tou	nou	lou	gou	kou	hou				zou	cou	sou	zhou	chou	shou	rou
an	ban	pan	man	fan	dan	tan	nan	lan	gan	kan	han				zan	can	san	zhan	chan	shan	ran
en	ben	pen	men	fen	den		nen		gen	ken	hen				zen	cen	sen	zhen	chen	shen	ren
ang	bang	pang	mang	fang	dang	tang	nang	lang	gang	kang	hang				zang	cang	sang	zhang	chang	shang	rang
eng	beng	peng	meng	feng	deng	teng	neng	leng	geng	keng	heng				zeng	ceng	seng	zheng	cheng	sheng	reng
ong					dong	tong	nong	long	gong	kong	hong				zong	cong	song	zhong	chong		rong
er																					
i	bi	pi	mi		di	ti	ni	li				ji	qi	xi	zi	ci	si	zhi	chi	shi	ri
ia								lia				jia	qia	xia							
ie	bie	pie	mie		die	tie	nie	lie				jie	qie	xie							
iao	biao	piao	miao		diao	tiao	niao	liao				jiao	qiao	xiao							
iu			miu		diu		niu	liu				jiu	qiu	xiu							
ian	bian	pian	mian		dian	tian	nian	lian				jian	qian	xian							
in	bin	pin	min				nin	lin				jin	qin	xin							
iang							niang	liang				jiang	qiang	xiang							
ing	bing	ping	ming		ding	ting	ning	ling				jing	qing	xing							
iong												jiong	qiong	xiong							

u	bu	pu	mu	fu	du	tu	nu	lu	gu	ku	hu				zu	cu	su	zhu	chu	shu	ru
ua									gua	kua	hua							zhua	chua	shua	rua
uo					duo	tuo	nuo	luo	guo	kuo	huo				zuo	cuo	suo	zhuo	chuo	shuo	ruo
uai									guai	kuai	huai							zhuai	chuai	shuai	
ui					dui	tui			gui	kui	hui				zui	cui	sui	zhui	chui	shui	rui
uan					duan	tuan	nuan	luan	guan	kuan	huan				zuan	cuan	suan	zhuan	chuan	shuan	ruan
un					dun	tun		lun	gun	kun	hun				zun	cun	sun	zhun	chun	shun	run
uang									guang	kuang	huang							zhuang	chuang	shuang	
ueng																					
ü							n ü	l ü				ju	qu	xu							
üe							n üe	l üe				jue	que	xue							
üan												juan	quan	xuan							
ün												jun	qun	xun							

2. Rules of combination of initials and finals

The above sound chart indicates all possible combinations of initials and finals in Mandarin Chinese. From the sound chart, we can see that the combination of initials and finals follows some basic rules, which are:

> (1) *b, p, m, f* cannot combine with *u* group (except for *u*) and *ü* group;
>
> (2) *d, t, n, l* can combine with all groups with some exceptions;
>
> (3) *z, c, s, zh, ch, sh, r* cannot combine with *i* group (except for *i*) and *ü* group;
>
> (4) *j, q, x* can only combine with *i* group and *ü* group;
>
> (5) *g, k, h* cannot combine with *i* group and *ü* group.

Remembering the combination rules will help in spelling.

Exercise 1

Read aloud the following classroom expressions.

Xiànzài wǒmen kǎoshì. 现在我们考试。	Now let's begin the test.
Qǐng tóngxuémen bǎ kèzhuō shang de shūběn shōu qǐlái. 请同学们把课桌上的书本收起来。	Please put away your books on your desks.

Kǎoshì de shíhòu bù kěyǐ dàshēng shuōhuà hé jiāotóu-jiē'ěr. 考试的时候不可以大声说话和交头接耳。	No talking or whispering during the test.
Búyào wàngle zài kǎojuàn shang xiěshang míngzì. 不要忘了在考卷上写上名字。	Do not forget to write your name on the answer sheet.
Jiāojuàn yǐqián qǐng zǐxì jiǎnchá yí biàn dá'àn. 交卷以前请仔细检查一遍答案。	Please check your answers carefully before handing in the test paper.
Míngtiān xiàwǔ wǒmen jìnxíng shìjuàn jiǎngpíng. 明天下午我们进行试卷讲评。	Test critique will be held tomorrow afternoon.

Exercise 2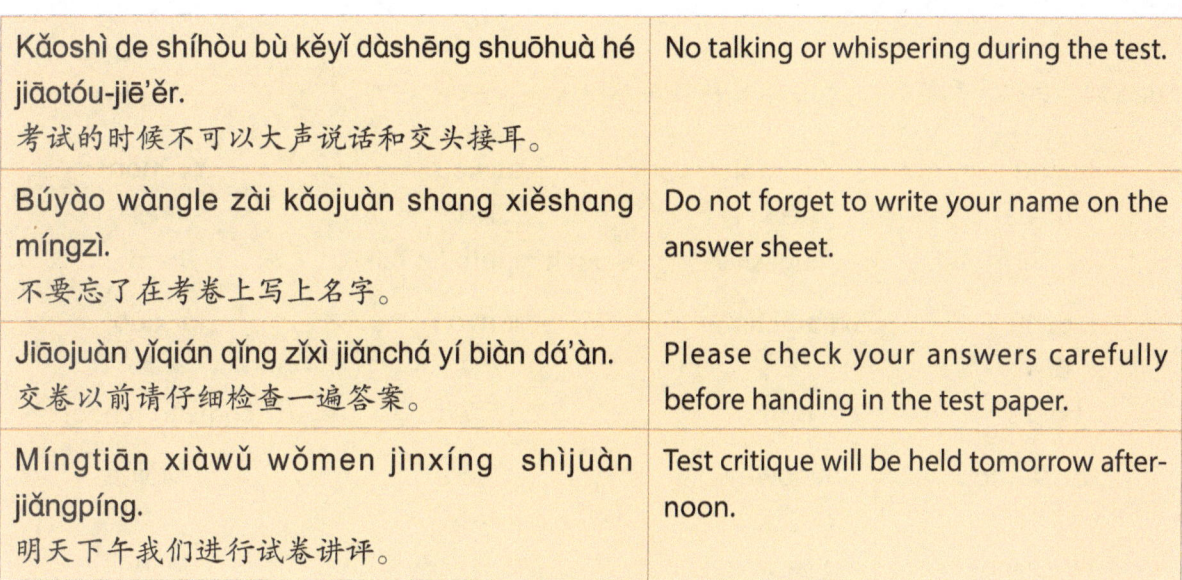

Read aloud the following sounds with the correct tones.

yuē			yuè
yīng	yíng	yǐng	yìng
jiāng		jiǎng	jiàng
gāo		gǎo	gào
	hái	hǎi	hài
shī	shí	shǐ	shì
pāo	páo	pǎo	pào
zhī	zhí	zhǐ	zhì
wān	wán	wǎn	wàn
fān	fán	fǎn	fàn
zuō	zuó	zuǒ	zuò
chēng	chéng	chěng	chèng
xuē	xué	xuě	xuè
sū	sú		sù
shē	shé	shě	shè
diān		diǎn	diàn
chī	chí	chǐ	chì

Exercise 3 📖

Read aloud the following combination of tones.

chūshēng 出生 be born	Yīngwén 英文 English	kāi kǒu 开口 open mouth (to talk)	Yuēhàn 约翰 John
túshū 图书 books	chángcháng 常常 often	nányǒu 男友 boyfriend	lái xiào 来校 come to school
Lǎo Zhāng 老张 Old Zhang	Xiǎowén 小文 Xiaowen	qǐzǎo 起早 get up early	Mǎlì 玛丽 Mary
kàn shū 看书 read books	dàxué 大学 university	diànyǐng 电影 movie	sùshè 宿舍 dorm

Exercise 4 📖

Read the following words aloud paying attention to the neutral tones.

tā de（他的）　　gēge（哥哥）

shéide（谁的）　　shénme（什么）

zǎoshang（早上）　wǎnshang（晚上）

duì ya（对呀）　　shì ba（是吧）

Exercise 5 📖

Read the following three-syllable words or phrases aloud.

Zhōngwénkè 中文课 Chinese lesson	nánpéngyou 男朋友 boyfriend	nǔpéngyou 女朋友 girlfriend	zuò zuòyè 做作业 do homework
Yīngwénxì 英文系 English Department	xué Zhōngwén 学中文 study Chinese	hěn gāoxìng 很高兴 very happy	qù shítáng 去食堂 go to the dining hall
chī wǎnfàn 吃晚饭 eat dinner	túshūguǎn 图书馆 library	hǎopéngyou 好朋友 good friend	Jiùjīnshān 旧金山 San Francisco

四、汉字 Chinese Characters

1. New characters in this lesson

序号	拼音	简 / 繁	部件	构词
1	ba	吧	口 + 巴	介绍一下吧 / 是你吧
2	bù	步	止 + 少	跑步 / 步行 / 大步走
3	cháng	常	尚 (⺌ + 冖 + 口) + 巾	常常 / 经常
4	chī	吃	口 + 乞	吃饭 / 吃东西 / 很好吃
5	cóng	从 / 從	人 + 人	从台湾来 / 从家到学校
6	diàn	电 / 電	电	电影 / 电视 / 电话 / 电灯
7	fàn	饭 / 飯	饣 + 反	吃晚饭 / 做饭
8	gāo	高	亠 + 口 + 冂 + 口	高兴 / 高个子 / 高楼
9	guǎn	馆 / 館	饣 + 官 (宀 + 𠂤)	图书馆 / 中国饭馆 / 餐馆
10	hái	孩	子 + 亥	女孩 / 男孩 / 小孩子
11	huí	回	囗 + 口	回家 / 回学校 / 回来
12	jiè	介	介	介绍 / 介入
13	jīn	金	金	旧金山 / 美金
14	jiù	旧 / 舊	丨 + 日	旧金山 / 旧衣服
15	kàn	看	手 + 目	看电影 / 看医生 / 看朋友
16	kè	课 / 課	讠 + 果	中文课 / 上课
17	lái	来 / 來	来	他来了 / 来上学
18	měi	每	⺈ + 母	每天 / 每个人 / 每次
19	nà	那	冄 + 阝	那是 / 那里 / 那些
20	nǚ	女	女	女朋友 / 女孩 / 女老师
21	pǎo	跑	𧾷 + 包 (勹 + 巳)	跑步 / 他跑了
22	qǐ	起	走 + 己	一起 / 起来
23	qù	去	土 + 厶	去上课 / 去学校 / 出去
24	rèn	认 / 認	讠 + 人	认识 / 认字
25	shān	山	山	旧金山 / 山上 / 高山

26	shào	绍 / 紹	纟 + 召 (刀 + 口)	介绍
27	shéi	谁 / 誰	讠 + 隹	他是谁 / 谁叫约翰
28	shí	识 / 識	讠 + 只	认识 / 学识
29	shí	食	人 + 良	食堂 / 粮食
30	shì	室	宀 + 至	室友 / 办公室 / 教室
31	shū	书 / 書	书	图书馆 / 书本 / 看书
32	táng	堂	尚 (小 + 冖 + 口) + 土	食堂 / 天堂
33	tiān	天	天	每天 / 天天 / 白天
34	tú	图 / 圖	囗 + 冬	图书馆 / 地图 / 中国地图
35	wǎn	晚	日 + 免	晚上 / 每晚
36	wèi	位	亻 + 立	这位老师 / 那位同学
37	xì	系	一 + 糸 (幺 + 小)	中文系 / 英文系
38	xià	下	下	下午 / 下课 / 上下
39	xìng	兴 / 興	丷 + 一 + 八	高兴 / 兴奋
40	ya	呀	口 + 牙	什么呀 / 我没有钱呀
41	yè	业 / 業	业	作业 / 工业
42	yǐng	影	景 (日 + 京) + 彡	看电影 / 电影院
43	zhè	这 / 這	文 + 辶	这是 / 这里 / 这儿
44	zuò	做	亻 + 故 (古 + 攵)	做功课 / 做作业 / 做工

Exercise 1 ✍

Copy the following single-component characters with correct stroke order in the spaces provided.

diàn	电	丨 冂 冋 日 电			
gāo	高	丶 一 亠 古 古 宁 高 高 高			
jiè	介	丿 人 介 介			

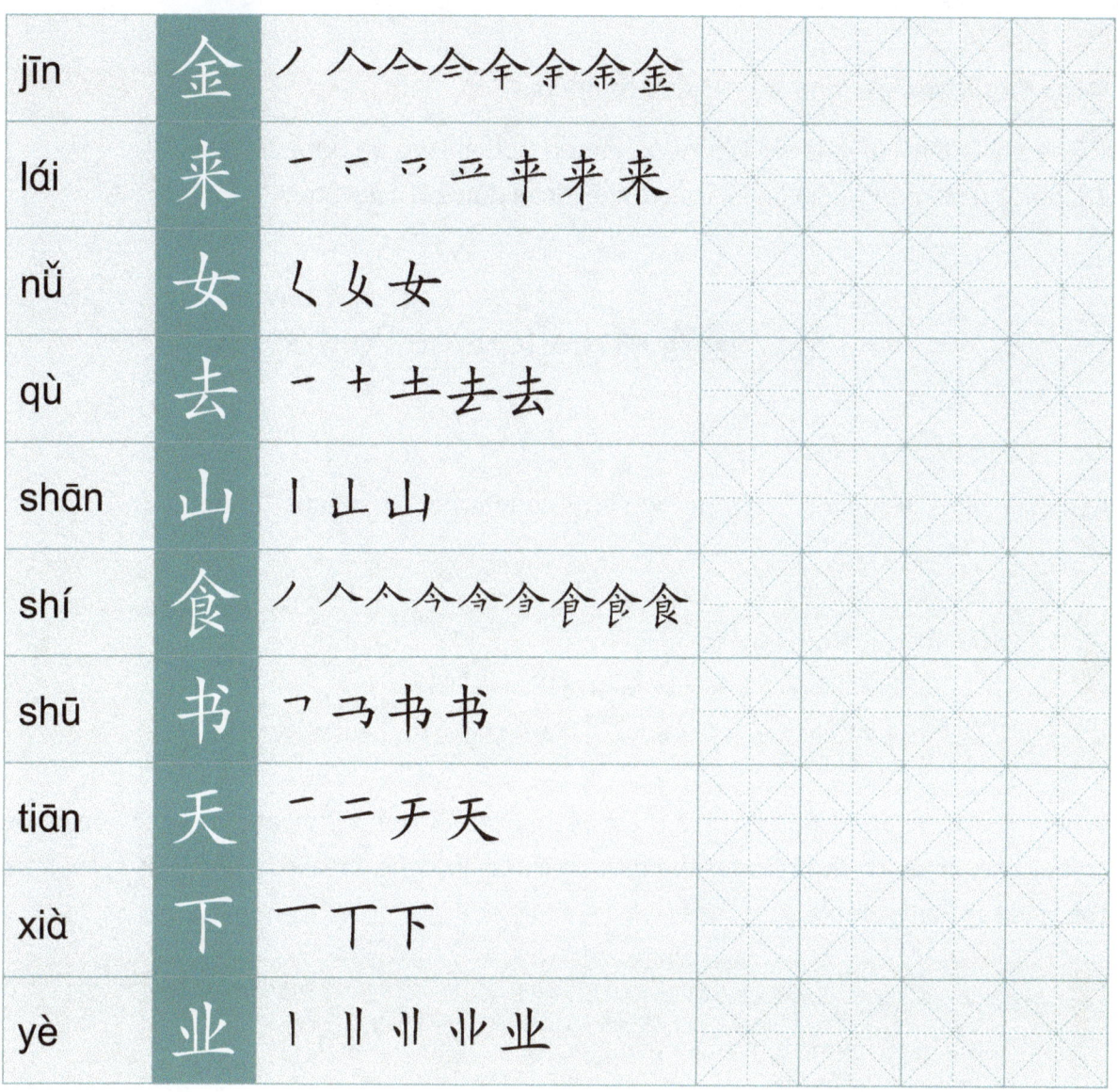

jīn	金	ノ 人 今 今 全 余 金 金		
lái	来	一 〒 〒 亜 平 来 来		
nǚ	女	く 女 女		
qù	去	一 十 土 去 去		
shān	山	丨 山 山		
shí	食	ノ 人 今 今 令 令 食 食 食		
shū	书	⁊ ⁊ 书 书		
tiān	天	一 二 干 天		
xià	下	一 丁 下		
yè	业	丨 ⅡⅠ ⅢⅠ 业 业		

2. Writing Chinese characters with a computer

While it is important to learn how to hand-write Chinese characters, it is even more important to learn how to write Chinese with computers in this Internet Age.

There are many ways to input Chinese characters into a computer. For foreign learners, the pinyin-based method is more practical and convenient since all personal computers, from Windows systems to Apple computers, are equipped with pinyin input methods now. One can easily input Chinese characters as long as the pinyin spelling is correct. After the pinyin is entered, several homonyms will appear. Selecting the right character is a character recognition exercise as well. Starting from this lesson, character-typing exercises will be provided for students to master the Chinese typing skills needed in each lesson.

Type the following characters on your computer.

1. Zhè shì Chén Yǔ, zhè shì Lín Huá, tāmen dōu shì wǒ de hǎopéngyou.

2. Chén Yǔ shì cóng Táiwān lái de, tā de jiārén dōu zài Táiwān.

五、语言点 Language Points

1. The use of 来 and 去

As a main verb, 来 means "to come" while its counterpart 去 means "to go".

> (1) 林华是从台湾来的。
> Lin Hua came from Taiwan.
> (2) "小红,去哪儿啊?""我去图书馆。"
> "Xiaohong, where are you going?" "I am going to the library."

When 来 and 去 are used before a main verb, both of them indicate an intention to do something, in which 来 indicates the motion is towards the speaker while 去 is away from the speaker. For example:

> (3) 来来来,我来介绍一下吧。
> Come here, let me introduce you quickly.
> (4) 你是来看电影的吗?
> Did you come to see a movie?
> (5) 早上我们一起去跑步。
> In the morning, we go jogging together.
> (6) 不跟你多说了。我得去吃午饭。
> I cannot talk with you anymore. I have to go to eat lunch.

2. The measure word for verb: 一下

一下, the measure word for verb, indicates a short duration of an action. It also softens the tone to make the action sound casual. For example:

> (1) 我来介绍一下。 Let me introduce you quickly.
> (2) 我来看一下。Let me take a look.

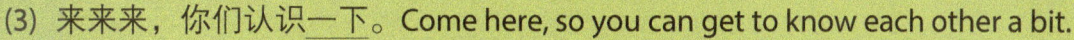

(3) 来来来，你们认识一下。Come here, so you can get to know each other a bit.

3. The question word 谁

The question word 谁 is equivalent to "who" and "whom" in English. Note that in the following two sentences, the question word 谁 comes where the answer comes. This illustrates that Chinese uses the same word order for questions and statements. For example:

(1) "谁是玛丽？""她就是玛丽。"
"Who is Mary?" "She is Mary."

(2) "这位女孩是谁？""她是我的同学玛丽。"
"Who is this girl?" "She is my classmate Mary."

4. The adverbs 常常 and 一起

The adverb 常常 means "often" and 一起 means "together". Like all other adverbs in Chinese, 常常 and 一起 should be put before the verb and never put at the beginning of a sentence. For example:

(1) 他常常回家看他的父母。
He often goes home to see his parents.

(2) 早上我们一起去跑步，晚上一起去吃晚饭。
In the morning, we go running together, and in the evening, we eat dinner together.

(3) 约翰、林华和我常常一起在图书馆做作业。
John, Lin Hua, and I often do homework together in the library.

(4) 玛丽是英文系的学生，我们不常在一起做作业。
Mary is a student in the English Department, so we don't do homework together often.

5. Verbs in series

Similar to English, a Chinese sentence may have two or more verbal expressions in a predicate. Note that usually there is only a main verb in a sentence and other verbal expressions may indicate the purpose, means, or result of the main action. For example:

(1) 你是来看电影的吗？ （看 main verb; 来 indicating the direction of the action）
Did you come to see a movie?

(2) 我来<u>介绍</u>一下吧。（介绍 main verb; 来 indicating the intention）
Let me introduce you quickly.

(3) 晚上我们一起<u>去</u>食堂<u>吃</u>晚饭。（吃 main verb; 去 indicating where the action takes place）
In the evening, we go to the dining hall together to eat dinner.

(4) 他常常<u>回家</u>看他的父母。（看 main verb; 回家 indicating means of the action）
He often goes home to see his parents.

Note that word order is very important in a sentence with verbs in a series. The general rule for word order is to follow the time sequence, that is: the action that happens first will be put first. A change in the word order will cause a change in the meaning of the sentence.

6. The time expression

As a general rule in Chinese, an adverbial time expression should be put before the verb. It can be put before or after the subject. For example:

(1) 我们<u>每天</u>一起上中文课。
We go to Chinese class together every day.

(2) <u>早上</u>我们一起去跑步。
In the morning, we went running together.

(3) <u>晚上</u>我们一起去食堂吃晚饭。
In the evening, we went to the dining hall to have dinner together.

(4) 约翰、林华和我<u>晚上</u>常常一起在图书馆做作业。
In the evening John, Lin Hua and I often go to library together to do homework.

Exercise 1 👂 🗣

Listen to the following short dialogs and answer the questions orally in Chinese.

Dialog 1
1. Who is the girl?
2. Where is she from?

Dialog 2
3. Who is the boy?
4. Where was he born?

Exercise 2 📖 ✎

Read the following sentences and fill in the blanks with the verb 来 or 去.

1. 我是中国人，我是从北京 _____ 的。

2. 我常常 _____ 小华家和他一起做作业。

3. 请问，你是 _____ 看玛丽的吗？她不在。

4. 我的女朋友常常 _____ 食堂吃饭。

5. 我 _____ 介绍一下我的家人。

6. 你的老师是从哪儿 _____ 的?

7. 我和我的室友常常一起 _____ 图书馆学习中文。

8. 小雨，晚上我们 _____ 哪儿看电影?

9. 玛丽的妈妈从英国 _____ 看她。

10. 李文，我 _____ 图书馆看书，你 _____ 吗?

Exercise 3

Choose the correct answer for each of the following sentences.

1. 丽莎，晚上你 _____ 我家和我一起做作业，好吗?

    a. 去   b. 回   c. 来

2. 你是和 _____ 一起看电影的?

    a. 哪儿   b. 谁   c. 哪人

3. 我们每天都一起 _____ 中文系上中文课。

    a. 来   b. 去   c. 去一下

4. 请问，你是从哪国 _____ 的?

    a. 人   b. 出生   c. 来

5. 她们两个 _____ 是江小姐?

    a. 谁   b. 哪   c. 这

6. 我来介绍 _____ ，这是我的女朋友小红。

    a. 她谁   b. 一下   c. 是谁

7. 这是 _____ 的家? 是大卫的家吗?

    a. 哪   b. 哪儿   c. 谁

8. 我去图书馆，你和我一起 _____ 吗?

    a. 那儿   b. 去   c. 来

Exercise 4 ✎

Translate the following sentences into English paying attention to the underlined parts.

1. 我<u>来</u>介绍一下，这是我的男朋友约翰。

_____

2. 你们是<u>来上</u>中文课的吗？

_____

3. 今天晚<u>上</u>我们去哪儿吃晚饭？

_____

4. 我可以<u>问</u> (wèn, to ask) 一<u>下</u>你的名字吗？

_____

5. 她是<u>从英国</u>来的，她的父母都在伦敦。

_____

6. 我和弟弟<u>每天</u>一起去跑步。

_____

7. 小雨，<u>请来</u>一<u>下</u>我家，好吗？

_____

8. 我和室友<u>常常</u>一起去图书馆做作业。

_____

9. 这位女孩是<u>谁</u>？她是你妹妹吗？

_____

10. 我学习很忙。我<u>不常</u>回家看父母。

_____

六、语言运用 Using the Language

Activity 1

**Your friend called you when you were not at home. He left a message on your phone. Listen to the message and answer the following questions.**

1. Why did your friend call you?

2. Who is Xiao Li?

3. What do your friend and Xiao Li often do together?

4. What family members does Xiao Li have? What do they do?

5. What will your friend and Xiao Li do?

Activity 2 📖 ✍

The following is a letter Wang Minghua's mother wrote to him. Read the handwritten letter and sum up the information about the person described here.

明华我儿：

近来好吧？今天写信是想给你介绍一个女朋友。她叫江丽丽，北京人。她今年28岁，身高1.62米，是小学老师。她人很好，常常来看我。她爸爸也是老师，妈妈是工程师。她还有一个妹妹，在北京上大学。我很喜欢丽丽。你下个周末回家的时候，我想介绍你们认识一下。

妈妈
十六日

Name	
Age	
Height	
Occupation	
Hometown	
Father	
Mother	
Siblings	

Activity 3 👂 🗣

Listen to a conversation and answer the following questions.

1. What is the occasion of this conversation?
2. Who is the man?
3. Who is Meili?
4. What does the man often do in the evening?
5. Why did the man never meet Meili?
6. What have they agreed to do together?

Activity 4

Role Play

Work in group of three. One student plays the role of Xiao Wang, who is your classmate. Another student plays the role of Xiao Liu, who is your girlfriend/boyfriend. Your girlfriend/boyfriend is a student of the English Department. You and your girlfriend/boyfriend run into Xiao Wang at the movie theater. Introduce your classmate Xiao Wang to your girlfriend/boyfriend.

Activity 5

Write a dialog in characters to describe the following pictures. Be creative about the identities of the people and their relationships. Type it out on your computer and act it out with your classmates.

Activity 6

What do you say?

1. You want to ask if somebody is coming here to watch the movie.
2. You want to introduce your friend to a guest.
3. You are introduced to a new friend.
4. You want to report the birthplace of your friend.
5. You wonder if a person is your friend's boyfriend or girlfriend.
6. You want to say you often do things together with your friend.

第六课　日期
Lesson Six　**Dates**

一、导入 Lead-in

Exercise 1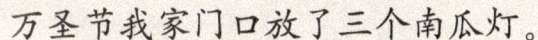

Look at the pictures below and talk about what you see in Chinese.

万圣节我家门口放了三个南瓜灯。

我们都有万圣节的面具。

十月二十七日是星期几？

After learning this lesson, you will be able to:

1. Ask and tell about the days and dates, and activities related to Halloween.
2. Pronounce the final "er" and the retroflex ending "-r" correctly.
3. Recognize the new characters in this lesson, and know how to consult a Chinese dictionary.
4. Use the aspectual particle 了, the adverb 没 (有), and the verb complements 完 and 在.

二、课文 Texts

课文（一）Text (1)

今天几号？

Xiaohua suddenly remembered something after she checked the date with John.

小华：约翰，今天几号？

Tips: how to ask about the date

约翰：我来看一下日历。

Tips: how to tell the date and day of the week

今天是十月二十九日，星期一。

小华：糟糕！后天就是万圣节，可我还没买我的面具呢！

约翰：没关系，你可以今天去买。

小华：约翰，今天晚上你能和我一块儿去买吗？

约翰：对不起，今晚不行，我还没做完我的作业呢。明天放学以后我们一起去，好吗？

小华：也行。那放学以后我去找你。

今天幾號？

Xiaohua suddenly remembered something after she checked the date with John.

小華：约翰，今天幾號？

约翰：我來看一下日歷。今天是十月二十九日，星期一。

小華：糟糕！後天就是萬聖節，可我還沒買我的面具呢！

約翰：沒關系，你可以今天去買。

小華：約翰，今天晚上你能和我一塊兒去買嗎？

約翰：對不起，今晚不行，我還沒做完我的作業呢。明天放學以後我們一起去，好嗎？

小華：也行。那放學以後我去找你。

Kèwén (yī) *Text (1)*

Jīntiān Jǐ Hào?

拼音版

Xiaohua suddenly remembered something after she checked the date with John.

Xiǎohuá: Yuēhàn, jīntiān jǐ hào?

Yuēhàn: Wǒ lái kàn yíxià rìlì. Jīntiān shì shí yuè èrshíjiǔ rì, Xīngqīyī.

Xiǎohuá: Zāogāo! Hòutiān jiù shì Wànshèngjié, kě wǒ hái méi mǎi wǒ de miànjù ne!

Yuēhàn: Méi guānxi, nǐ kěyǐ jīntiān qù mǎi.

Xiǎohuá: Yuēhàn, jīntiān wǎnshang nǐ néng hé wǒ yíkuàir qù mǎi ma?

Yuēhàn: Duìbuqǐ, jīnwǎn bù xíng, wǒ hái méi zuòwán wǒ de zuòyè ne. Míngtiān fàngxué yǐhòu wǒmen yìqǐ qù, hǎo ma?

Xiǎohuá: Yě xíng. Nà fàngxué yǐhòu wǒ qù zhǎo nǐ.

生词（一）*New Words (1)*

	简体（繁體）	拼音	词性	解释
1	今天	jīntiān	*n.*	today 今天几号了？/今天我不上学。
2	号（號）	hào	*n.*	date in a month 今天是三十号。

	简体（繁體）	拼音	词性	解释
3	日历（曆）	rìlì	n.	calendar 你有中文的日历吗?
4	月	yuè	n.	month 五月四号 / 六月一号 / 十月一号
5	日	rì	n.	day, date 一月一日
6	星期	xīngqī	n.	week 星期一 / 星期二
7	糟糕	zāogāo	adj.	too bad; terrible 糟糕! 我没做作业!
8	就	jiù	adv.	(adverb used to indicate emphasis) 后天就是万圣节了。
9	可	kě	conj.	but 后天就是万圣节，可我还没买面具呢!
10	买（買）	mǎi	v.	buy 买书 / 买课本 / 买东西
11	面具	miànjù	n.	mask 万圣节的面具哪儿有卖?
12	没关系（關係）	méi guānxi		It does not matter/It's OK. "对不起!" "没关系!"
13	可以	kěyǐ	a.v.	may, might 我今天可以去买面具。
14	能	néng	a.v.	can, may; capable of 你能和我一块儿去买面具吗?
15	一块儿（塊兒）	yíkuàir	adv.	together 我们一块儿去吧。
16	对（對）不起	duìbùqǐ		sorry; excuse me 对不起，请问你是小王吗? / 对不起，我不能和你去。
17	行	xíng	v.	OK, alright 行，我们一起做作业。
18	完	wán	v.	come to an end 电影完了。/ 我吃完饭了。/ 你做完作业了吗?
19	明天	míngtiān	n.	tomorrow 明天我们去看电影。/ 明天我们有考试。
20	放学（學）	fàngxué	v.	dismiss school 放学以后我们一起做作业。
21	以后（後）	yǐhòu	n.	after 晚饭以后我学中文。/ 放学以后我们一起做作业。
22	找	zhǎo	v.	look for; go to (someone) 我找我的面具。/ 放学以后我去找你。

专有名词 Proper Nouns			
1	万圣节（萬聖節）	Wànshèngjié	*pn.*	Halloween
2	小华（華）	Xiǎohuá	*pn.*	Xiaohua, a Chinese name

Exercise 1 👂

Listen to Text (1) and choose the correct answer for each of the following questions.

1. How can John tell the date?

    a. He keeps a diary.

    b. He has a calendar.

    c. He asked Xiaohua.

2. Why is Xiaohua worried?

    a. She missed a date.

    b. She handed in the wrong homework.

    c. She forgot to buy something.

3. What is John unable to do?

    a. Finish Xiaohua's homework.

    b. Accompany Xiaohua this evening.

    c. Buy Xiaohua the thing she needs.

4. How will Xiaohua's problem be solved?

    a. John will go with Xiaohua tomorrow.

    b. John will bring the thing Xiaohua needs.

    c. John will go help Xiaohua with her homework.

Exercise 2 📖 🗣

Read Text (1) and answer the questions orally in Chinese.

1. What day is Oct. 29th?

2. What date is Xiaohua concerned with and why?

3. Why cann't John fulfill Xiaohua's initial request?

4. What will the two do after school tomorrow?

Exercise 3 ✒

Translate the following Chinese phrases into English.

1. 看看日历　　_____

2. 真糟糕　　　_____

3. 万圣节面具　_____

4. 没关系　　　_____

5. 今天不行　　_____

6. 做作业　　　_____

Exercise 4 👂 🗣

Respond orally to the questions you hear in Chinese.

课文（二）Text (2)

万圣节

简体版

This is what David wrote as his weekly journal assignment for his Chinese class.

我这个星期很忙。星期一到星期五，我每天上下午都有课，晚上还要做很多作业。不过，这个星期也有高兴的事。星期五下午放学以后，我和妈妈去商店买万圣节的东西。我们买了很多糖，还买了一个很大的南瓜，做了一个南瓜灯，放在家门口。今年的万圣节，我要留在家里，给来要糖的孩子们发糖。

Tips: tell about activities related to Halloween

萬聖節

繁体版

This is what David wrote as his weekly journal assignment for his Chinese class.

我這個星期很忙。星期一到星期五，我每天上下午都有課，晚上還要做很多作業。不過，這個星期也有高興的事。星期五下午放學以後，我和媽媽去商店買萬聖節的東西。我們買了很多糖，還買了一個很大的南瓜，做了一個南瓜燈，放在家門口。今年的萬聖節，我要留在家裏，給來要糖的孩子們發糖。

Kèwén (èr) *Text (2)*

Wànshèngjié

拼音版

This is what David wrote as his weekly journal assignment for his Chinese class.

Wǒ zhège xīngqī hěn máng. Xīngqīyī dào xīngqīwǔ, wǒ měi tiān shàng-xiàwǔ dōu yǒu kè, wǎnshang hái yào zuò hěn duō zuòyè. Búguò, zhège xīngqī yě yǒu gāoxìng de shì. Xīngqīwǔ xiàwǔ fàngxué yǐhòu, wǒ hé māma qù shāngdiàn mǎi Wànshèngjié de dōngxi. Wǒmen mǎile hěn duō táng, hái mǎile yí gè hěn dà de nánguā, zuòle yí gè nánguādēng, fàng zài jiā ménkǒu. Jīnnián de Wànshèngjié, wǒ yào liú zài jiā li, gěi lái yào táng de háizimen fā táng.

生词（二）New Words (2)

	简体（繁體）	拼音	词性	解释
1	到	dào	*prep.*	to 星期一到星期三
2	下午	xiàwǔ	*n.*	afternoon 今天下午我去图书馆。

	简体（繁體）	拼音	词性	解释
3	要	yào	a.v.	want to; need to 晚上我要做作业，还要复习。
4	多	duō	adj.	many, much 我们的作业很多。
5	不过（過）	búguò	conj.	but, however 他没有哥哥，不过他有两个姐姐。
6	事	shì	n.	matter, thing 做事 / 办事 / 一件高兴的事 / 什么事？
7	商店	shāngdiàn	n.	store, shop 去商店买东西 / 在商店买东西
8	东（東）西	dōngxi	n.	thing, stuff 那里有很多东西。
9	糖	táng	n.	sugar, sweets, candy 吃糖 / 糖果
10	南瓜灯（燈）	nánguādēng	n.	jack-o-lantern 你会做南瓜灯吗？
11	放	fàng	v.	put, place 我的书放在宿舍了。
12	门（門）口	ménkǒu	n.	doorway 门口有个南瓜灯。
13	留	liú	v.	stay, remain 我不要留在家里。
14	里	lǐ	n.	inside 在家里 / 在宿舍里
15	给（給）	gěi	prep.	to 给他介绍一个朋友
16	要	yào	v.	want, ask 孩子们要了很多糖。 / 弟弟要一个面具。
17	孩子	háizi	n.	child 你有几个孩子？
18	发（發）	fā	v.	give, issue 给小孩子发糖

Exercise 5 🎧

Listen to Text (2) and decide whether the following statements are true or false.

1. David has classes in the mornings and evenings.	( )
2. David is busy, especially this week because of his school work.	( )
3. Now it is late autumn.	( )
4. David's mother bought a ready-made decorative object.	( )
5. David will go out to have fun on the festival day.	( )

Exercise 6 📖🗣

Read Text (2) and answer the questions in Chinese orally.

1. Is David free in the evenings after school? Why?

2. What was David's most pleasant experience this week?

3. What festival is mentioned? What do people usually do for this festival?

4. What is David's plan for the festival?

Exercise 7 📖

Match the verbs in Column I with the nouns in Column II according to Text (2).

Column I	Column II
(　　) 1. 做	a. 糖
(　　) 2. 去	b. 南瓜灯
(　　) 3. 发	c. 商店
(　　) 4. 留在	d. 家里

Exercise 8 👂✏

Listen to a passage with partial text below and fill in the blanks in pinyin with tone marks.

　　我每天都 ＿＿＿＿＿＿。上午上三节课，下午上三节课。晚上 ＿＿＿＿＿＿。万圣节快到了。今天放学后我要和朋友去买 ＿＿＿＿＿＿。我还要买很多糖，发给要糖的 ＿＿＿＿＿＿。我还要做一个 ＿＿＿＿＿＿。孩子们一定很 ＿＿＿＿＿＿。

三、语音 Phonetics

1. The final "er"

From the Chart of Combination of Initials and Finals, we know that the final "er" always forms a syllable by itself without combining with any initial. Here are some examples:

> nǚ'ér 女儿 (daughter)　　　érzi 儿子 (son)　　　ěrduo 耳朵 (ear)

2. The retroflex ending "-r"

Sometimes the final "er" is attached to another final and becomes the retroflex ending "-r". The retroflex ending "-r" is the only nonsyllabic suffix in Mandarin Chinese. It merges with the syllable preceding it to form a new syllable ending in the retroflex sound. For example: kòng + ér → kòngr "空儿" (free time). In actual writing, the character 儿 is added to the character preceding it. Here are more examples of syllables with the retroflex ending "-r":

> nǎr "哪儿" (where)　　wánr "玩儿" (to play)　　huàr "画儿" (picture)
> shìr "事儿" (thing)　　yìdiǎnr "一点儿" (a little bit)

Exercise 1 📖

Read the following classroom expressions aloud.

Jīntiān de zuòyè míngtiān zǎoshang jiāo. 今天的作业明天早上交。	Today's homework should be handed in tomorrow morning.
Qǐng tóngxuémen fùxí yíxià kèwén. 请同学们复习一下课文。	Please review the texts.
Míngtiān bié wàngle dài tīnglì kèběn. 明天别忘了带听力课本。	Don't forget to bring your listening textbooks tomorrow.
Zhège zì shéi huì xiě? 这个字谁会写？	Who knows how to write this character?

Exercise 2 📖

Read the following sounds with correct tones.

jī	jí	jǐ	jì
hāo	háo	hǎo	hào
			rì
	lí	lǐ	lì
zāo	záo	zǎo	zào
gāo		gǎo	gào
jiū		jiǔ	jiù
yāo	yáo	yǎo	yào
fāng	fáng	fǎng	fàng
zhū	zhú	zhǔ	zhù
fū	fú	fǔ	fù

xī	xí	xǐ	xì
	máng	mǎng	
xīng	xíng	xǐng	xìng
	nán	nǎn	nàn

Exercise 3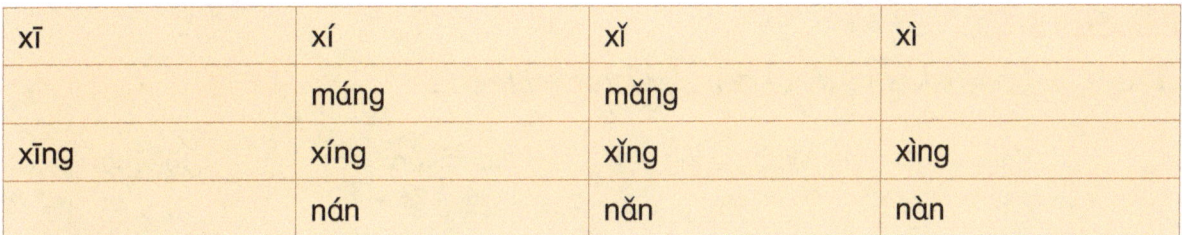

Read the following combination of tones.

xīngqī 星期 week	hē chá 喝茶 drink tea	jīnwǎn 今晚 tonight	bāngzhù 帮助 to help
míngtiān 明天 tomorrow	méi wán 没完 not finished	nín hǎo 您好 How are you?	búguò 不过 however
Běijīng 北京 Beijing	běnrén 本人 self	xǐzǎo 洗澡 to bathe	kǎoshì 考试 test
bàngbīng 棒冰 popsicle	shùlín 树林 woods	xiàwǔ 下午 afternoon	rìlì 日历 calendar

Exercise 4

Read aloud the following words paying attention to the retroflex ending "-r".

qìshuǐr 汽水儿 soda	bīnggùnr 冰棍儿 popsicle	xiǎoháir 小孩儿 kid	yàofāngr 药方儿 prescription
yíkuàir 一块儿 together	huàhuàr 画画儿 paint a picture	dàhuǒr 大伙儿 everybody	chàdiǎnr 差点儿 almost
guāzǐr 瓜子儿 melon seed	jìn ménr 进门儿 enter the door	xiǎoqǔr 小曲儿 folk music piece	kèběnr 课本儿 textbook
lǎotóur 老头儿 old man	shuǎ hóur 耍猴儿 monkey show	zìgěr 自个儿 self	méizhǔnr 没准儿 probably
yārlí 鸭儿梨 pear	yérliǎng 爷儿俩 father and son	míngrgè 明儿个 tomorrow	xiànrbǐng 馅儿饼 meat pie

Exercise 5 📖

Read aloud the following three-syllable words or phrases.

xiǎotíqín 小提琴 violin	Wángfǔjǐng 王府井 Wangfujing	jiàshǐyuán 驾驶员 driver	pūkèpái 扑克牌 poker
yòu'éryuán 幼儿园 kindergarten	sīlìngbù 司令部 headquarters	wěiyuánhuì 委员会 committee	jīguānqiāng 机关枪 machinegun
tíkuǎnjī 提款机 ATM	qìguǎnyán 气管炎 chronic bronchitis	zìxíngchē 自行车 bicycle	liánhuānhuì 联欢会 party

Exercise 6 📖

Read the following Beijing children's folk rhyme.

xiǎo xiǎozir, zuò méndūnr, kūzhe hǎnzhe yào xífùr. Yào xífùr gàn má ya? Diǎn dēng shuōhuàr, xī dēng zuòbànr, míngr zǎochen qǐlái shū xiǎobiànr.

小小子儿，坐门墩儿，哭着喊着要媳妇儿。要媳妇儿干嘛呀？点灯说话儿，熄灯做伴儿，明儿早晨起来梳小辫儿。

A little boy sat at the door and cried for a wife. What does he need a wife for? He needs a wife to talk to and to be his companion. He needs a wife so that he can braid her pigtails.

四、汉字 Chinese Characters

1. New characters in this lesson

序号	拼音	简 / 繁	部件	构词
1	dào	到	至 + 刂	七点到九点 / 到来 / 我到了
2	dēng	灯 / 燈	火 + 丁	南瓜灯 / 电灯
3	diàn	店	广 + 占	商店 / 旅店 / 饭店
4	dōng	东 / 東	东	东西 / 东面 / 东方 / 东京
5	duì	对 / 對	又 + 寸	对了 / 不对

6	fā	发 / 發	发	发糖 / 发生 / 发明
7	fàng	放	方 + 攵	放下 / 放在家里 / 放学
8	gāo	糕	米 + 羔（羊 + 灬）	糟糕 / 年糕 / 糕点
9	gěi	给 / 給	纟 + 合	给孩子发糖 / 给钱 / 给你
10	guā	瓜	瓜	南瓜 / 西瓜 / 瓜果
11	guān	关 / 關	丷 + 天	关系 / 开关 / 关门
12	guò	过 / 過	寸 + 辶	不过 / 过去 / 过来
13	hào	号 / 號	口 + 丂	三十号 / 号码
14	hòu	后 / 後	后	后天 / 晚饭以后 / 后来
15	jì	记 / 記	讠 + 己	日记 / 周记
16	jié	节 / 節	艹 + 卩	万圣节 / 节日 / 过节
17	jiù	就	京 + 尤	五点就起床 / 吃完饭就去
18	jù	具	具	面具 / 家具 / 工具
19	kě	可	可	可是 / 可以
20	kuài	块 / 塊	土 + 夬	一块儿 / 几块钱
21	lǐ	里 / 裡	里	在家里 / 在宿舍里
22	lì	历 / 曆	厂 + 力	日历 / 月历 / 年历
23	liú	留	卯 + 田	留在家里 / 留言 / 留下
24	mǎi	买 / 買	乛 + 头	买书 / 买课本 / 买东西
25	mén	门 / 門	门	门口 / 大门 / 门外
26	miàn	面	面	面具 / 外面 / 里面
27	míng	明	日 + 月	明天 / 明年 / 明亮
28	nán	南	冂 + 羊	南瓜灯 / 南方 / 南面
29	néng	能	厶 + 月 + 匕 + 匕	能不能 / 可能
30	qī	期	其 + 月	星期一 / 日期 / 过期
31	rì	日	日	一月一日 / 日月 / 日期
32	shāng	商	亠 + 八 + 口	商店 / 商场 / 商业
33	shèng	圣 / 聖	又 + 土	万圣节 / 圣诞节
34	shì	事	事	高兴的事 / 急事 / 没事

35	táng	糖	米 + 唐	发糖 / 买糖 / 巧克力糖
36	wán	完	宀 + 元（二 + 儿）	完了 / 吃完饭 / 做完作业
37	wàn	万 / 萬	万	万圣节 / 千万 / 一万元
38	wǔ	午	午	中午 / 下午 / 午饭
39	xī	西	西	东西 / 西方 / 西边
40	xīng	星	日 + 生	星期 / 星星
41	yào	要	西 + 女	要做作业 / 要复习 / 要不要
42	yǐ	以	𠄌 + 人	以后 / 以前 / 可以 / 不可以
43	yuè	月	月	五月 / 十月 / 日月 / 月亮
44	zāo	糟	米 + 曹	糟糕 / 糟了
45	zhǎo	找	扌 + 戈	找你 / 找钱 / 找资料
46	zhōu	周 / 週	冂 + 土 + 口	周记 / 周末 / 下周三考试
47	zi	子	子	孩子 / 裤子 / 筷子 / 样子

Exercise 1

Copy the following single-component characters with correct stroke order in the spaces provided.

dōng	东	一 𠂇 车 东 东					
fā	发	𠂉 ナ 方 发 发					
guā	瓜	㇒ 厂 兀 瓜 瓜					
hòu	后	㇒ 厂 𠂆 斤 后 后					
lǐ	里	丨 冂 冃 日 旦 甲 里					
mén	门	丶 丨 门					

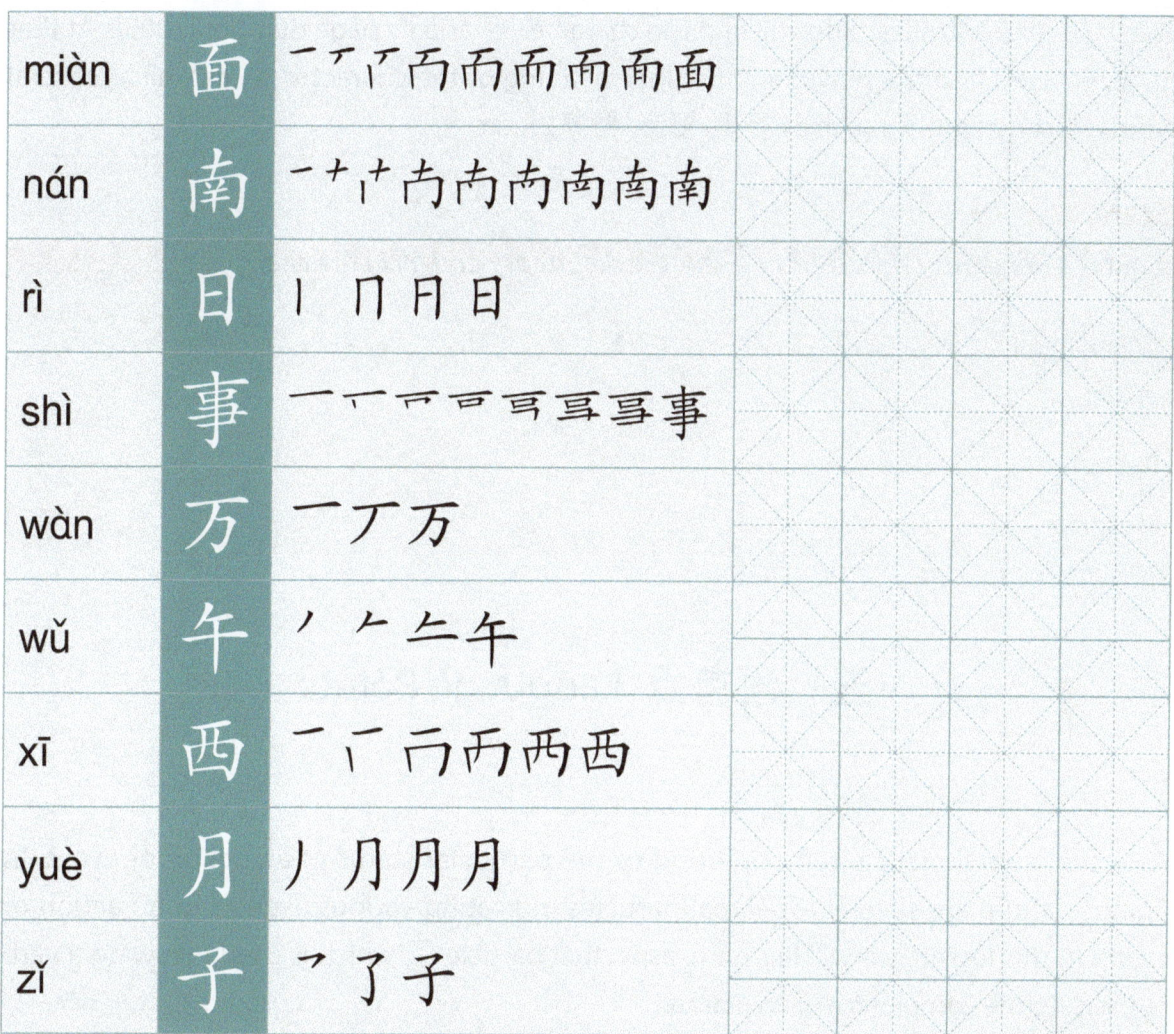

miàn	面	一 ナ 兀 而 而 而 面 面
nán	南	一 ナ 汁 内 内 两 南 南
rì	日	丨 冂 冃 日
shì	事	一 一 戸 戸 写 写 写 事
wàn	万	一 丁 万
wǔ	午	丿 ㇒ 仁 午
xī	西	一 一 厂 两 两 西
yuè	月	丿 刀 月 月
zǐ	子	㇇ 了 子

2. How to consult a Chinese dictionary

Traditional Chinese dictionaries arrange characters first under the radicals (indexing components), and then by stroke count. In order to look up a character in a traditional dictionary, one has to first locate the radical of the character in the Radical Index（部首目录）, and then count the number of strokes of the rest of the character to find it within its group（部）. Knowledge about the Chinese radical system will definitely save you much trouble in this time comsuming process.

For instance, to find the character 娶 in the *Chinese-English Dictionary* (Revised Edition, 2002, Beijing), first you need to determine that the bottom part of the character 女, is the radical. Count the number of strokes in radical 女: it has three strokes. You will find the radical 女 and its sequence number (65) in the Radical Index（部首目录）under 三 画 (three strokes). Then use the sequence number to locate the page number (32) for radical 女 in the Index of Characters（检字表）. Count the stroke number of the rest part 取, excluding the radical 女. You get eight counts. Finally, in the Index of Characters, under the radical 女

and 八画 (eight strokes), you will find the character 娶 and its page number (1005). At that page, you will find the pinyin and English meaning of the character 娶, as well as several words starting with 娶, such as 娶妻, 娶亲, 娶媳妇, etc.

Exercise 2 ✍

Find the following characters in a Chinese dictionary and fill in the chart.

Character	迟	时	街	刻	始	睡	忘
Pinyin							
Radical							
Meaning							

五、语言点 Language Points

1. The aspectual particle 了

Aspect is a grammatical term referring to the particular status of an action or event. In Chinese, there are several aspectual particles indicating various aspects of an action or event. In this lesson, we will learn the aspectual particle 了, which is used following a verb to indicate the completion of an action.

> **Subject + Verb + 了 + Object**

> (1) 我们买了很多糖。
> We bought a lot of candy.
>
> (2) 我们还买了一个很大的南瓜，做了一个南瓜灯，放在家门口。
> We also bought a big pumpkin, made a jack-o-lantern, and put it in front of our house.

Unlike the past tense marker "-ed" in English, the aspectual particle 了 can be used for future actions.

> (3) 明天放学以后，我们买了糖再回家。
> After school tomorrow, we will buy some candy before we go home.

To form a question with the aspectual particle 了, we can simply add the question marker 吗 to the end of the sentence.

> **Subject + Verb + 了 + Object + 吗？**

> Example: 他们买了很多糖。→ 他们买了很多糖吗？
>
> They bought a lot of candy. → Did they buy a lot of candy?

2. The negative adverb 没（有）

In Lesson 4, we learned the verb 没（有）("do not have" or "there is/are not"). Note that a noun is followed by the verb 没（有）. For example:

> 我有一个弟弟，我没（有）哥哥。
>
> I have a younger brother. I do not have an elder brother.

In this lesson, we will learn about the negative adverb 没（有）, which is used before a verb to indicate that an action "didn't" take place. 有 is optional here, and the aspectual particle 了 should not be used.

> **Subject + 没（有）+ Verb + Object**

> (1) 后天就是万圣节，可我还没（有）买我的面具呢！
>
> The day after tomorrow is Halloween, but I still have not bought the Halloween costumes yet.
>
> (2) 今晚不行，我还没（有）做完我的作业呢！
>
> It won't work tonight. I haven't finished my homework yet.

Same as the verb 没（有）, the negative adverb 没（有）can also be used to form affirmative-negative questions. The simplest way is to add an affirmative-negative phrase 有没有 before a verb:

> **Subject + 有没有 + Verb + Object？**

> Example: 我们买了很多糖。→ 你们有没有买很多糖?
>
> We bought a lot of candy. → Did you buy a lot of candy?

Another way to form an affirmative-negative questions is to add 没有 to the end of an affirmative sentence:

Subject ＋ Verb ＋ 了 ＋ Object ＋ 没有？

> Example: 我们买了很多糖。→ 你们买了很多糖没有?
>
> We bought a lot of candy. → Did you buy a lot of candy?

3. The verb complements: 完 and 在

In Chinese, a monosyllabic verb may become a compound verb by adding another verb or adjective to it. The first syllable of the compound verb indicates the action itself while the second one, which is called a verb complement, provides extra information such as the result or the description of the action. In this lesson, we will learn 完 and 在 as a verb complement to indicate the result of the action.

Verb ＋ 完 (finish) → Verb Complement Compound ＋ (Object)

做 ＋ 完 → 做完 (do something and finish)
吃 ＋ 完 → 吃完 (eat and finish)
说 ＋ 完 → 说完 (say something and finish)

(1) 对不起，今晚不行，我还没做完我的作业呢。
Sorry, it won't work tonight. I haven't finished my homework yet.

(2) 吃完晚饭以后，我可以跟你一起去。
I may go with you after I finish eating my dinner.

(3) 对不起，我还没说完呢!
Sorry, I haven't finished (my speech) yet.

Verb ＋ 在 (be in, at, on) → Verb Complement Compound＋ (Object)

飞跃——汉语初级教程学生用书　上册

放 + 在 → 放在 (put something in a place)

留 + 在 → 留在 (stay in a place)

生 + 在 → 生在 (born in a place)

(1) 我们还买了一个很大的南瓜，做了一个南瓜灯，<u>放在</u>家门口。

We also bought a big pumpkin, made a jack-o-lantern, and put it in front of our house.

(2) 今年的万圣节，我要<u>留在</u>家里，给来要糖的孩子们发糖。

This Halloween, I want to stay at home and give candy to the trick-or-treaters.

(3) 他<u>生在</u>美国，可是父母都是中国人。

He was born in the U.S., but his parents are Chinese.

4. Months, dates, and days in Chinese

The Chinese language has a unique way to state months, dates, and days.

Jan.	Feb.	Mar.	Apr.	May	June	July	Aug.	Sept.	Oct.	Nov.	Dec.
一月	二月	三月	四月	五月	六月	七月	八月	九月	十月	十一月	十二月
yīyuè	èryuè	sānyuè	sìyuè	wǔ-yuè	liù-yuè	qī-yuè	bā-yuè	jiǔ-yuè	shí-yuè	shíyī-yuè	shí'èr-yuè

Monday	Tuesday	Wednesday	Thursday	Friday	Saturday	Sunday
星期一	星期二	星期三	星期四	星期五	星期六	星期日 / 星期天
Xīngqīyī	Xīngqī'èr	Xīngqīsān	Xīngqīsì	Xīngqīwǔ	Xīngqīliù	Xīngqīrì / Xīngqītiān

To say dates in Chinese, we just add 年, 月, 日 to a cardinal number. Note that in Chinese, we often state big things first. So, the word order in saying a certain date is year, month, and date. For example:

二〇一二年十月二十九日，星期一：Monday, 29th October 2012.

〇二年二月十二号，星期二 : Tuesday, February 12th, 2002.

九八年十月四号，星期天：Sunday, 4th October 1998.

5. The use of 要

要 can serve as a main verb meaning "ask for". For example:

(1) 今年万圣节的时候，很多孩子们来我家要糖。

On Halloween this year, many children came to my house asking for candy.

(2) "你要什么？" "我要糖，不要面具。"

"What do you want?" "I want candy, not a costume."

要 can also be used as an auxiliary verb, meaning "want to do something". For example:

(3) 今年的万圣节，我要留在家里，给来要糖的孩子们发糖。

This Halloween, I want to stay home and give candy to the trick-or-treaters.

(4) 后天就是万圣节，我要和妈妈去商店买万圣节的东西。

The day after tomorrow is Halloween. I want to go with my mom to buy things for Halloween.

6. The time word 以后

The time word 以后 means "after". It follows other time or action words to form time expressions. Note that the word order to form a Chinese time expression is different from its counterpart in English.

a. Action words + 以后： 放学以后—after school

下课以后—after class

回家以后—after coming home

吃晚饭以后—after having dinner

b. Time words + 以后： 晚饭以后—after dinner

星期三以后—after Wednesday

万圣节以后—after Halloween

Exercise 1

Listen to the short dialogs and answer the questions in Chinese characters or pinyin with tone marks.

Dialog 1 Questions: 今天是几月几号？ 星期几？	Answer:
Dialog 2 Questions: 玛丽是哪年哪月哪日出生的？ 她是在哪儿出生的？	Answer:

飞跃——汉语初级教程学生用书 上册

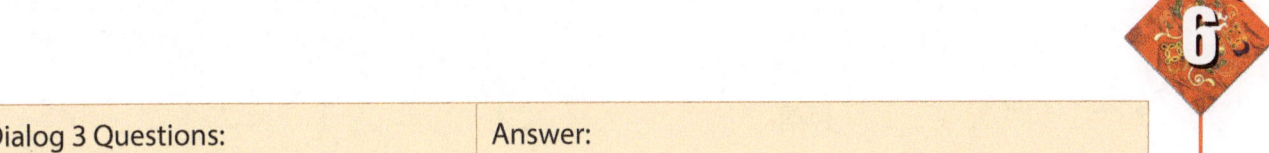

Dialog 3 Questions:	Answer:
吃完晚饭以后大卫要做什么？ 他家的南瓜灯放在哪儿？	

Exercise 2

Translate the following phrases into Chinese using the word 以后.

1. after school _____

2. after running _____

3. after Wednesday _____

4. after October 11th _____

5. after making the pumpkin lamp _____

6. after finishing my homework _____

Exercise 3

Complete the following dialogs by using 了 to indicate completion of an action.

1. A：放学以后你和妈妈去商店买了什么？

　　B：_____。(a big pumpkin)

2. A：你们今天上了什么课？

　　B：_____。(Chinese and English)

3. A：今晚你在图书馆做了什么作业？

　　B：_____。(Chinese course)

4. A：昨天你看了一个什么电影？

　　B：_____。(a film about Halloween)

Exercise 4

Change the following sentences first into affirmative-negative questions with 有没有 . Then give them negative answers with 没（有）+ Verb + Object.

Example:　小丽吃了早餐。

　　　　　小丽有没有吃早餐？　小丽没（有）吃早餐。

1. 大卫在商店买了很多糖。

_____ ? _____ 。

2. 约翰放学后去了小华家。

_____ ? _____ 。

3. 大卫和约翰买了面具和糖。

_____ ? _____ 。

4. 他们十月三十号回到了老家。

_____ ? _____ 。

Exercise 5

Translate the following sentences into English paying attention to the different usages of the word 要.

1. 大卫要了一个大南瓜，我要了很多糖。

_____

2. 这个星期六我要回家看看父母。

_____

3. 约翰要了三本日历和六本书。

_____

4. 今天晚上我要去看电影，你要和我一起去吗？

_____

六、语言运用 Using the Language

Activity 1

Look at this calendar and ask each other what month it is and what day a certain date is.

Activity 2 🗣

In addition to the Gregorian calendar, the Chinese also have a lunar calendar, the dates of which do not match those of the Gregorian calendar. In China, calendars show both Chinese and Western dates. The Chinese also have special names for each month of the year, but the most commonly known is for the first month 正月 (zhēngyuè), and the twelfth month 腊月 (làyuè). The Chinese also have special characters for 20 and 30: 廿 (niàn) and 卅 (sà). For the first ten days in the lunar calendar, the Chinese put 初 (chū) before the number.

Have a conversion discussing the differences between Chinese dates and Western dates using the following calendar pages.

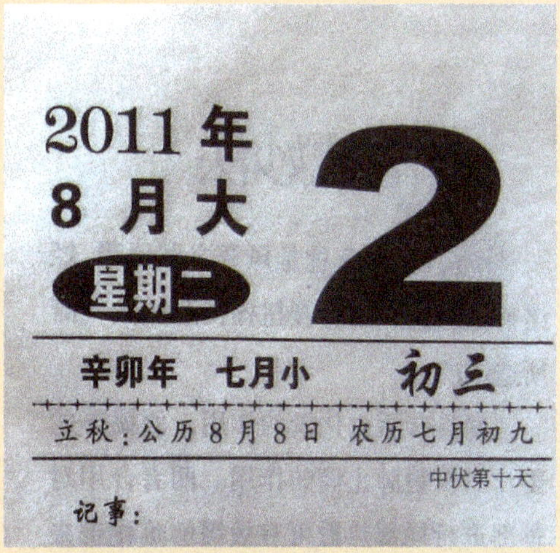

Lunar calendar: 七月初三

Lunar calendar: 正月二十日

Lunar calendar: 十二月初九

Lunar calendar: 十二月十二

Activity 3 🎧 🗣️

Listen to a conversation between two teachers, Zhang and Li, and answer the following questions.

New words:

考试 kǎoshì, test; take a test

讲 jiǎng, to explain; to tell

1. What are they talking about?
2. When will this be arranged?
3. When will they explain it to students?
4. What season of the year is it now?

Activity 4 📖 🗣️

Read the following passage with the help of the glossary and give a brief summary of its contents in English.

New words:

平均 píngjūn, on average

周 zhōu, week, cycle

　　日历里，一年是三百六十五天，有十二个月，五十二个星期。一个月三十天或三十一天（二月二十八天或二十九天），一个星期七天。星期也叫"周"。星期一也可以叫做"周一"，星期二可以叫做"周二"。星期的第七天不叫"星期七"，叫"星期日"，也叫"周日"。

Activity 5 📖 🗣️

Read the following notice about a Chinese school and answer the questions.

中文学校通知

　　因为这个周末是节日长周末，很多父母说要带孩子外出，不能来上课。中文学校决定，本周末不上课。下周末上课时间不变。上个周末的作业，请父母们看一看。

中文学校通知

　　因为这个周末是节日长周末，很多父母说要带孩子外出，不能来上课。中文学校决定，本周末不上课。下周末上课时间不变。上个周末的作业，请父母们看一看。

Questions:

1. What did some parents say about this weekend?

2. What has the school decided?

3. What is mentioned about the following weekend?

4. What is said about homework?

Activity 6 ✎

Xiao Zhang likes to use the calendar to plan his daily activities. Write a few sentences in pinyin with tone marks and/or characters about his schedule.

Example: 小张星期日上午 9 点去商店。

	1 月 8 日星期日	1 月 9 日星期一	1 月 10 日星期二	1 月 11 日星期三
8 am		上课	复习	上课
9 am	去商店			
10 am				
11 am			考试	
12 pm	去饭馆			去书店
1 pm		午饭		
2 pm		上课		上课
3 pm	图书馆复习			
4 pm				
5 pm		篮球比赛		去小华家
6 pm				
7 pm	做晚饭，吃饭			看电影

Activity 7 👄

What do you say?

1. You want to know what day it is today.

2. You want to know today's date.

3. You have not done something that should have been done.

4. Despite some bad things happening, there are also things to be happy about.

第七课 Lesson Seven **时 间** Time

一、导入 Lead-in

Exercise 1 📖 💬

Look at the pictures below and talk about what you see in Chinese.

> 现在是几点几分?

> 现在是九点钟。

> 我常去咖啡店做作业。

> 我们在中国城逛街。

After learning this lesson, you will be able to:

1. Ask and tell the time of a day, and daily routine activities.

2. Master the Chinese pinyin system including initials, finals, and tones.

3. Recognize the new characters in this lesson, and know the internal structure of characters.

4. Use the modal particle 了, structural particle 得, and adverbs 就 and 才.

二、课文 Texts

课文（一）Text (1)

现在几点了？

简体版

John meets Xiaohong on campus after morning classes.

约翰：小红，去哪儿啊？

小红：去图书馆。

约翰：你来得正好。我忘了带手表了，不知道时间。现在几点了？

> **Tips:** how to ask about the time

小红：我看看手机啊。现在是十一点五十六分。

约翰：差四分就到十二点了，我下午第一节有课，不跟你多说了。我得先去吃午饭。

> **Tips:** how to tell time

小红：哎，别忘了下午图书馆放电影。

约翰：是四点整开始吗？

小红：对，四点到五点三刻。可别迟到啊。

约翰：好，那下午见！

小红：下午见！

现在幾點了？

繁体版

John meets Xiaohong on campus after morning classes.

約翰：小紅，去哪兒啊？

小紅：去圖書館。

約翰：你來得正好。我忘了帶手錶了，不知道時間。現在幾點了？

小紅：我看看手機啊。現在是十一點五十六分。

約翰：差四分就到十二點了，我下午第一節有課，不跟你多說了。我得先去吃午飯。

小紅：哎，別忘了下午圖書館放電影。

約翰：是四點整開始嗎？

小紅：對，四點到五點三刻。可別遲到啊。

約翰：好，那下午見！

小紅：下午見！

Kèwén (yī)　*Text (1)*

Xiànzài Jǐ Diǎn le?

拼音版

John meets Xiaohong on campus after morning classes

Yuēhàn: Xiǎohóng, qù nǎr a?

Xiǎohóng: Qù túshūguǎn.

Yuēhàn: Nǐ lái de zhènghǎo. Wǒ wàngle dài shǒubiǎo le, bù zhīdào
　　　　shíjiān. Xiànzài jǐ diǎn le?

Xiǎohóng: Wǒ kànkan shǒujī a. Xiànzài shì shíyī diǎn wǔshíliù fēn.

Yuēhàn: Chā sì fēn jiù dào shí'èr diǎn le, wǒ xiàwǔ dì-yī jié yǒu kè,
　　　　bù gēn nǐ duō shuō le. Wǒ děi xiān qù chī wǔfàn.

Xiǎohóng: Āi, bié wàngle xiàwǔ túshūguǎn fàng diànyǐng.

Yuēhàn: Shì sì diǎn zhěng kāishǐ ma?

Xiǎohóng: Duì, sì diǎn dào wǔ diǎn sān kè. Kě bié chídào a.

Yuēhàn: Hǎo, nà xiàwǔ jiàn!

Xiǎohóng: Xiàwǔ jiàn!

生词（一）　*New Words (1)*

	简体（繁體）	拼音	词性	解释
1	得	de	*part.*	verb complement marker 来得正好 / 他中文说得很好。

简体（繁體）		拼音	词性	解释
2	正好	zhènghǎo	*adv.*	at the right moment 来得正好 / 正好在那儿 / 我这里正好有张电影票。
3	忘	wàng	*v.*	forget 我忘了带手表了。/ 我忘了做作业了。
4	带（帶）	dài	*v.*	bring 你的作业带来了吗？
5	手表（錶）	shǒubiǎo	*n.*	wrist watch 看看手表，几点了？ / 我的手表不走了。
6	知道	zhīdào	*v.*	know; be aware of 你不知道时间吗？ / 你知道他是谁吗？
7	时间（時間）	shíjiān	*n.*	time "现在是什么时间了？" "十点了。"
8	现（現）在	xiànzài	*n.*	now; at present 现在我没有时间。/ 我们现在就去。
9	点（點）	diǎn	*n.*	o'clock 三点钟 / 四点半 / 现在几点了？
10	手机（機）	shǒujī	*n.*	cell phone 我没有手机。/ 手机上有时间。
11	差	chà	*v.*	lack; be short of 五点差五分 / 现在差十分五点。
12	分	fēn	*n.*	minute 现在是四点十五分。
13	第	dì	*pref.*	(prefix indicating ordinal number) 第一 / 第二 / 第三
14	节（節）	jié	*m.*	(measure word for class session) 我们上午有三节课。
15	跟	gēn	*prep.*	with 我跟小王一起吃饭。/ 不跟你多说了。
16	说（說）	shuō	*v.*	speak 不跟你多说了。
17	得	děi	*a.v.*	must 我得找个北京的学生。/ 你得帮我。
18	先	xiān	*adv.*	firstly 我先去商店买东西，然后去图书馆学习。
19	别	bié	*adv.*	don't 别去那家商店买东西。/ 别去看电影了。
20	放	fàng	*v.*	show (movie) 今天放什么电影？
21	整	zhěng	*adj.*	exact (time, quantity) 现在是北京时间七点整。/ 这是二十块钱整。
22	开（開）始	kāishǐ	*v.*	begin 我们开始上课。/ 你们什么时候开始考试？
23	对（對）	duì	*adj.*	right 对，他就是小王。/ 你姓张吗？——对，我姓张。
24	刻	kè	*n.*	quarter (time) 五点一刻 / 十点三刻

	简体（繁體）	拼音	词性	解释
25	迟（遲）到	chídào	*v.*	arrive late 上课不要迟到。/ 我今天迟到了三分钟。
26	那	nà	*conj.*	then 好，那下午见！
27	见（見）	jiàn	*v.*	see, meet 我要见你。/ 明天见！

Exercise 1

Listen to Text (1) and decide whether the following statements are true or false.

1. Xiaohong does not know what time it is.	( )
2. John is on his way to lunch.	( )
3. They will meet in the library in the afternoon.	( )
4. The movie begins in the library at 4:45 pm.	( )

Exercise 2

Read Text (1) and answer the questions orally in Chinese.

1. Why does John ask about the time?

2. How can Xiaohong tell the time?

3. Why does John have to go?

4. What does Xiaohong remind David of?

Exercise 3

Match the Chinese phrases in Column I with their English equivalents in Column II.

Column I	Column II
( ) 1. 那明天见	a. begins at five sharp
( ) 2. 上课迟到了	b. don't forget about the movie in the library
( ) 3. 差七分八点	c. cell phone says it's two now
( ) 4. 别忘了图书馆放电影	d. won't keep on talking
( ) 5. 手机说现在两点	e. see you tomorrow then
( ) 6. 不多说了	f. It's 7 to 8 o'clock
( ) 7. 五点整开始	g. late for class

飞跃——汉语初级教程学生用书 上册

Exercise 4 📖 ✎

Read the following sentences and fill in the blanks with the correct characters according to the English given.

1. 我不能打电话，因为今天我忘了 _____(bring my cell phone with me)。
2. 现在是 _____(12 o'clock)，我要去吃饭了。
3. 电影不早不晚，_____(7 o'clock sharp) 开始。
4. 很多人用手机看时间，不看 _____(watch) 了。
5. 走路去一定会 _____ (be late)。
6. 我们去 _____(library) 看书。

Exercise 5 ✎

Translate the following sentences into Chinese using characters and/or pinyin.

1. I forgot I had a class on Tuesday.

   _____。

2. Please bring your watch.

   _____。

3. We are going to be late!

   _____。

4. They are going to show a movie at school on Friday.

   _____。

课文（二）Text (2)

日记

简体版

This is Li Wen's diary about his weekend.

今天是星期六，我睡到九点多才起床。起床以后，我先洗澡，然后吃早餐。十点半，我到学校附近的咖啡店做作业。我在那儿碰见了大卫。我们各买了一杯咖啡，在那里一直待到十二点多。

下午，我和大卫去了中国城。我们一起逛街，还去

书店买了几本书。然后我们在一家中国饭馆吃晚饭。我们回到宿舍的时候，已经是晚上十点三刻了。

日記

繁体版

This is Li Wen's diary about his weekend.

今天是星期六，我睡到九點多才起床。起床以後，我先洗澡，然後吃早餐。十點半，我到學校附近的咖啡店做作業。我在那兒碰見了大衛。我們各買了一杯咖啡，在那裏一直待到十二點多。

下午，我和大衛去了中國城。我們一起逛街，還去書店買了幾本書。然後我們在一家中國飯館吃晚飯。我們回到宿舍的時候，已經是晚上十點三刻了。

Kèwén (èr)   *Text (2)*

Rìjì

拼音版

This is Li Wen's diary about his weekend.

Jīntiān shì xīngqīliù, wǒ shuìdào jiǔ diǎn duō cái qǐchuáng. Qǐchuáng yǐhòu, wǒ xiān xǐzǎo, ránhòu chī zǎocān. Shí diǎn bàn, wǒ dào xuéxiào fùjìn de kāfēidiàn zuò zuòyè. Wǒ zài nàr pèngjiànle Dàwèi. Wǒmen gè mǎile yì bēi kāfēi, zài nàli yìzhí dāidào shí'èr diǎn duō.

Xiàwǔ, wǒ hé Dàwèi qùle Zhōngguóchéng. Wǒmen yìqǐ guàngjiē, hái qù shūdiàn mǎile jǐ běn shū. Ránhòu wǒmen zài yì jiā Zhōngguó fànguǎn chī wǎnfàn. Wǒmen huídào sūshè de shíhòu, yǐjīng shì wǎnshang shí diǎn sān kè le.

生词〔二〕 *New Words (2)*

	简体（繁體）	拼音	词性	解释
1	睡	shuì	*v.*	sleep 我睡到九点才起床。
2	才（纔）	cái	*adv.*	(adverb indicating the lateness of an action) 她周末十一点才起床。/ 他明天才到呢。
3	起床	qǐchuáng	*v.*	get up 我每天七点起床。
4	洗澡	xǐzǎo	*v.*	bathe, shower 小王天天洗澡。
5	然后（後）	ránhòu	*conj.*	then, afterwards 我先买东西，然后吃饭。
6	早餐	zǎocān	*n.*	breakfast 今天的早餐是牛奶和面包。
7	半	bàn	*n.*	half 九点半 / 十二点半 / 半本书
8	到	dào	*v.*	go to; arrive 我到咖啡店做作业。/ 你到我家来吧。万圣节快到了。
9	学（學）校	xuéxiào	*n.*	school 你在学校做作业吗？/ 我们学校很大。
10	附近	fùjìn	*n.*	vicinity 学校附近 / 我家附近有个商店。
11	咖啡店	kāfēidiàn	*n.*	coffee shop 开一家咖啡店 / 在咖啡店做作业
12	咖啡	kāfēi	*n.*	coffee 要一杯咖啡 / 他喜欢咖啡色的夹克。
13	碰见（見）	pèngjiàn	*v.*	run into 我在学校碰见王老师。
14	各	gè	*adv.*	each 我们各买了一杯咖啡。/ 我们各有各的作业要做。
15	杯	bēi	*n./m.*	glass, cup 杯子 / 一杯水 / 一杯牛奶
16	一直	yìzhí	*adv.*	straight, continuously 一直走就到了。/ 他在学校一直呆到下午两点。
17	待	dāi	*v.*	stay 星期天待在家里 / 他一天到晚总是待在图书馆。
18	中国（國）城	Zhōngguó-chéng	*n.*	Chinatown 旧金山的中国城比纽约的大。
19	逛街	guàngjiē	*v.*	window-shop; stroll down the street 考试以后我们逛街去吧。
20	书（書）店	shūdiàn	*n.*	bookstore 旧金山有中文书店。
21	几（幾）	jǐ	*num.*	several 我在书店买了几本书。

第七课 时间

简体（繁體）	拼音	词性	解释
22 本	běn	*m.*	(measure word for books) 一本书 / 一本字典
23 书（書）	shū	*n.*	book 买书 / 看书 / 书店 / 书市
24 家	jiā	*m.*	(measure word for shop, school, etc.) 一家商店 / 一家学校
25 饭馆（飯館）	fànguǎn	*n.*	restaurant 开饭馆 / 中国饭馆
26 宿舍	sùshè	*n.*	dormitory 男宿舍 / 女宿舍 / 学生宿舍
27 时（時）候	shíhòu	*n.*	time 我们回到宿舍的时候，已经是晚上十点三刻了。/ 现在都什么时候了，还不睡觉？
28 已经（經）	yǐjīng	*adv.*	already 已经是晚上十点了。/ 我已经去过中国了。

Exercise 6 🖐

Listen to Text (2) and choose the right answer for each of the following statements.

1. Today is _____.

    a. Monday   b. Friday   c. Saturday

2. The things Li Wen did after getting up in the correct order is _____.

    a. breakfast, homework, shower

    b. shower, homework, breakfast

    c. shower, breakfast, homework

3. Li Wen did homework at _____.

    a. the coffee shop   b. the school library   c. Tom's house

4. What is the thing that Li Wen did not do in the afternoon?

    a. Buy books.   b. Walk down the street.   c. Watch TV.

Exercise 7 📖 🗨

Read Text (2) and answer the questions orally in Chinese.

1. Where did she do her homework?

2. How many hours did she stay there?

3. What else did she do there?

4. Where did she go in the afternoon?

5. Make a list of things she did in the afternoon.

Exercise 8

Translate the following expressions into Chinese orally.

1. get up at 10 o'clock
2. first take a shower, then have breakfast
3. run into a friend in Chinatown
4. the coffee shop near the library
5. buy a cup of coffee
6. go window shopping

三、语音 Phonetics

Exercise 1

Read the following tones aloud.

dōng dóng dǒng dòng	kōng kóng kǒng kòng	mēng méng měng mèng
lōng lóng lǒng lòng	zhōng zhóng zhǒng zhòng	sōng sóng sǒng sòng
yōng yóng yǒng yòng	jiāng jiáng jiǎng jiàng	zhī zhí zhǐ zhì
shī shí shǐ shì	yī yí yǐ yì	jī jí jǐ jì
sī sí sǐ sì	lī lí lǐ lì	wēi wéi wěi wèi
fēi féi fěi fèi	yū yú yǔ yù	qū qú qǔ qù
jū jú jǔ jù	juē jué juě juè	kū kú kǔ kù
dū dú dǔ dù	wū wú wǔ wù	gū gú gǔ gù
xī xí xǐ xì	mī mí mǐ mì	jiē jié jiě jiè
xiā xiá xiǎ xià	bāi bái bǎi bài	hāi hái hǎi hài
gāi gái gǎi gài	gē gé gě gè	tāi tái tǎi tài
duī duí duǐ duì	duō duó duǒ duò	zhēn zhén zhěn zhèn
zhī zhí zhǐ zhì	sūn sún sǔn sùn	shūn shún shǔn shùn
rēn rén rěn rèn	rūn rún rǔn rùn	yīn yín yǐn yìn
xūn xún xǔn xùn	wēn wén wěn wèn	fēn fén fěn fèn
yuān yuán yuǎn yuàn	ruān ruán ruǎn ruàn	fā fá fǎ fà
wān wán wǎn wàn	fān fán fǎn fàn	gān gán gǎn gàn

huān huán huǎn huàn	huō huó huǒ huò	jiān jián jiǎn jiàn
xiān xián xiǎn xiàn	xiē xié xiě xiè	qiān qián qiǎn qiàn
juē jué juě juè	chuān chuán chuǎn chuàn	zhuān zhuán zhuǎn zhuàn
xiāo xiáo xiǎo xiào	xuē xué xuě xuè	liāo liáo liǎo liào
lüē lüé lüě lüè	jiāo jiáo jiǎo jiào	jiā jiá jiǎ jià
zuō zuó zuǒ zuò	xiā xiá xiǎ xià	zhāng zháng zhǎng zhàng
zhuō zhuó zhuǒ zhuò	rāng ráng rǎng ràng	ruō ruó ruǒ ruò
jiāng jiáng jiǎng jiàng	quē qué quě què	xiāng xiáng xiǎng xiàng
nuē nué nuě nuè	liū liú liǔ liù	liē lié liě liè
zōu zóu zǒu zòu	xiān xián xiǎn xiàn	qiā qiá qiǎ qià

Exercise 2 📖

Read the following initials and finals aloud, using the first tone.

ji-qi	xi-shi	jia-qia	ju-zhu	qu-chu	xu-shu
zhi-ji	chi-ri	shi-ri	yu-xu	wo-ou	zuo-zou
zi-ci	si-ci	zi-si	nü – lü	cui-zui-sui	chui-cui-shui
qiu-jiu	qie-jie	que-jue	xun-shun	chun-qun	zun-cun
nan-nar	hai-har	wan-war	kan-kar	shai-shar	tian-tiar

Exercise 3 📖

Read the 3rd tone sandhi aloud.

shuǐbīng 水兵	cǐshēng 此生	Běijing 北京	kǒnggāo 恐高	yǐngpiānr 影片儿	dǎchē 打车
jǐngchá 警察	nǔrén 女人	cǎorén 草人	lǔxíng 旅行	shuǐpíng 水平	huǒshén 火神
zǎodiǎn 早点	lǎoshǔ 老鼠	shuǐbiǎo 水表	xiǎngfǎ 想法	xiǎojiě 小姐	měihǎo 美好
shǒupà 手帕	shuǐbà 水坝	chǎnjià 产假	lǐbài 礼拜	qǐgài 乞丐	qǐngjià 请假
nǐmen 你们	wǒmen 我们	zǎoshang 早上	zuǐba 嘴巴	wěiba 尾巴	lǎoshi 老实

Exercise 4 📖

Read the tone sandhi with 一 and 不 aloud.

一 + 1st tone →4th + 1st:	yìbiān 一边	yìshēn 一身	yìshēng 一生	yì tiān 一天	yìxiē 一些
一 + 2nd tone →4th + 2nd:	yìshí 一时	yì míng 一名	yìzhí 一直	yìtóng 一同	yì rén 一人
一 + 3rd tone →4th + 3rd:	yì wěn 一吻	yìzhǔn 一准	yìqǐ 一起	yìzǎo 一早	yì kǒu 一口
一 + 4th tone →2nd + 4th:	yídìng 一定	yíbàn 一半	yígòng 一共	yí wèi 一位	yí dùn 一顿
不 + 4th tone →2nd + 4th:	búbì 不必	bú shuì 不睡	búcuò 不错	búyào 不要	búdàn 不但

Exercise 5 📖

Read the following words and phrases aloud paying attention to the neutral tones.

māma 妈妈	bàba 爸爸	gēge 哥哥	dìdi 弟弟	jiějie 姐姐		zhuōzi 桌子	yǐzi 椅子	pàngzi 胖子	shòuzi 瘦子
mèimei 妹妹	yéye 爷爷	nǎinai 奶奶	sūnzi 孙子	sūnnǚ 孙女					
wǒmen 我们	nǐmen 你们	tāmen 他们	rénmen 人们			shítou 石头	shétou 舌头	tiántou 甜头	kǔtou 苦头
lǎoshi 老实	hòushi 厚实	jiēshi 结实				gōngjia 公家	qìngjia 亲家	niángjia 娘家	pójia 婆家 / Zhāngjia 张家
hǎochu 好处	huàichu 坏处	chángchu 长处	duǎnchu 短处			shànglai 上来	xiàqu 下去	qǐlai 起来	guòlai 过来 / chuānshang 穿上

Exercise 6 📖

Read the following syllables aloud.

再见 zàijiàn	谢谢 xièxie	您早 nín zǎo	同学 tóngxué	您贵姓 nín guìxìng	姓名 xìngmíng
工作 gōngzuò	中国人 Zhōngguórén	老家 lǎojiā	几口人 jǐ kǒu rén	年纪 niánjì	多大了 duō dà le
今年 jīnnián	医生 yīshēng	工程师 gōngchéngshī	女朋友 nǚpéngyou	大学生 dàxuéshēng	中文系 Zhōngwénxì

介绍 jièshào	认识 rènshi	看电影 kàn diànyǐng	很高兴 hěn gāoxìng	室友 shìyǒu	跑步 pǎobù
食堂 shítáng	晚饭 wǎnfàn	图书馆 túshūguǎn	做作业 zuò zuòyè	今天几号 jīntiān jǐ hào	复习功课 fùxí gōngkè
有空 yǒukòng	考试 kǎoshì	商店 shāngdiàn	自己动手 zìjǐ dòngshǒu	万圣节 Wàn- shèngjié	南瓜灯 nánguā- dēng
要迟到 yào chídào	赶紧走 gǎnjǐn zǒu	学校附近 xuéxiào fùjìn	起床 qǐchuáng	洗澡 xǐzǎo	面包 miànbāo

Exercise 7 👂 ✍

Write down what you hear from left to right with correct spelling and tone marks.

四、汉字 Chinese Characters

1. New characters in this lesson

序号	拼音	简 / 繁	部件	构词
1	a	啊	口 + 阿（阝 + 可）	去哪儿啊
2	āi	哎	口 + 艾（艹 + 乂）	哎，干什么
3	bàn	半	半	九点半 / 半块 / 半个 / 一半
4	bēi	杯	木 + 不	杯子 / 一杯水 / 一杯牛奶

5	běn	本	本	书本 / 课本 / 本来
6	biǎo	表 / 錶	圭 + 长	手表 / 表面
7	bié	别	另（口 + 力）+ 刂	别忘了 / 别太快 / 别人
8	cái	才 / 纔	才	才起床 / 才到 / 才回来
9	cān	餐	歺 + 又 + 食（人 + 良）	早餐 / 午餐
10	chà	差	羊 + 工	八点差五分 / 差点儿
11	chéng	城	土 + 成	中国城 / 长城 / 城市
12	chí	迟 / 遲	尺 + 辶	迟到 / 迟睡 / 推迟
13	chuáng	床	广 + 木	起床 / 快起床 / 上床
14	dāi	待	彳 + 寺（土 + 寸）	待在家里 / 待在学校
15	dài	带 / 帶	卅 + 冖 + 巾	带来 / 带书包 / 领带
16	dào	道	首 + 辶	知道 / 味道 / 道路 / 大道
17	de/děi	得	彳 + 㝵（旦 + 寸）	来得正好 / 中文说得很好 / 我得走了 / 我得去吃午饭
18	dì	第	竹 + 弟	第一 / 第二 / 第三
19	diǎn	点 / 點	占 + 灬	三点钟 / 四点半
20	fēi	啡	口 + 非	咖啡 / 咖啡店 / 咖啡色
21	fēn	分	八 + 刀	24点15分 / 学分 / 分开
22	fù	附	阝 + 付（亻 + 寸）	学校附近 / 我家附近
23	gè	各	夂 + 口	全国各地 / 世界各地 / 各方面
24	gēn	跟	𧾷 + 艮	我跟小王 / 你跟我
25	guàng	逛	狂（犭 + 王）+ 辶	逛街 / 逛店 / 逛一逛
26	hòu	候	亻 + 丨 + 关	时候 / 等候
27	jī	机 / 機	木 + 几	手机 / 飞机 / 机车
28	jiān	间 / 間	门 + 日	时间 / 空间 / 房间
29	jiē	街	彳 + 圭 + 亍	逛街 / 上街 / 街上
30	jìn	近	斤 + 辶	附近 / 最近 / 很近
31	jīng	经 / 經	纟 + 圣	已经 / 经常 / 经过
32	kā	咖	口 + 加（力 + 口）	咖啡店 / 喝咖啡

33	kāi	开 / 開	开	开餐馆 / 开公司 / 打开盒子
34	kè	刻	亥 + 刂	五点一刻 / 立刻
35	pèng	碰	石 + 並	碰见 / 踫到
36	rán	然	夕 + 犬 + 灬	然后 / 当然 / 不然
37	shè	舍	人 + 舌（千 + 口）	学生宿舍
38	shí	时 / 時	日 + 寸	时间 / 时光 / 时候 / 那时
39	shǐ	始	女 + 台（厶 + 口）	开始 / 始终
40	shǒu	手	手	动手 / 两手
41	shuì	睡	目 + 垂	午睡 / 早睡早起 / 很晚才睡
42	shuō	说 / 說	讠 + 兑	说话 / 他说 / 我说
43	sù	宿	宀 + 亻 + 百	宿舍 / 男宿舍 / 女宿舍
44	wàng	忘	亡 + 心	别忘了 / 忘记 / 忘了
45	xǐ	洗	氵 + 先	洗澡 / 洗手 / 洗衣服
46	xiàn	现 / 現	王 + 见	现在 / 出现 / 现场 / 现金
47	xiào	校	木 + 交	学校 / 校园 / 校长
48	yǐ	已	已	已经 / 已然
49	zǎo	澡	氵 + 品 + 木	洗澡 / 澡堂
50	zhěng	整	敕（束 + 攵）+ 正	七点整 / 整齐
51	zhèng	正	正	正好 / 正在 / 正点 / 立正
52	zhī	知	矢 + 口	知道 / 知识 / 知情
53	zhí	直	直	一直 / 直到

Exercise 1 📖 ✍

Copy the following single-component characters with correct stroke order in the spaces provided.

bàn	半	丶 丷 丷 半 半				
běn	本	一 十 才 木 本				

cái	才	一 十 才
kāi	开	一 二 于 开
yǐ	已	一 コ 已
zhèng	正	一 丁 下 正 正
zhí	直	一 十 广 方 古 肖 直 直

2. A character with different pronunciations

A Chinese character usually has only one pronunciation. Some characters, however, have more than one pronunciation. Sometimes, different pronunciations share the same meaning; for example, 谁 can be pronounced as "shuí" or "shéi", 那 "nà" or "nèi". More often, different pronunciations suggest different meanings. For example, when 得 is pronounced "děi", it means "have to"; "dé" means "to get"; and "de" is a structural particle used to form a complement in a sentence.

3. The internal structure of characters

There are three basic forms of the internal structures of characters: top-bottom structure, left-right structure, and enclosed structure.

Internal Structures	Examples			
Top-bottom structure	爸	点	英	意
Left-right structure	朋	别	吗	谢
Enclosed structure	国	同	山	医

Exercise 2 ✎

With the help of a Chinese-English dictionary, find the different pronunciations and meanings for the following characters:

Character	Pronunciation 1	Meaning 1	Pronunciation 2	Meaning 2
还				
少				
没				
都				

五、语言点 Language Points

1. Telling time in Chinese

Times of the day	O'clock	Quarters	Minute
早上 early morning 上午 morning 中午 noon 下午 afternoon 晚上 evening 半夜 midnight	点（钟）diǎn (zhōng) 0:00—零点 1:00—一点（钟） 2:00—两点（钟） 3:00—三点（钟） 12:00—十二点（钟）	刻 kè 2:15—两点一刻 2:30—两点半（钟） 12:45—十二点三刻 12:00—十二点整	分 fēn 1st-9th minute: 2:05—两点零五分 / 两点过五分 / 两点五分 51th-59th minute: 2:55—三点差五分 / 差五分三点 / 两点五十五分

2. The modal particle 了

In lesson 6, we learned about the aspectual particle 了, which is used after a verb to indicate a completed action (e.g. 我们买了很多糖。) In this lesson, we will learn that 了 can also be used at the end of a sentence to express various moods (e.g. query, affirmation, and advice) of the speaker.

Subject ＋ Verb／Adjective（＋ Object）＋ 了

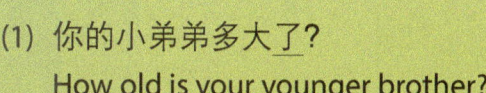

(1) 你的小弟弟多大**了**？

How old is your younger brother?

(2) 现在几点**了**？

What time is it now?

(3) 差四分就到十二点**了**。

It is four minutes to twelve.

(4) 我下午第一节有课，不跟你多说**了**。

I have a first period class this afternoon. I can't talk with you anymore.

(5) 我们回到宿舍的时候，已经是晚上十点三刻**了**！

When we got back to our dormitory, it was already 10:45 pm.

3. The use of 到

The verb 到 means "go to" or "to reach". For example:

(1) 十点半，我**到**学校附近的咖啡店做作业。

At 10:30, I went to the coffee shop near my school to do my homework.

(2) 差四分就**到**十二点了。

It is four minutes to (reach) twelve.

(3) 四点**到**五点三刻，在图书馆放电影。

A movie will be played in the library from 4 to 5:45.

The verb 到 can also be used as a verb complement in a compound verb.

> **Verb + 到 (to reach) → Verb Complement Compound**

回 ＋ 到 → 回到 (come back and reach a certain place)

睡 ＋ 到 → 睡到 (sleep until it reaches a certain time)

待 ＋ 到 → 待到 (stay until it reaches a certain time)

(4) 我们**回到**宿舍的时候，已经是晚上十点三刻了。

When we got back to our dormitory, it was already 10:45 pm.

(5) 今天是星期六，我**睡到**九点才起床。

Today is Saturday. I didn't get up until (it reached) nine o'clock.

(6) 我们在那里一直**待到**十二点多。

We stayed there until after twelve o'clock.

4. The adverb 就 (1)

The adverb 就 has many usages. One of its common usages is to indicate that something occurs quickly, or the interval of time/space is short. It is often used with the modal particle 了 at the end of the sentence.

> (1) 后天<u>就</u>是万圣节（了），可我还没买我的面具呢！
>
> The day after tomorrow is Halloween; however, I haven't bought my mask yet.
>
> (2) 差四分<u>就</u>到十二点了，我下午第一节有课，不跟你多说了。
>
> It is four minutes to 12 now. I have a first period class in the afternoon. I can't talk with you anymore.
>
> (3) 万圣节<u>就</u>要到了。
>
> Halloween is around the corner.

5. The auxiliary verb 得 děi

得 has different pronunciations with different meanings. In the combinations 觉得 and 来得正好, 得 is pronounced as de. When it is used before a verb serving as an auxiliary verb, it is pronounced děi, meaning "must; have to". For example:

> (1) 不跟你多说了，我<u>得</u>去吃午饭。
>
> I can't talk with you anymore. I have to go to eat lunch.
>
> (2) 上课的时间到了，我<u>得</u>走了！
>
> It is time for class. I have to go!
>
> (3) 要想知道时间，你<u>得</u>带手表。
>
> In order to know the time, you have to wear a watch.

6. The adverb 才 (1)

The adverb 才 is used after time words to indicate that something has taken place later than expected.

> (1) 今天是星期六，我睡到九点<u>才</u>起床。
>
> Today is Saturday. I didn't get up until 9:00 am.
>
> (2) 我们八点钟上课，都八点一刻了，你怎么现在<u>才</u>来?
>
> We have class at 8:00 and it is 8:15 now. How come you came so late?
>
> (3) 昨天下午放学后，我在图书馆做作业，一直到晚上九点<u>才</u>走。
>
> I did my homework in the library after class yesterday. I didn't leave there until 9:00 pm.

(4) 今天下午我和大卫去了中国城，一直到晚上十点多才回家。

This afternoon, I went to Chinatown with David. We didn't get home until after 10:00 pm.

Exercise 1 👂✍️

Listen to the following time expressions and write them down in English.

1. _____

2. _____

3. _____

4. _____

5. _____

6. _____

Exercise 2 ✍️

Translate the following dialogs into English paying attention to the use of the modal particle 了.

Dialog 1

A：小丽，你弟弟今年多大了？

B：我弟弟七岁了。

A：他上学了吗？

B：上学了。他是今年八月上学的。

_____
_____
_____
_____

Dialog 2

A：妈妈，现在几点了？

B：十点半了。

A：什么？都十点半了？

B：是啊，你得睡觉了，明天早上还要上课呢。

_____
_____
_____
_____

Dialog 3

A：大卫，谁来了？

B：小林来了。

A：他来这儿做什么？

B：他要和我们一起去跑步。

_____

_____

_____

_____

Exercise 3 ✍

Complete the following dialogs by using 得 to indicate obligation or necessity.

1. A：今天放学后四点钟我们一起去跑步好吗？

B：对不起，放学后 _____。

(I have to go to the store for shopping.)

A：那五点半可以吗？

B：好，我们五点半见。

2. A：明天是星期天，我们一起去中国城逛逛，好吗？

B：你要几点去？

A：上午九点半，怎么样？

B：上午不行，_____。

(I have to do my homework at home.)

A：那下午一点钟行不行？

B：行！

Exercise 4 📖

Choose the correct answer for each of the following sentences.

1. 我每天上午七点四十五分 _____ 学校。

　　a. 待　　　　　　　　　b. 到　　　　　　　　　c. 逛

2. 今天的电影是下午两点的, 你可 _____ 迟到啊 。

　　a. 不　　　　　　　　　b. 没　　　　　　　　　c. 别

3. 我星期一到五很早就睡了，可是星期六晚上十二点多 _____ 睡觉。

　　a. 得　　　　　　　　　b. 才　　　　　　　　　c. 就

4. "你们今天到哪儿去了？" "我们到旧金山去 _____ 。"

　　a. 了　　　　　　　　　b. 过　　　　　　　　　c. 得

飞跃——汉语初级教程学生用书　上册

5. 陈雨去书店买了 _____ 书?

    a. 几本   b. 几口   c. 几个

6. 我们每天上午八点 _____ 十一点上三节课。

    a. 和   b. 到   c. 过

7. 差五分就到八点了，我 _____ 去上课了。

    a. 能   b. 可   c. 得

8. 汤姆和我在咖啡店各买了 _____ 咖啡。

    a. 一位   b. 一个   c. 一杯

9. 星期六上午我常常 _____ 十点多才起床。

    a. 睡觉   b. 睡到   c. 睡了

10. 明天 _____ 是周末了，我要回家看我的爸爸妈妈。

    a. 到   b. 才   c. 就

Exercise 5

Translate the following sentences into English paying attention to the underlined parts.

1. 昨天我工作很忙，回到家已经是晚上八点了。

_____

2. 电影七点半开始，小红七点三刻才来。

_____

3. 差四分就到十二点了，约翰怎么还没有来？

_____

4. 万圣节就要到了，可我们家还没买南瓜呢！

_____

5. 下午三点图书馆放电影，你可别迟到啊。

_____

6. 王老师，你的女儿今年多大了？上学了吗？

_____

7. 对不起，我得去食堂吃午饭，下午再跟你说。

_____

8. 星期五晚上我常常到十一点钟才睡觉。

_____

9. "上课了吗？""快上课了，还有一分钟。"

_____

10. 我每天晚上七点半到九点做作业。

_____

六、语言运用 Using the Language

Activity 1 📖 🗣️

Look at Xiao Wang's calendar and talk about his activities. Take turns asking your partner what Xiao Wang will do at a particular time on a particular day.

24 星期日	25 星期一	26 星期二	27 星期三
晚上 7:00 看电影	下午 5:00 跟小明吃饭 下午 6:00 复习课文 晚上 8:00~9:00 看电视	下午 6:00 准备明天的考试 晚上 7:00 看电影	中午 12:00 出去吃饭 下午 6:00 去刘华家 晚上 7:00 复习生词
28 星期四	29 星期五	30 星期六	31 星期日
下午 5:00 我的生日晚会	下午 5:00 跟李华买书 下午 6:00 回家吃饭	上午 9:00 去红城咖啡店见约翰	上午 10:00~12:00 跟丽莎逛街，中午到丽华饭馆吃饭

Activity 2 👂 🗣️

You are David. Listen to the message left to you and answer the questions.

1. What has your friend not done yet?

2. What does he want you to do?

3. What did he say about his mother?

4. What are the three things you will do together this evening?

Activity 3 📖

Read the following passage and decide whether the statements are true or false.

　　张国华是一个学生。他的学习很忙，周一到周五每天都上课。上午上三节课，下午上两节课。每天晚上他还要做很多作业。每天早上他六点半起床。吃完早饭以后就去上学。中午十二点下课后，他在学校的食堂吃午饭。下午下课以后，他去图书馆做作业、复习。他六点钟吃晚饭。周末的时候他不忙。他星期六和星期天都睡到十点多才起来。周末的下午他去看电影或者去书店买书。有的时候他跟朋友去饭馆吃饭。

1. Zhang has five classes each day during the week.	( )
2. For two evenings a week he does not do homework.	( )
3. He goes home to have lunch.	( )

飞跃——汉语初级教程学生用书　上册

4. He does homework at a coffee shop.	( )
5. Sometimes, he goes to restaurants with friends on weekends.	( )
6. He has very relaxing weedends.	( )

Activity 4

A. Let's review how to express time. Look at the following pictures and write down in Chinese the time the watches indicate.

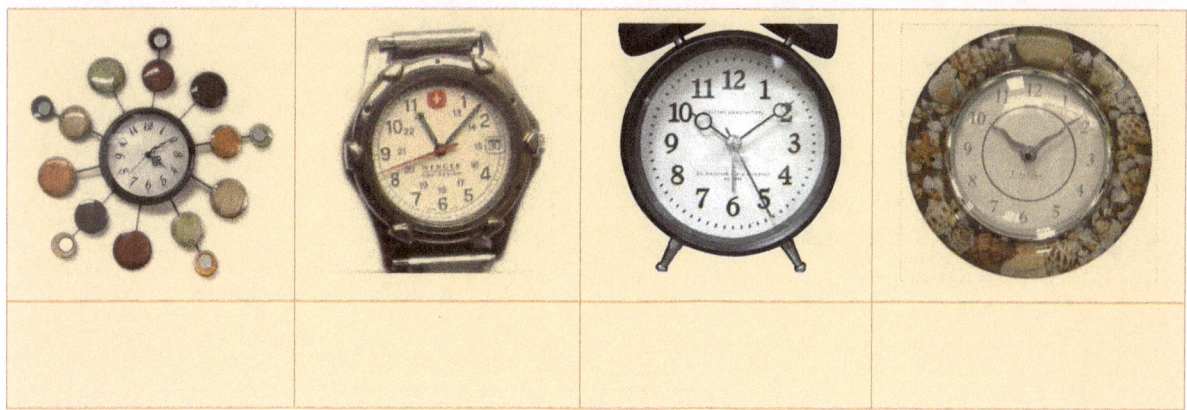

B. State the time in the following pictures and then write two sentences reporting the time for both the morning and the afternoon in Chinese, using the 24-hour system.

Activity 5

The United States is divided into five time zones. Using your knowledge of the time zones, fill in the chart below in Chinese characters, and then talk about the time differences with your partner in Chinese.

California 加州 Jiā Zhōu	Montana 蒙大拿州 Méngdàná Zhōu	Texas 德州 Dé Zhōu	Florida 佛罗里达州 Fóluólǐdá Zhōu	Main 缅因州 Miǎnyīn Zhōu
八点				
九点半				
十点二十五分				
十二点				
两点				
三点一刻				
四点三刻				

Activity 6

Role Play

You are a school newspaper reporter and you are interviewing a student about his/her school life. Speak with the student to find out about his/her weekly activities and the specific time of each activity.

Sentences you may need to use:

1. 请问你……做什么？ e.g. 请问你星期一上午做什么？
2. 你几点钟 ……? e.g. 你几点钟去图书馆？

Activity 7

What do you say?

1. You want to offer a reason why you need to ask about the time.
2. You want to cut short a conversation to do something else.
3. You want to remind someone of something.
4. You want to confirm the time of an activity.

第八课
Lesson Eight

打电话
Making a Phone Call

一、导入 Lead-in

Exercise 1 📖 🗣

Work in pairs. Look at the pictures below and discuss their contents.

小吃店有面包和牛奶。

我们在图书馆复习功课。

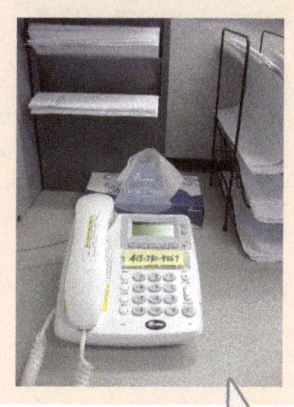

你的手机号码是多少？

请告诉我你办公室的电话号码。

After learning this lesson, you will be able to:

1. Use the language to make and answer phone calls, ask and tell people for phone numbers.

2. Talk about one's daily activities at school with common words related to school life.

3. Recognize new characters in this lesson, and understand how characters were created.

4. Use the adverb 在 to indicate an action in progress; use function words 给, 能, and 吧.

二、课文 Texts

课文（一）Text (1)

你的手机号码是多少？

Bill asks Lin Hua to do him a favor.

比尔：林华，能帮个忙吗？

Tips: how to ask for help

林华：什么忙？

比尔：我要找一个北京女孩。

林华：找女朋友？

比尔：什么呀，不是！我在学中文，想找一个辅导。

林华：哦，我认识一个女孩叫王红，她是北京人。

比尔：你有她的电话号码吗？

林华：没有，我得问她要。下午我在张老师的办公室能见到她。

比尔：那好，你找她要电话号码，然后你打电话告诉我。

林华：你的手机号码是多少？

Tips: how to ask for a phone number

比尔：756-4321。那你也给我你的手机号码吧。

林华：没问题，987-6543。

比尔：那我就等你的电话了。

你的手機號碼是多少？

Bill asks Lin Hua to do him a favor.

比爾：林華，能幫個忙嗎？

林華：什麼忙？

比爾：我要找一個北京女孩。

林華：找女朋友？

比爾：什麼呀，不是！我在學中文，想找一個輔導。

林華：哦，我認識一個女孩叫王紅，她是北京人。

比爾：你有她的電話號碼嗎？

林華：沒有，我得問她要。下午我在張老師的辦公室能
　　　見到她。

比爾：那好，你找她要電話號碼，然後你打電話告訴我。

林華：你的手機號碼是多少？

比爾：756-4321。那你也給我你的手機號碼吧。

林華：沒問題，987-6543。

比爾：那我就等你的電話了。

Kèwén (yī)　*Text (1)*

Nǐ de Shǒujī Hàomǎ Shì Duōshao?

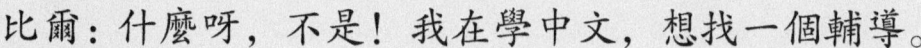

拼音版

Bill asks Lin Hua to do him a favor.

Bǐ'ěr:　Lín Huá, néng bāng ge máng ma?

Lín Huá: Shénme máng?

Bǐ'ěr:　Wǒ yào zhǎo yí gè Běijīng nǚhái.

Lín Huá: Zhǎo nǚpéngyou?

Bǐ'ěr:　Shénme ya, bú shì! Wǒ zài xué Zhōngwén, xiǎng zhǎo yí gè fǔdǎo.

Lín Huá: Ò, wǒ rènshi yí gè nǚhái jiào Wáng Hóng, tā shì Běijīngrén.

Bǐ'ěr:　Nǐ yǒu tā de diànhuà hàomǎ ma?

Lín Huá: Méiyǒu, wǒ děi wèn tā yào. Xiàwǔ wǒ zài Zhāng lǎoshī de bàngōngshì néng jiàndào tā.

Bǐ'ěr:　Nà hǎo, nǐ zhǎo tā yào diànhuà hàomǎ, ránhòu nǐ dǎ diànhuà gàosù wǒ.

Lín Huá: Nǐ de shǒujī hàomǎ shì duōshao?

Bǐ'ěr: Qī wǔ liù -sì sān èr yī. Nà nǐ yě gěi wǒ nǐ de shǒujī hàomǎ ba.

Lín Huá: Méi wèntí, jiǔ bā qī -liù wǔ sì sān.

Bǐ'ěr: Nà wǒ jiù děng nǐ de diànhuà le.

生词（一） *New Words (1)*

	简体（繁體）	拼音	词性	解释
1	帮（幫）忙	bāngmáng	*v.*	help 帮一个忙 / 帮她的忙 / 给他帮忙
2	想	xiǎng	*v.*	think; wish to; want to 我想学中文。/ 我想去中国。
3	辅导（輔導）	fǔdǎo	*n./v.*	tutor; to tutor 中文辅导 / 找一个辅导 / 老师辅导学生。
4	哦	ò	*intj.*	(interjection expressing understanding) 哦，小王就是你啊！
5	电话（電話）	diànhuà	*n.*	telephone; phone call 电话号码 / 公共电话 / 小王，有你的电话！
6	号码（號碼）	hàomǎ	*n.*	number 门牌号码 / 电话号码 / 衣服的号码
7	办（辦）公室	bàngōngshì	*n.*	office 请你来我的办公室。/ 张老师的办公室很大。
8	打	dǎ	*v.*	make (phone call) 打电话 / 打手机 / 请你给我打电话。
9	告诉（訴）	gàosu	*v.*	tell, inform 请你告诉我在哪儿坐地铁。
10	多少	duōshao	*pron.*	how many; how much 你的学校有多少学生？
11	给（給）	gěi	*v.*	give 请你给我你的电话号码。
12	问题（問題）	wèntí	*n.*	problem 帮你忙没问题！ / 你有问题吗？
13	就	jiù	*adv.*	then; in that case 我去找小王。小王不在，我就回来了。
14	等	děng	*v.*	wait 我等你。/ 我等你来。/ 我等你的电话。
专有名词 Proper Noun				
	比尔（爾）	Bǐ'ěr	*pn.*	Bill

Exercise 1 🔊

Listen to Text (1) and decide whether the following statements are true or false.

1. Bill wants to find a girlfriend.	(	)
2. Bill's Chinese is very good.	(	)
3. Lin Hua will see Wang Hong in the teacher's office.	(	)
4. Bill will wait for Lin Hua's call.	(	)

Exercise 2 📖 🗣

Read Text (1) and answer the questions orally in Chinese.

1. What kind of tutor does Bill want to find?

2. What did Lin Hua assume about Bill?

3. Where are Lin Hua and Wang Hong going to meet?

4. What will Bill probably do if Lin Hua does not call him?

Exercise 3 ✍

Fill in the blanks with the verbs listed below and translate the completed sentences into English.

a. 认识　b. 告诉　c. 打　d. 找　e. 要

1. 我看电影的时候 _____ 了一个北京女孩，我很高兴。

2. 我给她 _____ 了四次电话都占线，不知道她在跟谁说话。

3. 我的中文不好，想 _____ 一个中文辅导帮我补习（bǔxí, give a remedial course）。

4. 很多人跟她 _____ 电话号码，可是她不给。

5. 小张，能不能 _____ 我你的老师是谁?

Exercise 4 🗣

Translate the following expressions orally into Chinese.

1. do me a favor

2. Chinese tutor

3. find a girlfriend

4. in the teacher's office

5. wait for your phone call

6. cell phone number

You will hear three statements followed by three responses. Choose the most logical response to the statement.

1. a. 我想找一个北京女孩。

    b. 什么忙？

    c. 你的电话号码是什么？

2. a. 你有她的电话号码吗？

    b. 你也给我你的手机号码吧。

    c. 那我就等你的电话了。

3. a. 能帮个忙吗？

    b. 我也想找一个辅导。

    c. 下午我能见到她。

课文（二）Text (2)

你在跟谁说话呢？

简体版

Mary calls her boyfriend John and leaves a message.

喂，约翰，我是玛丽。我给你打了三次电话，都占线，你在跟谁说话呢？今天放学后李老师要帮我补习，我不能跟你一起吃晚饭了。我到小吃店吃两块面包，吃个鸡蛋，喝杯牛奶就行了。然后，我会在图书馆复习到九点左右，你八点三刻开车来接我吧。来以前给我发个短信，我在图书馆门口等你。你晚上开车得小心点儿，别太快了。再见！

課文〔二〕 Text (2)

你在跟誰說話呢？

繁体版

Mary calls her boyfriend John and leaves a message.

喂，約翰，我是瑪麗。我給你打了三次電話，都占綫，你在跟誰說話呢？今天放學後李老師要幫我補習，我不能跟你一起吃晚飯了。我到小吃店吃兩塊面包，吃個鷄蛋，喝杯牛奶就行了。然後，我會在圖書館復習到九點左右，你八點三刻開車來接我吧。來以前給我發個短信，我在圖書館門口等你。你晚上開車得小心點兒，別太快了。再見！

Kèwén (èr)　 *Text (2)*

Nǐ zài gēn Shéi Shuōhuà ne?

拼音版

Mary calls her boyfriend John and leaves a message.

Wèi, Yuēhàn, wǒ shì Mǎlì. Wǒ gěi nǐ dǎle sān cì diànhuà, dōu zhànxiàn, nǐ zài gēn shéi shuōhuà ne? Jīntiān fàngxué hòu Lǐ lǎoshī yào bāng wǒ bǔxí, wǒ bù néng gēn nǐ yìqǐ chī wǎnfàn le. Wǒ dào xiǎochīdiàn chī liǎng kuài miànbāo, chī ge jīdàn, hē bēi niúnǎi jiù xíng le. Ránhòu, wǒ huì zài túshūguǎn fùxí dào jiǔ diǎn zuǒyòu, nǐ bā diǎn sān kè kāichē lái jiē wǒ ba. Lái yǐqián gěi wǒ fā ge duǎnxìn, wǒ zài túshūguǎn ménkǒu děng nǐ. Nǐ wǎnshang kāichē děi xiǎoxīn diǎnr, bié tài kuài le. Zàijiàn!

生词〔二〕 New Words (2)

简体（繁體）	拼音	词性	解释
1　喂	wèi	*intj.*	hello, hi (in making phone call) 喂，喂，是小王吗？

	简体（繁體）	拼音	词性	解释
2	次	cì	m.	(measure wrod for the happening of actions) 打了三次电话 / 去了一次图书馆
3	占线（線）	zhànxiàn	v.	(telephone) be busy 你的电话老是占线。
4	在	zài	adv.	(adverb used before the verb to indicate an on-going action) 你在跟谁说话呢？ / 他在吃饭呢。 / 我在看书的时候，他来电话了。
5	说话（說話）	shuōhuà	v.	talk 你能用中文跟中国人说话吗？
6	帮（幫）	bāng	v.	assist, support, help 我帮约翰复习中文。 / 请你帮帮我。
7	补习（補習）	bǔxí	v.	take a remedial course 我三天没来上课，你帮我补习补习好吗？
8	小吃店	xiǎochīdiàn	n.	snack restaurant 我每天早上在小吃店吃早饭。
9	两	liǎng	num.	two 两块面包 / 两个人
10	块（塊）	kuài	m.	piece 一块面包 / 一块石头 / 一块糖
11	面（麵）包	miànbāo	n.	bread 一片面包 / 一块面包 / 烤面包
12	鸡（雞）蛋	jīdàn	n.	chicken egg 煮鸡蛋 / 炒鸡蛋 / 鸡蛋汤
13	喝	hē	v.	drink 喝水 / 喝茶 / 喝酒 / 喝汽水
14	牛奶	niúnǎi	n.	cow milk 挤牛奶 / 煮牛奶 / 喝牛奶
15	会（會）	huì	a.v.	can; be possible to 我会等你。 / 我以为他会来，可是他没有来。
16	复习（復習）	fùxí	v.	review 复习功课
17	左右	zuǒyòu	n.	about; or so 500块钱左右 / 人口一百万左右
18	开（開）	kāi	v.	drive 开车 / 开飞机 / 开车要小心。
19	车（車）	chē	n.	cart, vehicle 购物车 / 小车 / 自行车 / 汽车
20	接	jiē	v.	pick up (a person) 到学校接孩子回家 / 到机场接朋友
21	以前	yǐqián	n.	before 你来以前给我打个电话。 / 上大学以前我在小学教书。
22	短信	duǎnxìn	n.	text message 发短信 / 查短信
23	小心	xiǎoxīn	adj.	careful 开车的时候要小心。 / 他很小心。

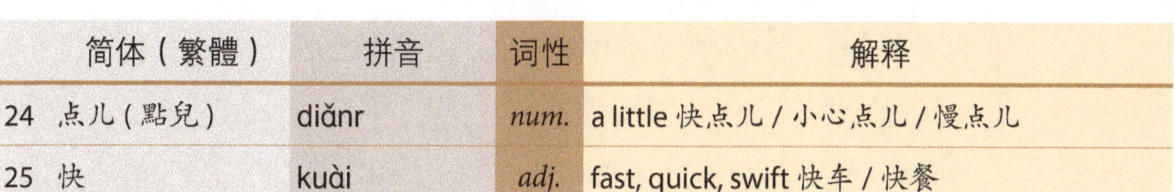

简体（繁體）	拼音	词性	解释
24 点儿（點兒）	diǎnr	num.	a little 快点儿 / 小心点儿 / 慢点儿
25 快	kuài	adj.	fast, quick, swift 快车 / 快餐

Exercise 6 👂

Listen to Text (2) then select the best answer for each of the following statements.

1. Mary called John _____.
   a. twice   b. three times   c. four times

2. Mary thought John was _____.
   a. shopping   b. busy with something   c. chatting with someone

3. Mary cannot have dinner with John because she will _____.
   a. have dinner with a friend   b. meet her teacher   c. work in the library

4. John is required to _____.
   a. meet Mary at the library   b. bring dinner to the library   c. bring her a cell phone

5. Mary warned John against _____.
   a. being late   b. being careless   c. being lazy

Exercise 7 📖 🗨

Read Text (2) and answer the questions orally in full Chinese sentences.

1. What happened to the line when Mary called John?

2. What will Mary and the teacher do after school?

3. What time does Mary want John to pick her up?

4. What is Mary's advice to John?

Exercise 8 ✍

Complete the following sentences in Chinese characters or pinyin with tone marks according to the English clues.

1. 我已经 _____(called you four times)。

2. 我现在很忙。每天 _____(help my friend review his lessons)。

3. 明天我要 _____ (study at school until 7 pm)。

4. 每天她下午三点钟 _____(go to school to pick up her little sister)。

5. 周末的时候开车的人很多，_____ (you have to be very careful when driving)。

6. 星期五早上我要去小吃店 _____(buy bread)。

第八课　打电话

165

三、汉字 Chinese Characters

1. New characters in this lesson

序号	拼音	简 / 繁	部件	构词
1	bàn	办 / 辦	办	办公室 / 办事 / 办法
2	bāng	帮 / 幫	邦（丰＋阝）＋巾	帮帮我 / 帮助 / 帮忙
3	bāo	包	勹＋巳	面包 / 烤面包 / 包子
4	bǐ	比	㇒＋匕	比尔 / 比如 / 比较
5	bǔ	补 / 補	衤＋卜	补习 / 补课 / 补衣服
6	chē	车 / 車	车	开车 / 开快车 / 汽车 / 上车
7	cì	次	冫＋欠	三次 / 每次 / 多次 / 下次
8	dǎ	打	扌＋丁	打电话 / 打手机 / 打车
9	dàn	蛋	疋＋虫	鸡蛋 / 蛋糕
10	dǎo	导 / 導	巳＋寸	辅导 / 领导
11	děng	等	竹＋寺（土＋寸）	我等你 / 等我 / 等等
12	duǎn	短	矢＋豆	假期很短 / 长短 / 短命
13	ěr	尔 / 爾	尔（𠂉＋小）	比尔
14	fǔ	辅 / 輔	车＋甫	辅导
15	fù	复 / 復	𠂊＋日＋夂	复习
16	gào	告	生＋口	告诉 / 告知 / 报告
17	hē	喝	口＋曷（日＋匃）	喝牛奶 / 喝水 / 喝茶
18	huà	话 / 話	讠＋舌（千＋口）	电话 / 说话 / 听话
19	huì	会 / 會	人＋云	我会 / 聚会 / 会议 / 开会
20	jī	鸡 / 雞	又＋鸟	鸡蛋 / 公鸡 / 火鸡 / 宫保鸡丁
21	jiē	接	扌＋妾（立＋女）	接孩子回家 / 接我 / 接送
22	kuài	快	忄＋夬	快点 / 我快看完这本书了。
23	liǎng	两 / 兩	两	两块 / 两个人
24	mǎ	码 / 碼	石＋马	电话号码 / 门牌号码
25	niú	牛	牛	牛奶 / 牛羊 / 奶牛

26	ò	哦	口＋我	哦，是你啊！／哦，多美啊！
27	qián	前	丷＋月＋刂	商店前／门前／前面／前进
28	shǎo	少	少	多少人／多少事
29	sù	诉／訴	讠＋斥	告诉／上诉
30	tí	题／題	是（日＋疋）＋页	问题／课题／题目
31	wèi	喂	口＋畏（田＋ ）	喂，是小王吗？／喂，找谁？
32	wèn	问／問	门＋口	请问／提问／学问／问题
33	xí	习／習	习	复习／学习／练习
34	xiàn	线／線	纟＋戋	占线／电话线／线路
35	xiǎng	想	相（木＋目）＋心	我想学中文／我想去中国
36	xīn	心	心	小心点／不小心
37	xìn	信	亻＋言	信纸／平信／挂号信／送信
38	yòu	右	𠂇＋口	左右／右边／右手
39	zhàn	占／佔	卜＋口	占线
40	zuǒ	左	𠂇＋工	左手／左边／左转／左右

Exercise 1 ✎

Copy the following single-component characters with correct stroke order in the spaces provided.

bàn	办	フ 力 办 办				
chē	车	一 𠂇 车 车				
liǎng	两	一 丆 丌 両 丙 两 两				
niú	牛	ノ 𠂉 二 牛				
shǎo	少	丨 亅 小 少				

| xí | 习 | ㄱ 习 习 | | | | | |
| xīn | 心 | 丶 心 心 心 | | | | | |

2. Creation of characters (1): pictographic characters

Traditionally, Chinese people created Chinese characters in four different ways, thus Chinese characters fall into four basic categories: pictographic, self-explanatory, associative compound, and pictophonetic characters.

Pictographic characters are simplified pictures of objects. The following characters with their original forms in brackets, belong to this group:

日（⊖）rì	月（☽）yuè	口（▽）kǒu
sun, day	moon, month	mouth; measure word for family members

3. Creation of characters (2): self-explanatory characters

Self-explanatory characters are symbols of abstract ideas. The following characters together with their original forms fall into this category:

上（⌐）shàng	下（⌐）xià
above	below

Exercise 2 ✎

Use your imagination to guess the meaning of the following pictographic and self-explanatory characters. Consult your instructor to check your answer.

1. ♡	2. ʔ	3. 中	4. 夨	5. 本

飞跃——汉语初级教程学生用书 上册

四、语言点 Language Points

1. The auxiliary verb 能

The auxiliary verb 能 is put before a verb to mark a person's ability or situational possibility to carry out an action. It is equivalent to "can" in English. The affirmative form is:

> **Subject ＋ 能 ＋ Verb （＋ Object）**

(1) 下午我在张老师的办公室能见到她。
　　This afternoon, I can see her in Instructor Zhang's office.
(2) 今天晚上我能跟你一起做作业。
　　I can do homework with you this evening.

The negative form is:

> **Subject ＋ 不 ＋ 能 ＋ Verb （＋ Object）**

(3) 今天放学后李老师要帮我补习，我不能跟你一起吃晚饭了。
　　Instructor Li will help me make up lessons after school today. So, I cannot have dinner with you.
(4) 我下午有课，不能去图书馆看电影。
　　I have classes this afternoon. I cannot go to the library to see the movie.

There are two ways to form a question with 能：

> **Subject ＋ 能 ＋ Verb （＋ Object）＋ 吗?**

or

> **Subject ＋ 能不能 ＋ Verb （＋ Object）?**

(5) 林华，能帮个忙吗？ / 林华，能不能帮个忙？

Lin Hua, can you do me a favor?

(6) 约翰，今天晚上你能和我一块儿去买东西吗？ /

约翰，今天晚上你能不能和我一块儿去买东西？

John, can you go shopping with me this evening?

2. The use of 给

The verb 给 (to give) often carries two objects after it.

Subject ＋ 给 ＋ Somebody ＋ Something

(1) 那你也给我你的手机号码吧。

Then please give me your cell phone number, too.

(2) 万圣节那天晚上，我给了孩子们很多糖。

On Halloween night, I gave children a lot of candy.

给 can also be used as a preposition, meaning "to; for the benefit of".

Subject ＋ 给 ＋ Pronoun / Noun ＋ Main Verb ＋ Object

(3) 我给你打了三次电话。

I called you three times.

(4) 你来以前要给我发个短信。

Before you come, you need to send me a short message.

(5) 我能给你发个短信。

I can send you a short message.

3. The adverb 在 indicating an action in progress

In Chinese, the ongoing aspect is marked by putting the adverb 在 or 正在 before a verb. The modal particle 呢 at the end of a sentence is optional.

Subject ＋（正）在 ＋ Verb ＋（呢）

(1) 我给你打了三次电话，都占线。你在跟谁说话呢？
I called you three times and always got busy signals. Who were you talking to?

(2) "小红，你在哪儿？""我在（商店）买东西呢。"
"Xiaohong, where are you?" "I am at the store shopping."

(3) 你给我打电话的时候，我正在给你发短信。
When you called me, I was sending you a short message.

4. The time word 以前

The time word 以前 means "before". Same as the time word 以后（"after"）that we learned about in Lesson 6, 以前 can also follow other time or action words to form time expressions. Note that the word order in a Chinese time expression with 以前 is the opposite to its counterpart in English.

(1) 你来以前给我发个短信。
Before you come, please send me a short message.

(2) 你做作业以前得先复习。
You must review (your lessons) before you do homework.

(3) 我每天七点半以前到学校。
I arrive at school before 7:30 everyday.

(4) 我们家万圣节以前得去买很多糖。
Our family has to buy a lot of candy before Halloween.

5. The modal particle 吧 (1)

The modal particle 吧 is used at the end of a sentence to indicate a suggestion or a request. The use of 吧 also softens the tone of the suggestion or request.

(1) 来来来，我来介绍一下吧。
Come here, let me introduce you quickly.

(2) 那你也给我你的手机号码吧。
Then, please give me your cell phone number, too.

(3) 你八点三刻开车来接我吧。
Please drive here to pick me up at 8:45.

6. The comparison of 两 and 二

Both 两 and 二 refer to "two"; however their usages are not the same. Basically 两 is used before measure words while 二 is used in counting numerals, including cardinal and ordinal numbers. For example:

> 两：
> 两个学生 (two students)　两块面包 (two pieces of bread)　下午两点钟 (2:00 pm)
> 二：
> 十二 (12)　二十二 (22)　五百零二 (502)　零点二 (0.2)　二分之一 (1/2)
> 第二 (second)　二哥 (second elder brother)

Exercise 1 👂 ✍

Listen to three short dialogs and answer the questions in Chinese characters or pinyin with tone marks.

Dialog 1 Question: 小文在做什么？	Answer:
Dialog 2 Question: 玛丽在做什么？	Answer:
Dialog 3 Question: 汤姆在做什么？	Answer:

Exercise 2 ✍

Change the following sentences into questions. Then give them negative answers.

Example:　大卫能说中文。

　　　　　大卫能说中文吗？ / 大卫能不能说中文？

　　　　　大卫不能说中文。

1. 小雨能在下午两点钟回到家。

　　_____？ /_____？

　　_____。

2. 约翰能教小丽学英文。

　　_____？ /_____？

　　_____。

3. 林华能帮比尔找到一个中文辅导。

　　_____？ /_____？

　　_____。

4. 他们能一块儿去商店买东西。

_____? / _____?

_____。

Exercise 3 🖎

第八课　打电话

Rearrange the words or phrases into correct sentences paying special attention to the usage of the verb 给.

1. 一块手表　昨天　爸爸　给了　我

_____。

2. 玛丽　给　写信　妈妈　常常

_____。

3. 怎么　我　给　打电话　中国的朋友

_____?

4. 小王　新手机　买了　女朋友　给　一个

_____。

Exercise 4 🗣️🖎

Look at the pictures below and answer the questions first orally, then in characters or pinyin with tone marks. Use 在 / 正在 to indicate an action in progress.

1. A：他们（正）在做什么?

B：_____。

2. A：她（正）在做什么?

B：_____。

3. A：他们在图书馆做什么?

B：_____。

(doing homework)

4. A：昨天下午三点你在做什么?

B：_____。

5. A：他们正在做什么？

B：＿＿＿＿＿＿＿＿＿＿＿＿＿。

6. A：他们在做什么？

B：＿＿＿＿＿＿＿＿＿＿＿＿＿。

Exercise 5 📖 ✍

Read the following dialogs aloud and then translate them into English.

Dialog 1

A：小文，我能在图书馆吃面包吗？

B：不能。

A：那我能不能在图书馆喝咖啡？

B：也不能。

＿＿＿＿＿＿＿＿＿＿＿＿＿＿＿＿＿＿＿＿＿＿＿＿＿

＿＿＿＿＿＿＿＿＿＿＿＿＿＿＿＿＿＿＿＿＿＿＿＿＿

＿＿＿＿＿＿＿＿＿＿＿＿＿＿＿＿＿＿＿＿＿＿＿＿＿

＿＿＿＿＿＿＿＿＿＿＿＿＿＿＿＿＿＿＿＿＿＿＿＿＿

Dialog 2

A：妈妈，你在做什么？

B：我在吃晚饭。

A：什么？都九点了，你还在吃晚饭？

B：是啊，八点半才回家。

＿＿＿＿＿＿＿＿＿＿＿＿＿＿＿＿＿＿＿＿＿＿＿＿＿

＿＿＿＿＿＿＿＿＿＿＿＿＿＿＿＿＿＿＿＿＿＿＿＿＿

＿＿＿＿＿＿＿＿＿＿＿＿＿＿＿＿＿＿＿＿＿＿＿＿＿

＿＿＿＿＿＿＿＿＿＿＿＿＿＿＿＿＿＿＿＿＿＿＿＿＿

Dialog 3

A：小文，我给你买了一个手机。

B：爸爸，你为什么要给我买手机？

A：有了手机，你可以常常给爸爸妈妈打电话呀！

B：对，还可以给女孩子们发短信！

_____

_____

_____

_____

Dialog 4

A：小华，这个星期你很忙吧？

B：是啊，我们每天上下午都有课，昨天星期五又有一个考试。

A：那今天下午我们去旧金山玩玩吧，怎么样？

B：好啊，可是下午一点钟以前不行，一点以后我可以跟你一起去。

A：那我们就一点半坐地铁去吧。

_____

_____

_____

_____

_____

Exercise 6 ⏻☀

Translate the following sentences into Chinese orally. Use the Chinese in the parentheses as a clue.

1. Do you often call your parents?（给）

2. Can you introduce your family members in Chinese?（能……吗 / 能不能）

3. David was having dinner at 7:00 pm yesterday evening.（正在）

4. Let's go to the coffee shop to do our homework after school.（以后，吧）

5. I can meet Xiao Li in the library at two o'clock this afternoon.（两，能）

6. I lived with my grandparents in Shanghai before I was twelve years old.（十二，以前）

7. "What is John doing now?" "He is making a jack-o-lantern."（正在）

8. I already gave David my cell phone number: 254-3202.（给）

9. You cannot eat in the library, you can't drink coffee there either.（不能）

10. Give me a call before you come to my house tomorrow afternoon.（以前，给，吧）

五、语言运用 Using the Language

Activity 1

In saying telephone numbers, the number "one" is often read as "yāo". Listen to the following statements and write down the phone numbers.

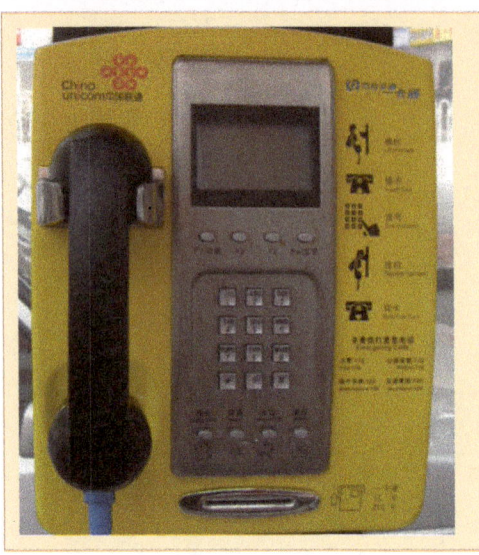

1.
2.
3.
4.
5.

Activity 2

Read the following notes and answer the questions below.

1.

约翰：
　　今天李英不能来上课。请你下课后到她家帮她复习今天的英语课。祝好！
　　　　　　　　玛丽

What did Mary ask John to do?

2.

小丽：
　　我到张妈妈家去了，晚上七点才回来。你放学回来先喝杯牛奶，吃两块面包吧。
　　　　　　　　妈妈

What should Xiaoli do when she gets back from school?

Activity 3 👂 ✎

Listen to a message and sum up its main idea.

_____

_____

_____

Activity 4 ✎

Write a message for Li Wen as a reply to Lin Hua according to Activity 3. Explain to Lin Hua why he missed her phone calls. Tell her he will do as she told him. He will call her when he is coming to pick her up. Type it out on your computer.

Activity 5 📖 🗣

Read the following blog by a foreign student named John who is learning Chinese in Beijing, and answer the questions.

　　我在学中文，想找一个辅导。我的同学大卫有个辅导，是个北京人。我问大卫能不能帮我找一个北京人做辅导。大卫说他有一个朋友，叫李英华，她的老家就在北京附近。大卫给了我她的电话号码。我给李英华打了一个电话。英华说很高兴给我辅导中文。可是她也说了，她想请我给她补习英文。我说没问题。今天早上，我们去了图书馆附近的咖啡店吃早点。我给她要了三片法国面包，两个鸡蛋和一杯牛奶。李英华说她很爱吃。

Questions:

1. What does John need?

2. Where is David's tutor from?

3. Where is Li Yinghua from?

4. How can John help Li Yinghua?

5. What did John and Li Yinghua do this morning? Be specific.

Activity 6 🗣

Role Play

You are learning Chinese. Call your friend to ask him/her to help you find a tutor. Your friend knows a Beijinger. Ask for his/her phone number.

Sentences you may need to use:

我需要一个辅导。能给我他 / 她的电话号码吗？

Activity 7 🗣

What do you say?

1. You wonder if your friend can help you with something.
2. You need the cell phone number of someone.
3. You want to tell someone you will wait for his/her phone call.
4. You want to say it will be OK if someone does something in a certain way.

一、导入 Lead-in

Exercise 1

Look at the pictures below and describe them in Chinese.

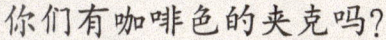
你们有咖啡色的夹克吗?

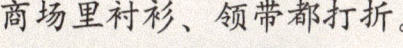
商场里衬衫、领带都打折。

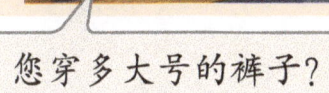
您穿多大号的裤子?

我买了一双白色的球鞋。

After learning this lesson, you will be able to:

1. Use Chinese to shop, talk about prices, and ask for a discount.

2. Talk about common colors, clothes, measure words, and the Chinese monetary system.

3. Recognize new characters in this lesson, and understand how most characters were created.

4. Use 还是 to form choice questions, use the idiomatic expression 打...折 and the 的 phrase.

二、课文 Texts

课文（一）Text (1)

多少钱？

Li Wen and his younger brother are in a clothing store.

李　文：小姐，我想买件西装上衣。

售货员：好。您要多大号的？

李　文：中号的。

售货员：要黑色的还是灰色的？

李　文：有蓝色的吗？

售货员：有。您看这件怎么样？

弟　弟：哥，还是要那件灰色的吧。

售货员：灰色的？好，您试试。

李　文：好像小了点儿。

售货员：您得穿大号的。看看这件行不行？

李　文：我看还行。多少钱？　**Tips:** how to ask about the price

售货员：六百块。　**Tips:** how to ask for a discount

弟　弟：不便宜啊！可不可以打个折？

售货员：您要可以给您打八折。

李　文：那我再来两件衬衫，一件咖啡色的，一件蓝色的，
　　　　也打八折吧。

售货员：好的。衬衫一百二十五块钱一件，两件
　　　　二百五十，加上西装六百，一共八百五十块，
　　　　八折是六百八十块。还要别的吗？

李　文：不要了。这是七百。

售货员：找您二十块。谢谢，欢迎再来！

简体版

多少錢？

繁体版

Li Wen and his younger brother are in a clothing store.

李　文：小姐，我想買件西裝上衣。

售貨員：好。您要多大號的？

李　文：中號的。

售貨員：要黑色的還是灰色的？

李　文：有藍色的嗎？

售貨員：有。您看這件怎麼樣？

弟　弟：哥，還是要那件灰色的吧。

售貨員：灰色的？好，您試試。

李　文：好像小了點兒。

售貨員：您得穿大號的。看看這件行不行？

李　文：我看還行。多少錢？

售貨員：六百塊。

弟　弟：不便宜啊！可不可以打個折？

售貨員：您要可以給您打八折。

李　文：那我再來兩件襯衫，一件咖啡色的，一件藍色的，
　　　　也打八折吧。

售貨員：好的。襯衫一百二十五塊錢一件，兩件
　　　　二百五十，加上西裝六百，一共八百五十塊，
　　　　八折是六百八十塊。還要別的嗎？

李　文：不要了。這是七百。

售貨員：找您二十塊。謝謝，歡迎再來！

Duōshao Qián?

Li Wen and his younger brother are in a clothing store.

Lǐ Wén: Xiǎojiě, wǒ xiǎng mǎi jiàn xīzhuāng shàngyī.

Shòuhuòyuán: Hǎo. Nín yào duō dà hào de?

Lǐ Wén: Zhōng hào de.

Shòuhuòyuán: Yào hēisè de háishì huīsè de?

Lǐ Wén: Yǒu lánsè de ma?

Shòuhuòyuán: Yǒu. Nín kàn zhè jiàn zěnmeyàng?

Dìdi: Gē, háishì yào nà jiàn huīsè de ba.

Shòuhuòyuán: Huīsè de? Hǎo, nín shìshi.

Lǐ Wén: Hǎoxiàng xiǎole diǎnr.

Shòuhuòyuán: Nín děi chuān dà hào de.

　　　　　　　Kànkan zhè jiàn xíng bu xíng?

Lǐ Wén: Wǒ kàn hái xíng. Duōshao qián?

Shòuhuòyuán: Liùbǎi kuài.

Dìdi: Bù piányi a! kě bu kěyǐ dǎ ge zhé?

Shòuhuòyuán: Nín yào kěyǐ gěi nín dǎ bā zhé.

Lǐ Wén: Nà wǒ zài lái liǎng jiàn chènshān, yí jiàn kāfēisè de, yí jiàn

　　　　　lánsè de, yě dǎ bā zhé ba.

Shòuhuòyuán: Hǎo de. Chènshān yìbǎi èrshíwǔ kuài qián yí jiàn,

　　　　　　　liǎng jiàn èrbǎi wǔshí, jiāshang xīzhuāng liùbǎi,

　　　　　　　yígòng bābǎi wǔshí kuài, bā zhé shì liùbǎi bāshí

　　　　　　　kuài. Hái yào bié de ma?

Lǐ Wén: Bú yào le. Zhè shì qībǎi.

Shòuhuòyuán: Zhǎo nín èrshí kuài. Xièxie! Huānyíng zài lái!

生词（一） *New Words (1)*

	简体（繁體）	拼音	词性	解释
1	件	jiàn	*m.*	(measure word for clothes) 一件蓝衣服 / 一件西装
2	西装（裝）	xīzhuāng	*n.*	Western suit 你穿西装很好看。/ 西装有成套的，也有单件的。
3	上衣	shàngyī	*n.*	upper outer garment; jacket 上衣和裤子
4	售货员（貨員）	shòuhuòyuán	*n.*	shop clerk; salesperson 我姐姐是售货员。
5	号（號）	hào	*n.*	size 小号 / 中号 / 大号 / 多大号？
6	中	zhōng	*adj.*	middle 中号 / 中学 / 中等
7	黑	hēi	*adj.*	black 黑色 / 天黑 / 黑西装
8	色	sè	*n.*	color 红色 / 黑色 / 白色 / 蓝色
9	还（還）是	háishì	*conj./ adv.*	or/ had better 你要灰色的还是蓝色的？/ 还是要那件灰色的吧。
10	灰	huī	*adj.*	gray 灰衣服 / 天灰灰的。
11	蓝（藍）	lán	*adj.*	blue 蓝领 / 蓝色的夹克
12	怎么样（麼樣）	zěnmeyàng	*pron.*	how 这个怎么样？/ 我们一起复习，怎么样？/ 最近你怎么样？
13	试（試）	shì	*v.*	test, try 试衣服 / 试穿 / 试用 / 试一试
14	好像	hǎoxiàng	*adv.*	as if; seem 他看起来好像病了。/ 这件衣服好像大了点儿。
15	穿	chuān	*v.*	wear; put on 穿衣服 / 穿鞋 / 穿上衣服
16	钱（錢）	qián	*n.*	money 零钱 / 钱包 / 有钱人
17	块（塊）	kuài	*m.*	(colloquial word for Chinese yuan and the U.S. dollar) 两块钱 / 三块两毛五
18	便宜	piányi	*adj.*	cheap, inexpensive 这本书很便宜。/ 便宜的衣服不好。
19	打折	dǎzhé	*v.*	make a discount 打八折 / 给我打个折。
20	衬（襯）衫	chènshān	*n.*	shirt 一件衬衫 / 灰色的衬衫
21	加上	jiāshang		add; plus 上衣加上衬衫一共五百块。

第九课　买东西

183

简体（繁體）	拼音	词性	解释
22 一共	yígòng	*adv.*	altogether; in sum 一共五块钱 / 一共买了两件西装
23 别的	bié de		other 还要别的吗？ / 你买了别的东西没有？
24 欢（歡）迎	huānyíng	*v.*	welcome 欢迎新同学 / 欢迎再来
25 再	zài	*adv.*	again 今天我很忙，你明天再来吧。

Exercise 1

Listen to Text (1) and decide whether the following statements are true or false.

1. Li Wen wanted to buy a T-shirt.	(	)
2. Li Wen's brother preferred a different color.	(	)
3. Li Wen spent 900 kuai at the store.	(	)
4. The store clerk was not friendly.	(	)

Exercise 2

Read Text (1) and answer the questions orally in Chinese.

1. What did Li Wen want to buy?

2. How did Li Wen's brother feel about what was shown to Li Wen?

3. What happened when he tried on the second item?

4. What were the colors of the other two items?

5. How much change did he get?

Exercise 3

Read the following dialogs and fill in each blank with the verbs and adjectives below.

喜欢　　穿　　试试　　要　　便宜　　打折　　找

A：这件衣服您 _____ 吗？

B：我 _____ 上 _____ 看。还行，挺合适 (héshì, fitting) 的。

A：您想要吗？

B：九百四十，太贵 (guì, expensive) 了。要是 _____ 一点儿就好了。
　　能不能 _____ ？

A：最多打八折。

B：七百五十二块。我 _____ 了。这是八百。

A：_____ 您四十八块。请拿好。

Exercise 4 🎧 📖

Listen to the following dialog and decide whether the following statements are true or false.

1. 男士要买西装。	(	)
2. 他要买中号的。	(	)
3. 他要买蓝色的。	(	)
4. 他花了九十块钱。	(	)
5. 女士找给他钱。	(	)

课文（二）Text (2)

那些东西很便宜！

简体版

Xiao Wang writes about his shopping experience last weekend.

上个周末，我和朋友逛街的时候，看见有人在自己家的院子里卖东西，有衣服、鞋、书、家具、日用品等。那些东西价钱都很便宜。比如一条裤子只要两三美元，一件衬衫也只要三四美元。虽然是旧衣服，但是都很干净。有的才穿了几天，像新的一样。我买了一件夹克，只要八美元。我的朋友买了一双球鞋和一条红色的领带，才六美元。他说在商场，这些东西减价的时候，也还是有点儿贵。

那些东西很便宜！

繁体版

Xiao Wang writes about his shopping experience last weekend.

上個周末，我和朋友逛街的時候，看見有人在自己家的院子裏賣東西，有衣服、鞋、書、家具、日用品等。那些東西價錢都很便宜。比如一條褲子祇要兩三美元，一件襯衫也祇要三四美元。雖然是舊衣服，但是都很幹淨。有的才穿了幾天，像新的一樣。我買了一件夾克，祇要八美元。我的朋友買了一雙球鞋和一條紅色的領帶，才六美元。他説在商場，這些東西減價的時候，也還是有點兒貴。

Kèwén (èr)   *Text (2)*

Nàxiē Dōngxi Hěn Piányi !

拼音版

Xiao Wang writes about his shopping experience last weekend.

Shàngge zhōumò, wǒ hé péngyou guàngjiē de shíhou, kànjiàn yǒu rén zài zìjǐ jiā de yuànzi lǐ mài dōngxi, yǒu yīfu, xié, shū, jiājù, rìyòngpǐn děng. Nàxiē dōngxi de jiàqian dōu hěn piányi. Bǐrú yì tiáo kùzi zhǐ yào liǎng-sān Měiyuán, yí jiàn chènshān yě zhǐ yào sān-sì Měiyuán. Suīrán shì jiù yīfu, dànshì dōu hěn gānjìng. Yǒu de cái chuānle jǐ tiān, xiàng xīn de yíyàng. Wǒ mǎile yí jiàn jiākè, zhǐ yào bā Měiyuán. Wǒ de péngyou mǎile yì shuāng qiúxié hé yì tiáo hóngsè de lǐngdài, cái liù Měiyuán. Tā shuō zài shāngchǎng, zhèxiē dōngxi jiǎnjià de shíhòu, yě háishì yǒudiǎnr guì.

飞跃——汉语初级教程学生用书　上册

生词（二） *New Words (2)*

简体（繁體）	拼音	词性	解释
1　上	shàng	*n.*	previous, last 上个月 / 上个星期
2　周（週）末	zhōumò	*n.*	weekend 过周末 / 周末晚会
3　逛	guàng	*v.*	walk around in streets, malls, etc. 逛街 / 逛商店 / 逛公园
4　自己	zìjǐ	*pron.*	self 我的小弟弟会自己穿衣服了。/ 我给自己买了一件西装。
5　院子	yuànzi	*n.*	yard 美国的院子和中国的院子不一样。
6　卖（賣）	mài	*v.*	sell 商店里有很多衣服卖。/ 这件上衣怎么卖？
7　衣服	yīfu	*n.*	clothes 穿衣服 / 衣服的号码
8　鞋	xié	*n.*	shoe 皮鞋 / 球鞋 / 你穿多大号码的鞋？
9　家具	jiājù	*n.*	furniture 家具店 / 旧家具
10　日用品	rìyòngpǐn	*n.*	daily use articles 日用品商店
11　等	děng	*part.*	so on and so forth; etc. 我喜欢看电影、看电视、读书等。
12　价钱（價錢）	jiàqian	*n.*	price 这件衣服的价钱很贵。
13　比如	bǐrú	*v.*	for example 比如一条裤子只要二三十块钱。
14　裤（褲）子	kùzi	*n.*	trousers, pants 一条裤子 / 穿裤子
15　虽（雖）然	suīrán	*conj.*	although 虽然这件衣服很便宜，但是我不喜欢。
16　但是	dànshì	*conj.*	but 二手店虽然便宜，但是我不喜欢。
17　干净（淨）	gānjìng	*adj.*	clean 二手店的衣服都是洗干净了的。
18　新	xīn	*adj.*	new 像新的一样 / 新学年 / 新年 / 新书
19　像…一样（樣）	xiàng…yíyàng		same as… 这本旧书看起来像新的一样。
20　夹（夾）克	jiākè	*n.*	jacket 买夹克 / 穿夹克
21　双（雙）	shuāng	*m.*	pair 一双球鞋 / 一双袜子 / 一双筷子
22　球鞋	qiúxié	*n.*	sneakers 打球需要穿球鞋。
23　领带（領帶）	lǐngdài	*n.*	tie 一条领带 / 戴领带
24　商场（場）	shāngchǎng	*n.*	market, mall 他在商场工作。/ 商场几点开门？

简体（繁體）		拼音	词性	解释
25	些	xiē	*m.*	some, few, several 有些人 / 这些东西不贵。
26	减价（減價）	jiǎnjià	*v.*	cut prices; sell on discount 周末大减价 / 减价出售
27	贵（貴）	guì	*adj.*	expensive 这家店的东西很贵。
专有名词 Proper Noun				
	美元	Měiyuán	*pn.*	US dollar

Exercise 5 🦻 📖

Listen to Text (2) and select the correct word/phrase that best completes each sentence.

1. 他们看见有人在 _____ 卖家里的东西。

　　a. 商场　　　　　　b. 院子里　　　　　　c. 街上

2. 他们卖的东西 _____。

　　a. 价格跟商场一样　b. 很便宜　　　　　　c. 打三四折

3. 他们卖的衣服 _____。

　　a. 很干净　　　　　b. 都是新的　　　　　c. 都穿了很长时间

4. 我的朋友买的球鞋 _____。

　　a. 不到六十块钱　　b. 九十块钱　　　　　c. 打了八折

5. 商场的东西 _____。

　　a. 减价也贵　　　　b. 好像不花钱　　　　c. 便宜很多

Exercise 6 📖 ✍

Read Text (2) and fill in the chart with information from the text.

Topic	Information
What did Xiao Wang and his friend do last weekend?	
What did they see at someone's yard?	
What did his friend buy?	
What did Xiao Wang buy?	

Exercise 7 📖 ✍

Read the following sentences and rearrange them into a meaningful paragraph.

1. 有衣服、鞋、家具、日用品等。

2. 我周末喜欢逛街。

3. 我为什么喜欢去那些地方买东西？

4. 但是在院子里卖的东西都很便宜。

5. 逛街时可以看到有人在自己家的院子里卖旧东西。

6. 商场的东西减价的时候也还是有点儿贵。

7. 因为那些地方的东西很便宜。

Exercise 8 👂 📖

Listen to the four statements followed by three responses. Choose the most logical response to the statement.

1. a. 你家的院子里有商店吗？

   b. 你得穿大号的衣服。

   c. 周末有很多人在院子里卖东西吗？

2. a. 那些衣服都很干净。

   b. 那些衣服都很贵。

   c. 那些衣服都很小。

3. a. 打折也还贵。

   b. 我不喜欢到别人家里买东西。

   c. 我朋友买了一双鞋，打五折。

4. a. 周末逛商店去吧。

   b. 小姐，这个多少钱？

   c. 一双鞋和一条领带。

三、汉字 Chinese Characters

1. New characters in this lesson

序号	拼音	简 / 繁	部件	构词
1	bǎi	百	百	一百块 / 百万 / 百货商场
2	chǎng	场 / 場	土 + 昜	商场 / 一场电影 / 一场球
3	chèn	衬 / 襯	衤 + 寸	衬衫 / 白衬衣
4	chuān	穿	穴 + 牙	穿衣服 / 穿鞋 / 穿裤子
5	fú	服	月 + 艮	衣服 / 服装 / 服务员
6	gān	干 / 乾	干	干净
7	gòng	共	共	一共五块 / 共同 / 公共洗手间

飞跃——汉语初级教程学生用书 上册

8	hēi	黑	黑	黑色 / 黑板 / 黑笔 / 天黑了
9	huān	欢 / 歡	又 + 欠	喜欢 / 欢乐 / 欢笑
10	huī	灰	尢 + 火	灰色
11	huò	货 / 貨	化（亻+ 匕）+ 贝	百货商场 / 百货公司
12	jǐ	己	己	自己
13	jiā	加	力 + 口	参加 / 加上 / 加州
14	jiā	夹（夾）	夹	夹克 / 穿夹克 / 黑色夹克
15	jià	价 / 價	亻 + 介	价钱 / 高价 / 减价
16	jiǎn	减 / 減	冫 + 咸	大减价 / 减价出售
17	jiàn	件	亻 + 牛	一件衣服 / 两件衬衣
18	jìng	净 / 淨	冫 + 争	干净
19	kè	克	十 + 兄（口 + 儿）	夹克 / 克服
20	kù	裤 / 褲	衤 + 库（广 + 车）	裤子 / 长裤
21	lán	蓝 / 藍	艹 + 监（⺊ + 皿）	蓝色 / 蓝天 / 蓝海
22	lǐng	领 / 領	令 + 页	领带 / 领巾 / 蓝领
23	mài	卖 / 賣	十 + 买（乛 + 头）	烧卖 / 买卖 / 卖东西
24	mò	末	末	周末 / 期末 / 末日
25	pián	便	亻 + 更	便宜 / 价钱便宜 / 不便宜
26	pǐn	品	口 + 口 + 口	日用品 / 产品 / 出品
27	qián	钱 / 錢	钅 + 戋	零钱 / 钱包 / 金钱
28	qiú	球	王 + 求	球鞋 / 篮球 / 足球 / 气球 / 打球
29	rú	如	女 + 口	如果 / 如是
30	sè	色	夕 + 巴	咖啡色 / 红色 / 白色 / 蓝色
31	shān	衫	衤 + 彡	衬衫 / 衣衫 / 白衫
32	shì	试 / 試	讠 + 式（工 + 弋）	试衣服 / 试穿 / 试用
33	shòu	售	隹 + 口	售货员 / 出售
34	shuāng	双 / 雙	又 + 又	一双鞋 / 一双手 / 双亲
35	suī	虽 / 雖	口 + 虫	虽然
36	tiáo	条 / 條	夂 + 木	一条领带 / 一条河

37	xiàng	像	亻+象	好像 / 像片
38	xiē	些	此(止+匕)+二	一些 / 有些人
39	xié	鞋	革+圭(土+土)	球鞋 / 皮鞋
40	xīn	新	亲+斤	新学年 / 新年 / 新书
41	xíng	行	彳+亍	不行 / 行不行 / 我看还行
42	yàng	样/樣	木+羊	怎么样 / 这样 / 那样
43	yī	衣	衣	衣服 / 衣领
44	yi	宜	宀+且	便宜
45	yíng	迎	卬+辶	欢迎 / 迎接
46	yòng	用	用	日用品 / 信用卡 / 不用
47	yuán	员/員	口+贝	售货员 / 员工
48	yuàn	院	阝+完(宀+元)	医院 / 学院 / 院校 / 院子
49	zěn	怎	乍+心	怎么样 / 怎么办
50	zhé	折	扌+斤	打两折 / 给我打折
51	zhuāng	装/裝	壮(丬+士)+衣	西装 / 服装 / 装修
52	zì	自	自	自己 / 自从 / 自动

Exercise 1 ✎

Copy the following single-component characters with correct stroke order in the spaces provided.

bǎi	百	一　一　一　丁　百　百	
gān	干	一　二　干	
hēi	黑	丨　冂　冂　四　四　里　里，里　黑　黑　黑	
gòng	共	一　十　廿　井　共　共	
jǐ	己	一　コ　己	

jiā	夹	一 ｢ ｢ 冂 쭈 夹		
mò	末	一 ニ 丰 才 末		
sè	色	ノ ク ⺈ 乞 包 色		
yī	衣	丶 一 ㇗ 亢 产 衣		
yòng	用	ノ 冂 月 月 用		
zì	自	′ ⺊ 自 自 自 自		

2. Creation of characters (3): associative compound characters

An associative compound character is formed by two or more single characters, and its meaning is determined by the association of the meanings of each of the single characters. For example, the associative character 明 (明 míng), is formed by two single characters: 日 (rì, the sun), and 月 (yuè, the moon). Its original meaning is "bright". Some other meanings, like "plain", "to understand", and "tomorrow", are derived from its original meaning. Below are more associative characters:

好 = 女 + 子	林 = 木 + 木	明 = 日 + 月	男 = 田 + 力
hǎo, good	lín, forest	míng, tomorrow	nán, male
woman has a baby	two trees	tomorrow comes after a day and a night	people who work in the field

3. Creation of characters (4): pictophonetic characters

In modern Chinese, more than 80 percent of characters are pictophonetic characters. A pictophonetic character is formed by two parts: the meaning element (xíngpáng) and the sound element (shēngpáng). The meaning element, or radical, usually indicates the category the character belongs to while the sound element indicates its sound. Take 妈 (mā, mother) as an example, the radical 女 (nǚ, female), is the meaning element indicating that the character is related to female; while the sound element 马 (mǎ, horse) indicates the character's sound, with nothing to do with the character's meaning. Another example is the particle 吗, its radical 口 (kǒu, mouth) indicates that this character is related to speech while the sound element 马 hints at its sound. Note that many sound elements in pictophonetic characters do not accurately indicate the sound, and some meaning elements do not indicate the exact meaning either. In most cases though, they can still give us some hints at the character's sound and meaning.

Exercise 2 ✍

Use your imagination to guess the meaning of the following associative compound characters. Consult a Chinese-English dictionary to check your answer.

囚	从	晶	森	休

Exercise 3 ✍

Give the pinyin for the following characters and write the common sound element for each group inside the parenthesis:

1. 吧 _____ 把 _____ 爸 _____ (   )   2. 作 _____ 昨 _____ (   )
3. 很 _____ 银 _____ 跟 _____ (   )   4. 姓 _____ 星 _____ (   )

四、语言点 Language Points

1. The 的 construction

The structural particle 的 can be used to form the 的 construction, which functions as a noun. See the following examples from this lesson:

> A：小姐，我想买件西装上衣。Miss, I would like to buy a Western suit.
> B：好。您要多大号的？ What size (of suit) do you want?
> A：中号的。Medium.
> B：什么颜色？ What color?
> A：有黑色的吗？ Do you have black (color suit)?

In the above text, 多大号的, 中号的 and 黑色的 are 的 constructions. They all refer to the Western suit which was mentioned at the beginning of the text.

2. The use of 还是

A. Used as an alternative question marker

The conjunction 还是 can be used as an alternative question marker providing two or more choices for selection. Note that 还是 is put in front of the last choice. For example:

> (1) 你要灰色的还是蓝色的?
>
> What do you want? Gray color or blue color?
>
> (2) 你是中文系的、日文系的还是英文系的?
>
> Are you from the Chinese Department, Japanese Department, or English Department?

B. Used as an adverb in a statement

When used as an adverb, 还是 indicates either a suggestion meaning "it had better …" (examples 4 & 5) or simply a statement meaning "it is still the case" (examples 6 & 7):

> (3) 还是要那件灰色的吧。
>
> I think you had better take the gray one.
>
> (4) 你穿大号不合适,还是要中号的吧。
>
> A large is not suitable for you. You had better take the medium.
>
> (5) 我觉得还是有点儿贵。
>
> I think it is still a bit too expensive.
>
> (6) 今天早上妈妈要约翰早点儿起床,可是他还是迟到了。
>
> Mom told John to get up early this morning, but he was still late for school.

3. The separable verb-object compounds

In Chinese, some verb-object compounds are separable. A word or words can be inserted between the first and second syllables of the compound thus making it become a phrase.

> 打折 (make a discount) → 打个折 (give a discount)
>
> 打折 (make a discount) → 打八折 (give a 20% discount)
>
> 打折 (make a discount) → 打三折 (give a 70% discount)
>
> 打折 (make a discount) → 打很大的折 (give a very big discount)
>
> 吃饭 (have a meal) → 吃午饭 (have lunch)
>
> 吃饭 (have a meal) → 吃晚饭 (have dinner)
>
> 吃饭 (have a meal) → 吃中国饭 (have a Chinese meal)

4. Numbers from 1 to 10000

Numbers from 1-10000 in Chinese

0	10	100	1000	10000
零	十	百	千	万
líng	shí	bǎi	qiān	wàn

Count by 10:   十, 二十, 三十, 四十, 五十, 六十, 七十, 八十, 九十

Count by 100:   一百, 二百, 三百, 四百, 五百, 六百, 七百, 八百, 九百

Count by 1000: 一千, 两千, 三千, 四千, 五千, 六千, 七千, 八千, 九千

Examples:

> 1200: 一千二（百）　　　　1230: 一千二百三（十）　　　1234: 一千二百三十四
> yìqiān èr(bǎi)　　　　　　yìqiān èrbǎi sān(shí)　　　yìqiān èrbǎi sānshisì
>
> 1002: 一千零二　　　　　1203: 一千二百零三　　　　1034: 一千零三十四
> yìqiān líng èr　　　　　　yìqiān èrbǎi líng sān　　　yìqiān líng sānshísì

5. Monetary system and simple calculation

yuan	jiao	fen
块（元）	毛（角）	分
kuài (yuán)	máo (jiǎo)	fēn

Examples:

> ￥0.99: 九毛九（分）　￥2.99: 两块九毛九（分）　　　￥2.09: 两块零九（分）
> ￥12.00: 十二块　　　￥12.99: 十二块九毛九（分）　￥112.09: 一百一十二块零九（分）

Simple calculation: 加（jiā, plus）　　减（jiǎn, minus）　　等于（děngyú, equals to）

> 40 + 80=120 (sìshí jiā bāshí děngyú yìbǎi èrshí)
>
> 1200–300=900 (yìqiān èrbǎi jiǎn sānbǎi děngyú jiǔbǎi)

6. The adverb 才 (2)

The adverb 才 is also used before number measure words or time expressions, meaning "only".

(1) 有的才穿了几天，像新的一样。

It had been worn for only a few days and still looked new.

(2) 我的朋友买了一双球鞋和一条红色的领带，才六十块钱。

My friend bought a pair of tennis shoes and a red tie for only sixty kuai.

(3) 英文系有二十多个男学生，中文系才五个（男学生）。

There are more than 20 male students in the English Department, while there are only five in the Chinese Department.

(4) 现在才七点一刻，你开车别太快了。

It's only 7:15. Don't drive too fast.

Exercise 1 🦻 👄✳

Listen to the short dialogs and answer the following questions orally in Chinese. Pay attention to the numbers mentioned.

Dialog 1

1. 夹克卖多少钱？

2. 那套西服多少钱？

3. 那双白球鞋多少钱？

Dialog 2

1. 请问这个手机多少钱？

2. 那位小姐每个星期工作多少小时？

3. 她的大学有多少个学生在那儿打工？

Dialog 3

1. 四百三十加五千零七等于多少？

2. 八百九十五减二十二等于多少？

Exercise 2 ✍

Make alternative questions to each of the answers below with the conjunction 还是.

Example: A：你是英文系的学生还是中文系的（学生）？
            B：我不是英文系的，我是中文系的。

1. A：_____

   B：我不是英国人，我是美国人。

2. A：_____

   B：我不是学生，我是老师。

3. A：_____

   B：我们星期一没有中文课，星期三有（中文课）。

4. A：＿＿＿＿＿＿＿＿＿＿＿＿＿＿＿＿＿

　　B：我不是在中国出生的，我是在美国出生的。

5. A：＿＿＿＿＿＿＿＿＿＿＿＿＿＿＿＿＿

　　B：我不想买日历，我想买书。

6. A：＿＿＿＿＿＿＿＿＿＿＿＿＿＿＿＿＿

　　B：我不喜欢喝牛奶，我喜欢喝咖啡。

Exercise 3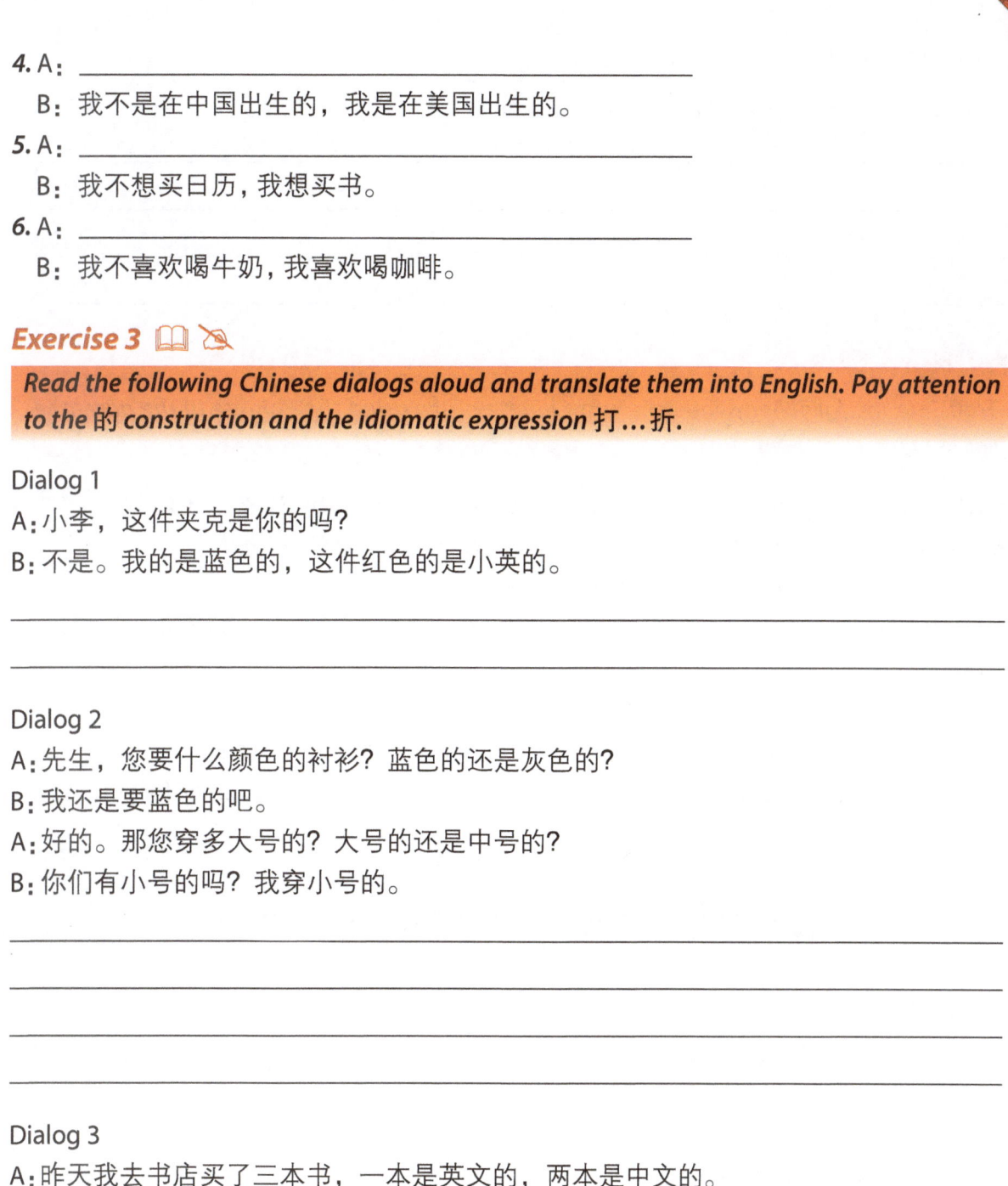

Read the following Chinese dialogs aloud and translate them into English. Pay attention to the 的 *construction and the idiomatic expression* 打…折.

Dialog 1

A：小李，这件夹克是你的吗？

B：不是。我的是蓝色的，这件红色的是小英的。

＿＿＿＿＿＿＿＿＿＿＿＿＿＿＿＿＿＿＿＿＿＿＿＿＿＿＿＿＿＿＿＿

＿＿＿＿＿＿＿＿＿＿＿＿＿＿＿＿＿＿＿＿＿＿＿＿＿＿＿＿＿＿＿＿

Dialog 2

A：先生，您要什么颜色的衬衫？蓝色的还是灰色的？

B：我还是要蓝色的吧。

A：好的。那您穿多大号的？大号的还是中号的？

B：你们有小号的吗？我穿小号的。

＿＿＿＿＿＿＿＿＿＿＿＿＿＿＿＿＿＿＿＿＿＿＿＿＿＿＿＿＿＿＿＿

＿＿＿＿＿＿＿＿＿＿＿＿＿＿＿＿＿＿＿＿＿＿＿＿＿＿＿＿＿＿＿＿

＿＿＿＿＿＿＿＿＿＿＿＿＿＿＿＿＿＿＿＿＿＿＿＿＿＿＿＿＿＿＿＿

Dialog 3

A：昨天我去书店买了三本书，一本是英文的，两本是中文的。

B：你花了多少钱买这两本书？有没有给你打折？

A：打了八折。英文书二十五块整，两本中文书三十七块八毛，一共是六十二块八毛。

＿＿＿＿＿＿＿＿＿＿＿＿＿＿＿＿＿＿＿＿＿＿＿＿＿＿＿＿＿＿＿＿

＿＿＿＿＿＿＿＿＿＿＿＿＿＿＿＿＿＿＿＿＿＿＿＿＿＿＿＿＿＿＿＿

＿＿＿＿＿＿＿＿＿＿＿＿＿＿＿＿＿＿＿＿＿＿＿＿＿＿＿＿＿＿＿＿

Dialog 4

A：我妈妈昨天买了两个南瓜灯，一个大的一个小的。

B：贵不贵？打折了吗？

A：因为明天就是万圣节了，商店给我们打了七折。

B：是吗？那我今天也去买两个南瓜灯。

_____

_____

_____

_____

Exercise 4 🗣

Translate the following sentences into Chinese orally using the Chinese in the parentheses as clues.

1. Whom are you writing to? Your elder sister or your elder brother?（在，还是）

2. We are students. Could you give us a 10 % discount?（能不能，打九折）

3. That blue coat is very cheap. It is only 80.（才）

4. Our university has eighteen departments with two thousand six hundred eighty-two students.（系，千，百，十）

5. "What do you want to drink, coffee or tea?" "I still prefer coffee."（还是）

6. Your hometown has a population of ninety thousand. Mine only has ten thousand.（万，才）

7. You had better buy this large size jacket. That medium size is a bit too small for you.（还是）

五、语言运用 Using the Language

Activity 1 🗣

Read the signs in the stores and answer the questions in Chinese orally.

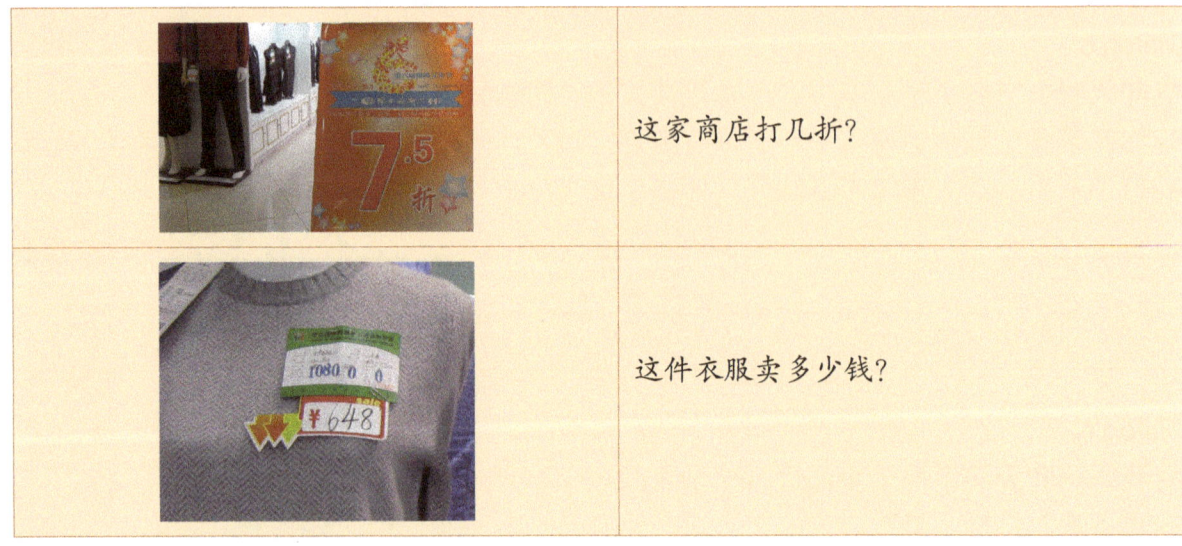

	这家商店打几折？
	这件衣服卖多少钱？

这家商店打几折？

Activity 2

At a local store you overheard the following conversation. Listen and answer the following questions orally in Chinese.

Questions:

1. How much is the first item at other stores?

2. Why did the woman buy the second item?

3. What discount did the woman get for the first and the second item respectively?

Activity 3

Read the following blog entry by Li Xiang and answer the questions.

New words:　考试 kǎoshì, take a test
　　　　　　另外 lìngwài, another
　　　　　　智能 zhìnéng, smart

　　昨天我在图书馆复习功课的时候，我的电话响了，是小文打来的。她问我："你忙什么呢？"我说："我复习功课呢。"小文说："别复习了！你快点儿来找我。我在商场呢。今天他们大减价，很多东西都打五折呢。""可是我明天就要考试了！""没关系，我们买好东西后到我家去。我帮你复习。"小文的学习很好。她帮助我复习，我的考试一定能考好。于是我就和她去了商场。商场里很多店都打折。 我们在商场从一个店走到另外一个店，不知道买什么好。最后我买了两套西服，一套运动服，三双皮鞋。小文买了不少电子游戏，还买了一个智能手机。

Questions:

1. What happened when I was in the library?

2. Where did Xiaowen want me to go? Why?

3. Was I willing to go, why?

4. Why did I finally go with her?

5. What did we buy?

Activity 4 📖

Xiao Li just came back from Chinatown. He posted some pictures with descriptions on his Facebook. Read them and decide whether the following statements are true or false.

我和同学们昨天去了唐人街。唐人街有很多商店和饭馆。很多商店里的东西都打折。

我先去书店买了几本中文书。书店里很多书都打折。小王让我给他买一本英文书。那本书很贵。我问书店能不能便宜点儿。他们说那是新的，不能打折。

中午的时候我和几个同学去中国饭馆吃中餐。饭馆里人不太多。

吃完饭以后，我们逛了几家中国商店。我买了一套学中国功夫的衣服和一双鞋，都是打七折的。

飞跃——汉语初级教程学生用书 上册

1. 小李昨天一个人去了唐人街。	( )
2. 唐人街的商店里很多东西都很便宜。	( )
3. 小李在唐人街去的第一个地方是书店。	( )
4. 书店里的中英文书都打折。	( )
5. 小李和同学们在一家中国饭馆吃午饭。	( )
6. 小李在中国商店里没有买到合适的衣服。	( )

Activity 5 ✎

Discuss the following photos with your partner and then write a description for them. Compare your descriptions with your classmates'.

Useful words: 装修 zhāngxiū, interior decoration
                特卖 tèmài, special sale
                平价 píngjià, low price
                销售 xiāoshòu, to sell

Activity 6 🗣✳

You are in Chinatown of San Francisco. You need to buy some clothes, shoes, and other things. Go to a store and ask if the store has them on sale and what discounts they have. If you are not satisfied with the style and color of the things shown to you, ask for another type. Your partner will play the role of shop clerk.

Sentences you may need to use:

请问你们的衣服打折吗?
能不能给我打……折?
这件衣服有点儿大 / 小。

Activity 7 🗣✳

What do you say?

1. You want to know the size of a piece of clothing.

2. You want to report your size.

3. You wish the price could be lower.

4. You want to complain about the high prices in the store, discount or not.

Cultural Tip

The Chinese monetary system has three units: yuan（元 / 块）, jiao（角 / 毛）and fen（分）and is based on the decimal system. 10 fen =1 jiao and 10 jiao=1 yuan. Banknotes come in denominations of 1, 5, 10, 20, 50, and 100 yuan, and coins come in 1 and 5 jiao, and 1 yuan. Fen coins are used infrequently and the issuance of the fen coins has ceased.

第十课 长周末
Lesson Ten · Long Weekend

一、导入 Lead-in

Exercise 1 📖 🗣

Look at the pictures below and describe the activities in Chinese.

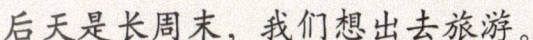

后天是长周末，我们想出去旅游。

冬天常常下雪，不太适宜露营。

上个周末，我们带了苹果、热狗和可乐去公园野餐。

After learning this lesson, you will be able to:

1. Tell and ask about weekend plans and activities, and talk about the weather.

2. Talk about four seasons and state temperatures in both Fahrenheit and Centigrade.

3. Recognize new characters in this lesson, know basic principles of character simplification.

4. Use the 一边…一边 and 只要…就 constructions, reduplicated verbs, and 想, 本来, 左右.

二、课文 Texts

课文（一）Text (1)

看看天气预报再说

简体版

Wang Hong, Lin Hua, David and Peter are making plans for the upcoming long weekend.

Tips: how to ask about a plan

王红：后天就是长周末了，你们想到哪儿去玩儿啊？

林华：还没想好呢。本来想出去旅游，后来觉得三天时间太少了。

Tips: how to give suggestions

彼得：我们一块儿去露营怎么样？

王红：我想，秋天去露营比较好，现在是冬天，不太合适。

大卫：对，冬天是滑雪的季节，我们去滑雪吧。

林华：滑雪太冷了，我不想去。

彼得：那么，去打网球吧。

王红：打网球？要是下雪怎么办？

林华：说了半天，到底去哪儿呀？

大卫：还是看看天气预报再说吧。要是下雪，就在家里睡觉好了。

看看天氣預報再說

繁体版

Wang Hong, Lin Hua, David and Peter are making plans for the upcoming long weekend.

王紅：後天就是長周末了，你們想到哪兒去玩兒啊？

林華：還沒想好呢。本來想出去旅游，後來覺得三天時間太少了。

彼得：我們一塊兒去露營怎麼樣？

王红：我想，秋天去露營比較好，現在是冬天，不太合適。

大衛：對，冬天是滑雪的季節，我們去滑雪吧。

林華：滑雪太冷了，我不想去。

彼得：那麼，去打網球吧。

王红：打網球？要是下雪怎麼辦？

林華：説了半天，到底去哪兒呀？

大衛：還是看看天氣預報再説吧。要是下雪，就在家裏睡覺好了。

Kèwén (yī) *Text (1)*

Kànkan Tiānqì Yùbào Zài Shuō

拼音版

　　Wang Hong, Lin Hua, David and Peter are making plans for the upcoming long weekend.

Wáng Hóng: Hòutiān jiù shì cháng zhōumò le, nǐmen xiǎng dào nǎr qù wánr a?

Lín Huá: Hái méi xiǎnghǎo ne. Běnlái xiǎng chūqù lǚyóu, hòulái juéde sān tiān shíjiān tài shǎo le.

Bǐdé: Wǒmen yíkuàir qù lùyíng zěnmeyàng?

Wáng Hóng: Wǒ xiǎng, qiūtiān qù lùyíng bǐjiào hǎo, xiànzài shì dōngtiān, bú tài héshì.

Dàwèi: Duì, dōngtiān shì huáxuě de jìjié, wǒmen qù huáxuě ba.

Lín Huá: Huáxuě tài lěng le, wǒ bù xiǎng qù.

Bǐdé: Nàme, qù dǎ wǎngqiú ba.

Wáng Hóng: Qù dǎ wǎngqiú? Yàoshì xiàxuě zěnme bàn?

Lín Huá: Shuōle bàntiān, dàodǐ qù nǎr ya?

Dàwèi: Háishì kànkan tiānqì yùbào zài shuō ba. Yàoshì xiàxuě, jiù zài jiā li shuìjiào hǎo le.

生词（一）New Words (1)

	简体（繁體）	拼音	词性	解释
1	后（後）天	hòutiān	n.	the day after tomorrow 今天星期一，明天星期二，后天星期三。
2	长（長）	cháng	adj.	long 长期 / 长时间 / 长周末
3	本来（來）	běnlái	adv.	originally 我本来想去旅游，可是天气不好，就没去。
4	出去	chūqù	v.	go out 出去旅游 / 出去找工作
5	旅游	lǚyóu	v.	travel, tour 到国外旅游 / 十一长假旅游的人很多。
6	觉（覺）得	juéde	v.	think, feel 你觉得中文好学吗？ / 我觉得三天旅游时间太少了。
7	少	shǎo	adj.	few, little 三天时间太少了，不能到外地旅游。
8	露营（營）	lùyíng	v.	go camping 他周末常常去露营。
9	秋天	qiūtiān	n.	autumn 北京秋天天气最好。
10	比较（較）	bǐjiào	adv.	comparatively, relatively 秋天去露营比较好。
11	冬天	dōngtiān	n.	winter 加拿大的冬天很长。 / 冬天可以滑雪。
12	合适（適）	héshì	adj.	suitable, decent 这件夹克你穿很合适。 / 你这样做不合适。
13	滑雪	huáxuě	v.	ski 我不喜欢滑冰，喜欢滑雪。
14	雪	xuě	n.	snow 大雪 / 小雪 / 白雪 / 雪人
15	季节（節）	jìjié	n.	season 一年有四个季节。
16	冷	lěng	adj.	cold 冷水 / 冷饭 / 今天很冷，请多穿衣服。
17	网球	wǎngqiú	n.	tennis 打网球
18	要是	yàoshì	conj.	if 要是下雪，我们周末就去滑雪。
19	下	xià	v.	fall (rain, snow, fog) 下雨 / 下雪 / 下雾
20	半天	bàntiān	nc.	a long time; quite a while 这里服务太慢，等了半天也没上菜。
21	到底	dàodǐ	adv.	after all 你到底去不去？
22	天气（氣）	tiānqì	n.	weather 天气预报 / 今天天气怎么样？

飞跃——汉语初级教程学生用书　上册

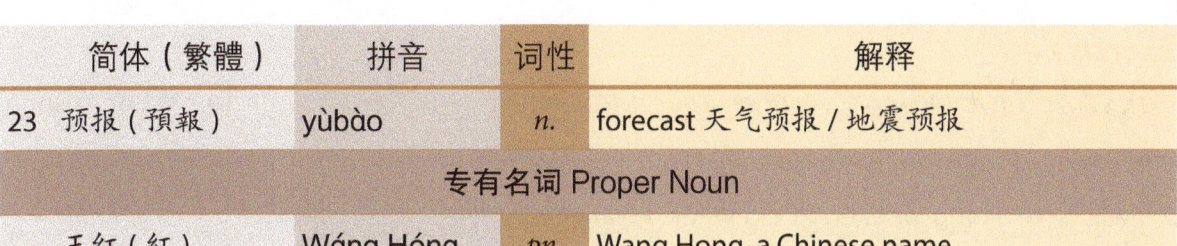

简体（繁體）	拼音	词性	解释
23 预报（預報）	yùbào	n.	forecast 天气预报 / 地震预报
专有名词 Proper Noun			
王红（紅）	Wáng Hóng	pn.	Wang Hong, a Chinese name

Exercise 1

Listen to Text (1) and check which of the following are mentioned.

1. a changed idea

2. weather conditions of the past three days

3. the best season for doing a certain activity

4. concerns about possible rain

5. the health condition of someone

6. a suggestion to postpone an activity

Exercise 2

Read Text (1) and decide whether the following statements are true or false.

1. A long weekend is not enough for traveling.	( )
2. Wang Hong suggested going camping.	( )
3. David agrees with Wang Hong.	( )
4. Lin Hua thinks it is too far to go skiing in the mountains.	( )
5. They finally agreed on a weekend plan.	( )

Exercise 3

Match the Chinese phrases in Column I with their English equivalents in Column II.

Column I	Column II
( ) 1. 长周末就要到了	a. originally wanted to play tennis
( ) 2. 本来想去打网球	b. after all this talking
( ) 3. 冬天露营太冷	c. just go traveling
( ) 4. 滑雪的季节	d. long weekend is coming
( ) 5. 去旅游好了	e. if it is cold
( ) 6. 要是天冷	f. it's too cold to go camping in the winter
( ) 7. 说了半天	g. skiing season

Exercise 4 🗣

Translate the following sentences orally into Chinese.

1. It was very cold and rainy yesterday.

2. I will have a long weekend next week. I want to travel.

3. Do you often go back to China to visit your parents?

4. Let's wait to see the weather forecast and then decide.

课文（二）Text (2)

野 餐

简体版

A diary by Wang Hong

12 月 9 日　　　　星期天　　　　晴天

今天我和几个同学在公园野餐，玩儿得很高兴。我们带了沙拉、可乐、果汁、苹果、面包和热狗，大家一边吃，一边聊天。野餐以后，我们一起玩儿游戏，还在公园里跑步。一直到下午五点半我们才回家。

我们这里的天气真好！春天很暖和，夏天不太热，秋天很凉快，冬天也不冷。现在已经是冬天了，可气温还在华氏六十度左右，还能在公园里野餐。我想起北京老家的冬天，最低气温要到摄氏零下二十度。我真喜欢这里的天气。

Tips: how to describe the activities at a picnic

Tips: how to describe the four seasons

野 餐

繁体版

A diary entry by Wang Hong

12 月 9 日　　　　星期天　　　　晴天

　　今天我和幾個同學在公園野餐，玩兒得很高興。我們帶了沙拉、可樂、果汁、蘋果、面包和熱狗，大家一邊吃，一邊聊天。野餐以後，我們一起玩兒游戲，還在公園裏跑步。一直到下午五點半我們才回家。

　　我們這裏的天氣眞好！春天很暖和，夏天不太熱，秋天很涼快，冬天也不冷。現在已經是冬天了，可氣溫還在華氏六十度左右，還能在公園裏野餐。我想起北京老家的冬天，最低氣溫要到攝氏零下二十度。我眞喜歡這裏的天氣。

Kèwén (èr)　**Text (2)**

Yěcān

拼音版

A diary entry by Wang Hong

12 yuè 9 rì　　　　xīngqītiān　　　　qíngtiān

　　Jīntiān wǒ hé jǐ gè tóngxué zài gōngyuán yěcān, wánr de hěn gāoxìng. Wǒmen dàile shālā, kělè, guǒzhī, píngguǒ, miànbāo hé règǒu, dàjiā yìbiān chī, yìbiān liáotiān. Yěcān yǐhòu, wǒmen yìqǐ wánr yóuxì, hái zài gōngyuán li pǎobù. Yìzhí dào xiàwǔ wǔ diǎn bàn wǒmen cái huíjiā.

　　Wǒmen zhèli de tiānqì zhēn hǎo! Chūntiān hěn nuǎnhuo, xiàtiān bú tài rè, qiūtiān hěn liángkuài, dōngtiān yě bù lěng. Xiànzài yǐjīng shì dōngtiān le, kě qìwēn hái zài Huáshì liùshí dù zuǒyòu, hái néng zài gōngyuán li yěcān. Wǒ xiǎngqǐ Běijīng lǎojiā de dōngtiān, zuì dī qìwēn yào dào Shèshì líng xià èrshí dù. Wǒ zhēn xǐhuan zhèli de tiānqì.

生词（二） New Words (2)

	简体（繁體）	拼音	词性	解释
1	晴天	qíngtiān	*n.*	clear sky; sunny day 如果周末是晴天，我就出去玩。
2	公园（園）	gōngyuán	*n.*	park 晴天的时候，我去公园散步。
3	野餐	yěcān	*v.*	go picnic 在公园野餐
4	玩儿	wánr	*v.*	play 孩子们在公园里玩儿。
5	沙拉	shālā	*n.*	salad 我喜欢水果沙拉。/ 你会做沙拉吗？
6	可乐（樂）	kělè	*n.*	cola 你喜欢喝可乐吗？
7	果汁	guǒzhī	*n.*	fruit juice 果汁对身体好。
8	苹（蘋）果	píngguǒ	*n.*	apple 野餐时，他吃了两个苹果。
9	热（熱）狗	règǒu	*n.*	hot dog 热狗很好吃。
10	一边（邊）…… 一边（邊）	yìbiān... yìbiān	*conj.*	while; at the same time as 我一边工作，一边学习。/ 他一边吃饭，一边看电视。
11	聊天	liáotiān	*v.*	chat 聊天室 / 我喜欢和朋友们聊天。
12	游戏（戲）	yóuxì	*n.*	game 玩游戏 / 做游戏 / 电子游戏
13	这里（這裡）	zhèli	*pron.*	here 我们这里的天气很好。
14	真	zhēn	*adv.*	really, truly 天气真好 / 这个电影真好看。
15	春天	chūntiān	*n.*	spring 北京的春天不长。/ 春天是春游的好时候。
16	暖和	nuǎnhuo	*adj.*	warm 春天的天气很暖和。/ 天冷了，穿暖和一点儿。
17	夏天	xiàtiān	*n.*	summer 北京的夏天很热。/ 加州的夏天很干。
18	热（熱）	rè	*adj.*	hot 热水 / 热气 / 热茶 / 今天的天气不太热。
19	凉快	liángkuai	*adj.*	cool 北京夏天热，秋天凉快。

简体（繁體）	拼音	词性	解释
20 气温（氣溫）	qìwēn	*n.*	air temperature 室内气温 / 晚上的气温比白天的低。
21 度	dù	*n.*	degree 360 度 / 高度 / 零度
22 想起	xiǎngqǐ		recall 我想起了他的名字。/ 我想不起他是谁了。
23 最	zuì	*adv.*	the most 最好 / 最高 / 最美 / 北京秋天天气最好。
24 低	dī	*adj.*	low 低温 / 最低气温 / 飞机飞得很低。
25 零下	líng xià		below zero 摄氏零下二十度。
26 喜欢（歡）	xǐhuan	*v.*	like; be fond of 喜欢学中文 / 喜欢吃食堂 / 喜欢逛街
专有名词 Proper Nouns			
1 华（華）氏	Huáshì	*pn.*	Fahrenheit
2 摄（攝）氏	Shèshì	*pn.*	Celsius, centigrade

第十课 长周末

Exercise 5 👂 🗨

Listen to Text (2) and answer the questions orally in Chinese.

1. How did I feel today?

2. What did we do while eating?

3. What two other things did we do?

4. What is the weather like here?

5. What is the weather like in Beijing?

6. How do I like the weather here?

Exercise 6 📖

Read Text (2) and decide whether the following statements are true or false.

1. We did not eat hamburger.	(	)
2. Someone brought his dog to the picnic.	(	)
3. We stayed at the park for a long time.	(	)
4. I almost forgot about my hometown.	(	)
5. I prefer a cold winter.	(	)

211

Exercise 7 ✎

Put the following words into the six groups below.

热狗　沙拉　游戏　公园　气温　暖和　凉快　果汁　可乐
聊天　晴天　度　华氏　想起　喜欢　玩　夏天　苹果　春天

Weather	Food	Season	Action/Attitude	Place	Temperature

Exercise 8 📖 ✎

Fill in the blanks in the following paragraph with the words given.

旅游　下雪　春天　下雨　老家　最好的　暖和

　　我的 _____ 在北京。北京四季分明。_____ 从三月到五月，时间不长。春天很 _____，是人们出去玩儿的季节。六月到八月是北京的夏天，常常 _____，不下雨的时候很热。九月到十一月是秋天，是北京 _____ 季节，不冷也不热。很多人喜欢在这个季节到北京 _____。十二月到二月是冬天。北京的冬天常常 _____。

三、汉字 Chinese Characters

1. New characters in this lesson

序号	拼音	简/繁	部件	构词
1	bào	报/報	扌+艮	天气预报/地震预报
2	bǐ	彼	彳+皮	彼得
3	biān	边/邊	力+辶	边吃边玩/一边跑，一边叫
4	cháng	长/長	长	长周末/长期/长时间
5	chūn	春	夫+日	春天/春风/春节
6	dī	低	亻+氐	低温/飞机飞得很低/高低
7	dǐ	底	广+氐	到底/底下
8	dōng	冬	夂+冫	冬天/冬白菜/冬瓜

9	dù	度	广+廿+又	二十度 / 温度 / 零度
10	gǒu	狗	犭+句	热狗 / 小狗
11	guǒ	果	果	果汁 / 水果 / 如果 / 结果
12	hé	合	合	合适 / 合作 / 合理
13	huá	滑	氵+骨	滑冰 / 滑雪 / 滑梯 / 滑道
14	jiào	较/較	车+交	比较 / 较量 / 较真
15	jiào/jué	觉/覺	龸+冖+见	睡觉 / 不想睡觉 / 觉得 / 不觉得
16	lā	拉	扌+立	沙拉 / 拉手 / 拉肚子
17	lè	乐/樂	乐	快乐 / 可乐 / 生日快乐
18	lěng	冷	冫+令	天气冷 / 很冷 / 冰冷
19	liáng	凉/涼	冫+京	天凉 / 秋凉 / 凉水 / 冰凉
20	liáo	聊	耳+卯	上网聊天 / 聊天室
21	líng	零	雨+令	零点 / 零下
22	lù	露	雨+路（𧾷+各）	露营 / 露水
23	lǚ	旅	方+㇏	旅游 / 旅行 / 旅店
24	nuǎn	暖	日+爰	暖和 / 暖暖和和 / 温暖
25	píng	苹/蘋	艹+平	苹果
26	qì	气/氣	气	天气 / 天气预报 / 生气 / 和气
27	qíng	晴	日+青（龶+月）	晴天 / 晴朗
28	qiū	秋	禾+火	秋天 / 秋风 / 秋雨
29	rè	热/熱	执（扌+丸）+灬	天气热 / 热水 / 热气 / 热茶
30	shā	沙	氵+少	沙拉 / 沙子
31	shè	摄/攝	扌+聂（耳+又+又）	摄氏 / 摄影 / 摄影机
32	shì	氏	氏	华氏 / 张氏 / 李氏
33	shì	适（適）	舌（千+口）+辶	合适 / 适当 / 适用
34	wán	玩	王+元	玩游戏 / 到朋友家玩 / 玩笑
35	wēn	温/溫	氵+昷（日+皿）	气温 / 温度 / 高温 / 低温
36	xǐ	喜	吉（士+口）+丷+口	喜欢 / 喜庆 / 喜日
37	xì	戏/戲	又+戈	做游戏 / 看戏 / 京戏
38	xià	夏	一+自+夂	夏天 / 夏季 / 夏日

39	xuě	雪	雨+彐	下雪／大雪／小雪／雪山
40	yě	野	里+予	野餐／野外
41	yíng	营／營	艹+冖+口+口	露营／营房
42	yóu	游／遊	氵+方+𠂉(𠂉+子)	旅游／游玩／游行
43	yù	预／預	予+页	预报／预约／预定／预防
44	yuán	园／園	口+元	公园／花园／园林
45	zhēn	真	真	真好／真好看／真忙
46	zhī	汁	氵+十	果汁／奶汁
47	zuì	最	日+取(耳+又)	最好／最高／最美／最大

Exercise 1 ✎

Copy the following single-component characters with correct stroke order in the spaces provided.

cháng	长	ノ 一 ⻓ 长	
guǒ	果	丨 冂 冂 日 旦 甲 果 果	
lè	乐	ノ 匚 午 斥 乐	
qì	气	ノ ノ 气 气	
shì	氏	ノ 丆 氏 氏	

2. Principles of character simplification (1)

The principles of character simplification that we introduce below will illustrate how simplified characters were created from traditional characters.

(1) Reduction of strokes

Some strokes of traditional characters were reduced while the basic structures of the characters remained the same. In this category, the most common way of simplification is using a simple symbol to replace various components of traditional characters.

對→对 (right)	歡→欢 (happy)	難→难 (difficult)
聖→圣 (holy)	戲→戏 (drama)	雞→鸡 (chicken)
會→会 (to meet; will)	動→动 (to move)	層→层 (layer)
覺→觉 (to feel)	學→学 (to study)	國→国 (country)

(2) Simplification of radicals

With the simplification of radicals, all characters with the same radical were simplified.

	繁体 Traditional Form	简体 Simplified Form
糹→纟	紅　綫	红　线
言→讠	語　誰　課	语　谁　课
食→饣	飯　館	饭　馆
金→钅	銀　鐘	银　钟

(3) Simplification of sound elements

The original sound elements of the traditional characters were replaced by simpler and more accurate sound elements in simplification.

| 遠→远 (far) | 鐘→钟 (clock) | 運→运 (to transport) |
| 圍→围 (garden) | 蘋→苹 (apple) | 華→华 (China) |

(4) Omission of components

Some components of the traditional characters are omitted, thus causing the original structure to be changed. For example:

| 開→开 (to open) | 醫→医 (doctor) | 盤→盘 (plate) |
| 聲→声 (sound) | 雖→虽 (although) | 復→复 (to repeat) |

Exercise 2 ✎

Using the principles of character simplification as a hint, fill in the following chart. Each column should have the same character in two forms.

学 鐘 医 丽 號 電 认 學 业 醫 号 業 開 习 电 开 習 認 麗 钟

Traditional										
Simplified										

215

四、语言点 Language Points

1. The 要是 … 就 construction

要是 + Phrase / Clause, Subject + 就 + Verb + (Object)

In the 要是 … (就) construction, 要是 is used in the first clause introducing a supposition or a hypothesis; and 就 in the second clause telling the result. Note that 就 is an adverb that must always be placed after the subject and before the verb.

(1) 要是下雨，（我们）就在家里睡觉好了。
    If it rains, we will sleep at home.
(2) 要是天气好，我们就去野餐。
    If the weather is good, we will have a picnic.
(3) 要是我有钱，我就去台湾旅游。
    If I had money, I would go to Taiwan for sightseeing.

2. The reduplication of verbs

Reduplication of a verb indicates a short duration of an action, or an action in a casual way. It has the same effect as "V + 一下". For example:

(1) 我看看手机啊。现在是十一点五十六分。(same as 我看一下手机啊。)
    Let me take a look at my cell phone. It is 11:56.
(2) 我来看看日历。(same as 我来看一下日历。)
    Let me take a look at the calendar.
(3) 我们还是看看天气预报再说吧，要是下雨，就在家里睡觉好了。(same as 看一下天气预报。)
    We had better take a look at the weather forecast first. If it rains, we'll sleep at home.

3. The 一边 … 一边 … construction

The 一边 … 一边 … construction is used to indicate two actions happening at the same time.

(1) 大家一边吃，一边聊天。
    We were chatting while we were eating.
(2) 他喜欢一边看电视，一边做作业。
    He likes watching TV while doing his homework.

4. The use of the adverb 本来

The adverb 本来 refers to an original plan or idea, which is later changed.

> (1) 我本来想出去旅游，后来觉得三天时间太少了。
>
> Originally I wanted to travel. Later I felt that three days was too short.
>
> (2) 昨天本来想去露营，可是下雨了，没有去。
>
> I originally wanted to go camping yesterday. However, I didn't go because it rained.

5. The use of the verb 想

When used as a verb, 想 means "to think".

> (1) 我想，秋天去露营比较好。
>
> I think it is better to go camping in the fall.
>
> (2) 我还没想好呢。
>
> I haven't thought it through yet.
>
> (3) 我想起北京老家的冬天，最低气温要到摄氏零下二十度。
>
> I recalled the weather in my hometown, Beijing, where the lowest temperature would reach 20 degrees Celsius below zero.

When used as an auxiliary verb, 想 means "would like to do something".

> (4) 我在学中文，想找一个辅导。
>
> I am learning Chinese now. I would like to find a tutor.
>
> (5) 小姐，我想买件西装上衣。
>
> Miss, I would like to buy a suit jacket.
>
> (6) 滑雪太冷了，我不想去。
>
> It is too cold to go skiing. I don't want to go.
>
> (7) 后天就是长周末了，你们想到哪儿去玩儿啊？
>
> The long weekend starts the day after tomorrow. Where would you like to go?
>
> (8) 我本来想出去旅游，后来觉得三天时间太少了。
>
> Originally I wanted to travel. Later I felt that three days was too short.

NOTE: When served as an auxiliary verb, 想 and 要 share the meaning of "want to". However, their focuses are different. "想 + Verb" means "would like to do something" or "consider doing something" while "要 + Verb" expresses a strong desire to do something.

6. The numeral 左右 indicating approximation

左右 is a special numeral used to indicate approximation, meaning "about", "or so". Note that 左右 is always used after a number.

> (1) 现在已经是冬天了，可气温还在华氏六十度左右。
>
> It is winter now, but the air temperature is still around 60 degrees Fahrenheit.
>
> (2) 我会在图书馆复习到九点左右。
>
> I will review my lessons in the library until 9:00 pm or so.
>
> (3) 我老家有两万人左右。
>
> There are about twenty thousand people in my hometown.

Exercise 1 👂 ✍

Listen to two short dialogs and answer the questions in Chinese characters or pinyin. Pay attention to the use of 想 and 本来.

Dialog 1 Question: 彼得这个长周末本来想做什么？	Answer:
Dialog 2 Question: 小张他们昨天去哪儿吃晚饭了？	Answer:
Dialog 3 Question: 小雨明天想做什么？	Answer:

Exercise 2 📖 🗨

Give the appropriate reduplicated form for each of the verbs below. Then read the following passage with the use of reduplicated verbs and orally translate the passage into English.

Example: 看书——看看书

    1. 喝咖啡——

    2. 看电影——

    3. 逛街——

    4. 玩游戏——

    5. 吃饭——

    6. 听 (tīng, listen to) 音乐 (yīnyuè, music)——

    7. 洗 (xǐ, to wash) 衣服 (yīfu, clothes)——

我的周末

　　星期六上午我常常睡到九点半才起床。我吃完早饭就洗洗衣服。星期六下午我喜欢跟朋友们去电影院看看电影、逛逛街，晚上再一起去饭馆吃吃中国饭。星期天我喜欢待在家里喝喝咖啡、听听音乐。星期天晚上我看看书，玩玩游戏，十点左右睡觉。

Exercise 3

Follow the example and rewrite the sentences using the construction of 一边 … 一边 ….

Example: 我每天学中文的时候听中国歌。——我每天一边学中文一边听中国歌。

1. 我喜欢喝咖啡的时候吃面包。

_____

2. 我和丽丽吃饭的时候聊天。

_____

3. 他喜欢跑步的时候听中文。

_____

4. 她告诉我不要在开车的时候发短信。

_____

Exercise 4

Use the 要是 … 就 construction to complete the following dialogs. Use the English in the parentheses as a clue.

Dialog 1
A：约翰，今天的野餐怎么样？你玩得高兴吗？
B：玛丽，要是你高兴，_____(I would be happy)。
A：_____ (If I am not happy)？
B：那我也就不高兴了。

Dialog 2
A：小林，这个周末，你想做什么？
B：_____ (If the weather is fine)，我就和朋友们一起去露营。
A：要是下雨呢？
B：要是下雨，_____(I will stay at home studying Chinese)。

Dialog 3
A：比尔，_____ (If you have ten days or so)，你想去哪儿旅游？

第十课　长周末

B：我想去北京和上海旅游。你呢？

A：要是我有十天左右的时间，_____ (I want to visit Britain and France)。

Dialog 4

A：小林，今年的圣诞节你要回台北吗？

B：_____ (If I can buy the plane ticket)，我就回家看看父母。

A：要是你买不到票呢？

B：_____ (I will spend Christmas at my classmate David's home)。

Exercise 5 📖 ✎

Translate the following sentences into English paying attention to the underlined parts.

1. 每次我们在一起野餐，都是<u>一边吃一边聊天</u>。

_____

2. 我<u>要是</u>想家，<u>就</u>给爸爸妈妈打电话。

_____

3. 约翰<u>本来</u>三点钟<u>左右</u>要来看我，可是<u>后来</u>他有事不能来了。

_____

4. 我弟弟喜欢<u>一边</u>开车，<u>一边</u>唱歌 (chànggē, sing a song)。

_____

5. 明天<u>要是</u>有时间，我们<u>就</u>坐火车去旧金山<u>逛逛</u>吧。

_____

6. <u>一边</u>吃饭<u>一边</u>看书不好。

_____

7. 你<u>要是</u>去小吃店，<u>就</u>给我买一杯咖啡和两个苹果。

_____

8. 每天早上我<u>一边</u>跑步<u>一边</u>听中文。

_____

9. 我<u>本来</u>想和小红一起去买东西，可是<u>后来</u>下雨了，<u>就</u>没有去。

_____

五、语言运用 Using the Language

Activity 1

Work in pairs. Listen to the following dialog about travel plans for a summer vacation. One student takes notes on the male speaker and the other student takes notes on the female speaker. After listening, tell each other what you have heard.

New words:

东北 Dōngběi, the Northeast   海南 Hǎinán, Hainan Province   海边 Hǎibiān, beach

Male	Female

Activity 2

Listen to the following passage and answer the questions.

1. 上海一年四季的天气怎么样?
2. 上海冬天不常有什么天气?
3. 到上海去的最好时间是什么?
4. 上海在几月份下雨比较多?
5. 上海什么时候天气变冷?

Activity 3

Look at the following pictures and read the following passages. Identify which passage describes which picture.

1

2

3

4

Passage 1

台湾的天气，从 3 月中到 4 月开始热起来，5~10 月都很热。李先生 5 月去了台湾。他说，5 月台湾的天气很热，狗 (gǒu, dog) 喜欢在地上睡觉。

Passage 2

今年冬天以来，这里已经下了两场雪。下雪以后，公园里每个地方都很好看。

Passage 3

纽约在美国的东北部。纽约的冬天常常下雪，下得很多。

Passage 4

每年春天，这个公园都把很多花放在外边。这是人们在看花。

Activity 4 📖🗣✳

Read the following photo descriptions and answer the questions.

1

2

北京的冬天很冷。冬天来的时候，院子里的树也要"穿衣服"。

What needs to be done about the trees in this yard in the winter?

张先生家在北京。秋天到来的时候，院子的地上都是树叶 (shùyè, tree leaves)。

Where is this yard located? What season is it?

Activity 5 🗣

Role Play

You met a new friend at school. He is from Nanjing, China. You are from New York. You both want to know about the climate and weather conditions of each other's hometown. Start a conversation with your friend on this topic. Change roles when you finish. You may need to do some online research to find information about these two places.

Sentences you may need to use:

你们老家的天气怎么样?

你们老家什么季节最好?

你们那里常常下雨 / 雪 / 雾吗?

Activity 6 🗣

What do you say?

1. You want to say you had an original travel plan that you later changed.

2. You want to suggest a picnic in a park during a long weekend.

3. You want to postpone something until after you watch the weather forecast first.

4. You want to say you like to chat with friends while watching a movie.

第十一课 圣诞快乐
Lesson Eleven
Merry Christmas

一、导入 Lead-in

Exercise 1 📖 🗣*

Look at the pictures below and talk about what you see in Chinese.

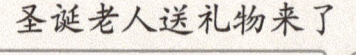

圣诞老人送礼物来了！

把礼物放在圣诞树下。

给家人朋友买圣诞礼物

After learning this lesson, you will be able to:

1. Tell and ask how people celebrate Christmas.

2. Talk about buying Christmas gifts and Christmas-related customs.

3. Recognize new characters in this lesson, know about the principles of character simplification.

4. Use the 把 sentence, the 又…又… construction, and the modal particles 啦 and 呀.

二、课文 Texts

课文（一）*Text (1)*

买圣诞礼物

简体版

　　Xiaohong and David are talking about the upcoming Christmas celebrations.

Tips: how to ask about recent activities

小红：大卫，你最近在忙什么呀？

大卫：圣诞节快到了，我正忙着买圣诞礼物呢。

小红：要买很多圣诞礼物吗？

大卫：当然啦！父母、兄弟、姐妹、朋友都得送。

小红：那够你忙的了。你到哪儿去买呢？

大卫：我喜欢在网上买，又便宜，又方便，不过得花点儿时间上网。

小红：我想，去商店买得花更多的时间。你喜欢圣诞节吗？

大卫：小的时候特别喜欢，因为可以收到很多礼物。

小红：现在呢？

大卫：现在还是喜欢圣诞节，因为圣诞节放假，不用上课。

小红：哈哈！我也是！

買聖誕禮物

Xiaohong and David are talking about the upcoming Christmas celebrations.

小紅：大衛，你最近在忙什麼呀？

大衛：聖誕節快到了，我正忙着買聖誕禮物呢。

小紅：要買很多聖誕禮物嗎？

大衛：當然啦！父母、兄弟、姐妹、朋友都得送。

小紅：那夠你忙的了。你到哪兒去買呢？

大衛：我喜歡在網上買，又便宜，又方便，不過得花點兒時間上網。

小紅：我想，去商店買得花更多的時間。你喜歡聖誕節嗎？

大衛：小的時候特別喜歡，因爲可以收到很多禮物。

小紅：現在呢？

大衛：現在還是喜歡聖誕節，因爲聖誕節放假，不用上課。

小紅：哈哈！我也是！

Kèwén (yī) *Text (1)*

Mǎi Shèngdàn Lǐwù

Xiaohong and David are talking about the upcoming Christmas celebrations.

Xiǎohóng: Dàwèi, Nǐ zuìjìn zài máng shénme ya?

Dàwèi: Shèngdànjié kuài dào le, wǒ zhèng mángzhe mǎi Shèngdàn lǐwù ne.

Xiǎohóng: Yào mǎi hěn duō Shèngdàn lǐwù ma?

Dàwèi: Dāngrán la! Fùmǔ, xiōngdì, jiěmèi, péngyou dōu děi sòng.

Xiǎohóng: Nà gòu nǐ máng de le. Nǐ dào nǎr qù mǎi ne?

Dàwèi: Wǒ xǐhuan zài wǎngshang mǎi, yòu piányi, yòu fāngbiàn, búguò děi huā diǎnr shíjiān shàngwǎng.

Xiǎohóng: Wǒ xiǎng, qù shāngdiàn mǎi děi huā gèng duō de shíjiān. Nǐ xǐhuan Shèngdànjié ma?

Dàwèi: Xiǎo de shíhòu tèbié xǐhuān, yīnwèi kěyǐ shōudào hěn duō lǐwù.

Xiǎohóng: Xiànzài ne?

Dàwèi: Xiànzài háishì xǐhuān Shèngdànjié, yīnwèi Shèngdànjié fàngjià, búyòng shàngkè.

Xiǎo hóng: Hāhā! Wǒ yě shì!

生词（一）*New Words (1)*

	简体（繁體）	拼音	词性	解释
1	最近	zuìjìn	*n.*	recently 最近我看了一本书。/ 最近我去了一次中国。
2	正	zhèng	*adv.*	in the process of (doing something) 他正上网时，女朋友来找他了。/ 小王来找我的时候，我正在吃饭。
3	着（著）	zhe	*part.*	(particle indicating continuation) 我正忙着买圣诞礼物呢。
4	礼（禮）物	lǐwù	*n.*	gift 买礼物 / 送礼物 / 礼物商店
5	当（當）然	dāngrán	*adv.*	of course 他不会中文，当然看不懂这本书。/ "你喜欢吃中餐吗？" "当然啦。"
6	啦	la	*part.*	(end of sentence particle or end of noun particle for a list of things) 他已经去中国啦！/ 课本啦，字典啦，我都买了。
7	兄弟	xiōngdì	*n.*	brothers 你有几个兄弟？/ 他家兄弟三人都是医生
8	姐妹	jiěmèi	*n.*	sisters 他的姐妹很多。/ 你有几个兄弟姐妹？

简体（繁體）	拼音	词性	解释
9　送	sòng	*v.*	give, send, accompany 我要送你一个礼物。/ 请你把这封信给他送去。/她早上送孩子上学。
10　够（夠）	gòu	*v.*	be enough 够用 / 够吃 / 够花 / 三十块钱够了。
11　又……又……	yòu … yòu …		both…and 上网买东西又便宜又快。/ 这个房间又大又暖和。
12　方便	fāngbiàn	*adj.*	convenient 上网买票很方便。/ 我们找一个方便的地方说话。
13　花	huā	*v.*	spend 花钱 / 花时间 / 花力气 / 花功夫
14　上网（網）	shàngwǎng	*v.*	go online 我每天都上网。/ 他常常上网买东西。
15　特别	tèbié	*adv.*	especially 我特别爱看中国电影。/ 他特别告诉我要请你来参加晚会。
16　因为（為）	yīnwèi	*conj.*	because 我能去看电影，因为我做完作业了。
17　收	shōu	*v.*	receive 收到一个礼物 / 收到一封信
18　放假	fàngjià	*v.*	have a holiday or vacation 放假的时候，学生不用上课。
19　不用	búyòng	*adv.*	don't need to 你不用来了。/你不用去商店买，在网上买就行。
20　哈	hā	*ono.*	(imitating laughing) 哈哈大笑
专有名词 Proper Noun			
圣诞（聖誕）	Shèngdàn	*pn.*	Christmas

Exercise 1 🎧 🗣

Listen to Text (1) and answer the questions orally in Chinese.

1. Why is David so busy?

2. Why does he need to do what he has been doing?

3. How does he do it?

4. What different reasons does David give for liking Christmas?

Exercise 2 📖

Read Text (1) and choose the right answer for each of the following statements.

1. Who is not intended as a receiver of David's presents?

    a. Family.   b. Friends.   c. Bosses.

2. According to David, the only disadvantage of shopping online is_____.

    a. that it takes much time   b. the goods are not timely delivered

    c. that there is no receipt

3. When David was a child, he liked _____.

    a. summer vacation   b. gifts   c. shopping

Exercise 3 📖

Match the following questions in Column I with the appropriate responses in Column II.

Column I	Column II
( )1. 你最近在忙什么？	a. 小的时候特别喜欢。
( )2. 你喜欢圣诞节吗？	b. 我想去商店买。
( )3. 你到哪儿去买圣诞礼物呢？	c. 我正忙着买圣诞礼物。
( )4. 要买很多圣诞礼物吗？	d. 不，只给我太太和两个孩子买。

Exercise 4 ✍

Translate the following sentences into Chinese in characters or pinyin with tone marks.

1. I am busy with studying Chinese.

_____

2. I have to buy gifts for many of my friends.

_____

3. Shopping online is both convenient and inexpensive.

_____

4. We have no class on Christmas Day.

_____

课文（二）*Text (2)*

过圣诞节

简体版

    Xiaohong writes a diary about how she celebrates Christmas.

    今年的圣诞节，我是在我的美国朋友家过的。圣诞前夜，我们一起装饰圣诞树，把礼物都放在圣诞树下。

Tips: describe Christmas related customs

然后，我和朋友一起聊天。我们还看了一部名叫《圣诞老人》的电影。一直到十二点多我们才睡觉。

圣诞节早上，我六点半就醒了。我朋友的两个孩子早就起床了，他们在圣诞树下打开自己的礼物，有说有笑，高兴极了。看到他们高兴的样子，我也很开心。现在我才明白为什么孩子们都喜欢圣诞节，为什么大家都说圣诞节快乐！

過聖誕節

Xiaohong writes a diary about how she celebrates Christmas.

今年的聖誕節，我是在我的美國朋友家過的。聖誕前夜，我們一起裝飾聖誕樹，把禮物都放在聖誕樹下。然後，我和朋友一起聊天。我們還看了一部名叫《聖誕老人》的電影。一直到十二點多我們才睡覺。

聖誕節早上，我六點半就醒了。我朋友的兩個孩子早就起床了，他們在聖誕樹下打開自己的禮物，有說有笑，高興極了。看到他們高興的樣子，我也很開心。現在我才明白爲什麼孩子們都喜歡聖誕節，爲什麼大家都說聖誕節快樂！

Kèwén (èr)　*Text (2)*

Guò Shèngdànjié

Xiaohong writes a diary about how she celebrates Christmas.

Jīnnián de Shèngdànjié, wǒ shì zài wǒ de Měiguó péngyou jiā guò de. Shèngdàn qiányè, wǒmen yìqǐ zhuāngshì Shèngdànshù, bǎ lǐwù dōu fàng zài Shèngdànshù xià. Ránhòu, wǒ hé péngyou yìqǐ liáotiān. Wǒmen hái kànle yí bù míng jiào "Shèngdàn Lǎorén" de diànyǐng.Yìzhí dào shí'èr diǎn duō wǒmen cái shuìjiào.

　　Shèngdànjié zǎoshang, wǒ liù diǎn bàn jiù xǐng le.Wǒ péngyou de liǎng gè háizi zǎo jiù qǐchuáng le, tāmen zài Shèngdàn-shù xià dǎkāi zìjǐ de lǐwù, yǒu shuō yǒu xiào, gāoxìng jí le. Kàndào tāmen gāoxìng de yàngzi, wǒ yě hěn kāixīn. Xiànzài wǒ cái míngbai wèi shénme háizimen dōu xǐhuan Shèngdànjié, wèi shénme dàjiā dōu shuō Shèngdànjié kuàilè!

生词（二） New Words (2)

	简体（繁體）	拼音	词性	解释
1	前夜	qiányè	n.	eve 圣诞前夜 / 新年前夜
2	装饰（裝飾）	zhuāngshì	v.	decorate 装饰圣诞树 / 装饰房间
3	树（樹）	shù	n.	tree 圣诞树 / 大树 / 种树 / 树上
4	把	bǎ	prep.	(preposition introducing the object in the 把 sentence) 我把书放在屋里了。/ 他把作业做完了。
5	下	xià	n.	under, below 书本下有一张地图。/ 你把它放在床下吧。
6	部	bù	m.	(measure word for movies, novels) 看了一部新电影 / 读了一部新书
7	睡觉（覺）	shuìjiào	v.	sleep 睡大觉 / 睡午觉 / 我十点睡觉。
8	就	jiù	adv.	(emphasizing the earliness or imminence of an action) 我五点钟就起床了。/ 我吃完饭就去。
9	醒	xǐng	v.	wake up 睡醒了 / 睡不醒 / 孩子醒了。
10	打开（開）	dǎkāi	v.	open 打开门 / 打开礼物 / 打开盒子
11	有说（說）有笑	yǒu shuō yǒu xiào		talk and laugh 老师上课总是有说有笑。
12	极（極）	jí	adv.	extremely 字写得极好 / 跑得极快

简体（繁體）	拼音	词性	解释
13 样（樣）子	yàngzi	*n.*	look, appearance 看你开心的样子！/ 那个礼物是什么样子的？
14 开（開）心	kāixīn	*adj.*	happy, pleased 收到礼物后，他开心极了。
15 明白	míngbai	*v.*	understand; be clear about 你明白这句话吗？/ 这件事我心里很明白。
16 为（為）什么（麼）	wèi shénme		why 你为什么喜欢圣诞节？
17 快乐（樂）	kuàilè	*adj.*	happy, merry 快乐的日子 / 祝你圣诞快乐。

Exercise 5

Listen to Text (2) and answer the questions orally in full Chinese sentences.

1. Where did Xiaohong stay during Christmas?

2. What did she do on Christmas Eve?

3. What did the children do on Christmas morning?

4. What did Xiaohong understand?

Exercise 6

Read Text (2) and decide whether the following statements are true or false.

1. Xiaohong spent Christmas at her brother's house.	( )
2. Xiaohong watched a movie.	( )
3. Xiaohong went to bed late on Christmas Eve.	( )
4. Xiaohong got up earlier than the kids on Christmas Day.	( )
5. Xiaohong learned something new on Christmas Day.	( )

Exercise 7

Match the following words and phrases in Column I with the Chinese expressions in Column II.

Column I	Column II
( ) 1. Santa Clause	a. 在朋友家过圣诞
( ) 2. chat with friends	b. 圣诞前夜
( ) 3. open gifts	c. 装饰圣诞树

( ) 4. Christmas Eve		d. 和朋友聊天
( ) 5. get up very early		e. 圣诞老人
( ) 6. spend Christmas at a friend's home		f. 早就起床了
( ) 7. Merry Christmas		g. 打开礼物
( ) 8. decorate Christmas tree		h. 有说有笑
( ) 9. talk and laugh		i. 很开心
( ) 10. very happy		j. 圣诞快乐

Exercise 8 📖 ✏️

Fill in the blanks with the given words.

礼物　　便宜　　大餐　　放假　　上网　　圣诞节

_____ 快到了。爸爸妈妈开始买圣诞 _____ 了。商店里很多东西都很 _____，但是去商店买东西要花很多时间，所以爸爸妈妈常常 _____ 买。我小的时候特别喜欢圣诞节。爸爸妈妈总是给我很好的礼物。现在我不需要礼物了。但是我还喜欢圣诞节，因为那天 _____，可以跟家人和朋友一起吃圣诞 _____。

三、汉字 Chinese Characters

1. New characters in this lesson

序号	拼音	简/繁	部件	构词
1	bǎ	把	扌+巴	我把书放下 / 他把作业做完
2	bái	白	白	明白 / 白天 / 白雪 / 白衬衫
3	biàn	便	亻+更	方便 / 又便宜，又方便
4	bù	部	咅（立+口）+阝	一部电影 / 部分
5	dàn	诞/誕	讠+延（正+辵）	圣诞节 / 诞生
6	dāng	当/當	⺌+彐	当然 / 当家
7	fāng	方	方	方便 / 方向 / 方面 / 正方
8	gèng	更	更	更多 / 更好 / 更热 / 更喜欢
9	gòu	够/夠	句+多（夕+夕）	够了 / 够用 / 够吃 / 够花

10	hā	哈	口+合	哈哈 / 哈哈大笑
11	huā	花	艹+化（亻+匕）	花钱 / 花时间 / 红花 / 开花
12	jí	极/極	木+及	极好 / 极快 / 极少
13	jià	假	亻+段	放假 / 暑假 / 假期 / 请假
14	la	啦	口+拉（扌+立）	太好啦 / 太快啦
15	lǐ	礼/禮	礻+乚	买礼物 / 礼节
16	shì	饰/飾	饣+𠂉+巾	装饰 / 装饰品
17	shōu	收	丩+攵	收到 / 收信 / 收礼物
18	shù	树/樹	木+对（又+寸）	圣诞树 / 大树 / 种树 / 上树
19	sòng	送	关+辶	送礼物 / 送信 / 送行 / 送别
20	tè	特	牛+寺（土+寸）	特别 / 特点 / 特有
21	wǎng	网/網	冂+乂+乂	上网 / 网上 / 网路 / 电网
22	wèi	为/為	为	因为 / 为什么
23	wù	物	牛+勿	购物中心 / 购物车
24	xiào	笑	𥫗+夭	有说有笑 / 欢笑 / 大笑
25	xǐng	醒	酉+星（日+生）	睡醒了 / 睡不醒
26	xiōng	兄	口+儿	兄弟 / 兄长
27	yè	夜	亠+亻+夂	前夜 / 半夜 / 年夜饭
28	yīn	因	囗+大	因为 / 原因
29	yòu	又	又	又来了 / 又要 / 又大又圆
30	zhe	着/著	𦍌+目	忙着 / 想着 / 写着

Exercise 1 ✍

Copy the following single-component characters with correct stroke order in the spaces provided.

bái	白	′ ′ ′ 白 白				
fāng	方	′ 亠 方 方				

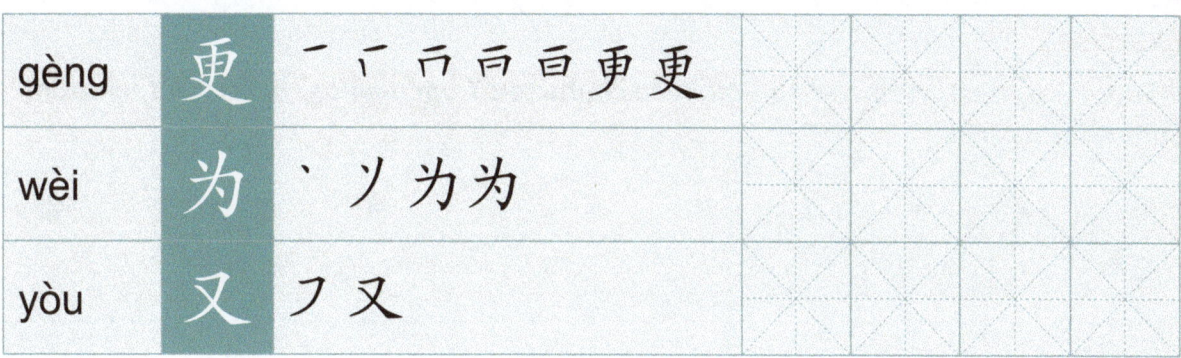

gèng	更	一 T T 百 百 更 更			
wèi	为	、ソ为为			
yòu	又	フ又			

2. Principles of character simplification (2)

(1) Creation of new pictophonetic characters

In the process of simplification, some new pictophonetic characters were made with a complete new radical and new sound element.

| 驚→惊 (be frightened) | 罷→吧 (a particle) |
| 響→响 (sound) | 護→护 (to protect) |

(2) Reduction of homonym characters

Two or more homonym characters were replaced by a simpler homonym character, thus reducing the number of homonyms.

Traditional	Simplified
後 hòu (behind); 后 hòu (queen)	后 hòu (behind, queen)
幾 jǐ (how many); 几 jī (small table)	几 jī/jǐ (small table/how many)
穀 gǔ (grains); 谷 gǔ (ravine)	谷 gǔ (grains, ravine)
颳 guā (to blow); 刮 guā (to scrape)	刮 guā (to blow, to scrape)
鬆 sōng (loose); 松 sōng (pine)	松 sōng (loose; pine)

(3) Adoption of the cursive

Some simplified characters were created by adopting the cursive writing that was developed over a thousand years ago.

| 書→书 (book) | 東→东 (east) | 寫→写 (to write) |
| 專→专 (special) | 鳥→鸟 (bird) | 見→见 (to see) |

Write down the corresponding simplified characters from memory based on their traditional forms given.

繁體	書	見	後	銀	學	從	語	幾	麗	醫
简体										

四、语言点 Language Points

1. The aspectual particle 着 (1)

The aspectual particle 着 is attached to a verb to indicate a progressive action or a continuous state. It is similar to the verb suffix "–ing" in English. Here is an example in this lesson:

> A：大卫，你最近在忙什么呀？
> David, what have you been busy doing recently? (忙: verb; 什么: nominal object)
> B：圣诞节快到了，我正忙着买圣诞礼物呢。(买圣诞礼物: verbal object)
> Christmas is almost here. I have been busy buying Christmas gifts.

Below is the pattern with more examples:

> **Subject +（正）+ Verb + 着 + Object (nominal or verbal phrase) +（呢）**

> (1) 现在你别去找张老师，他正忙着呢！
> Don't look for Mr. Zhang now. He is busy doing something.
> (2) 请你别跟他说话，他正开着车呢！
> Please don't talk with him. He is driving now.
> (3) 我看见他的时候，他正跟他女朋友说着话呢。
> When I saw him, he was talking with his girlfriend.
> (4) 外面下着雨，我们就别去了。
> It is raining now. Let's not go.

NOTE:

Not all verbs can use this pattern to indicate an action in progress. Only the verbs expressing the continuation of an action can use this pattern.

2. The 又 … 又 … construction

The 又 … 又 … construction means "both … and …".

> ### Subject + 又 + Adjective + 又 + Adjective

(1) 我喜欢在网上买，又便宜，又方便。
I like shopping online. It is both inexpensive and convenient.

(2) 他做作业做得又快又好。
He does his homework both quickly and well.

(3) 这个公园又大又干净。
This park is both large and clean.

(4) 这家商店卖的衣服又便宜又好看。
The clothes in this shop are both inexpensive and stylish.

3. The 把 construction

The 把 construction is used to indicate how the subject (a person or a thing) deals with an object and causes it to change. The change is indicated with a verb complement (verb followed by an adjective, or a certain number plus measure word.) The pattern is:

> ### Subject + 把 + Object + Verb + Complement (adjective, etc.)

(1) 我们一起装饰圣诞树，把礼物都放在圣诞树下。
We decorated the Christmas tree together, putting all gifts under the tree.

(2) 妈妈早就把圣诞礼物买好了。
Mom has done shopping for Christmas gifts.

(3) 我们把两个南瓜灯放在我们家前面。
We put two jack-o-lanterns in front of our house.

(4) 我把作业都做完了。
I have finished all of my homework.

(5) 请你把你的手机号码告诉我。

Please give me your cell phone number.

(6) 我把她的短信看了三遍，还不知道她在说什么。

I read her message three times and still didn't know what she was talking about.

The negative form of the 把 construction is formed by placing the negative markers 没, 不 or 别 before 把. Note that 没, 不 and 别 are all adverbs indicating negation; however, they are used differently. 没 indicates "did not"; 不 means "will not" or "do not"; while 别 means "don't" in an imperative sentence. When 没 is used, no aspectual particle, such as 了, is used at the end of the sentence.

(7) 妈妈还没把圣诞礼物买好。

Mom hasn't bought Christmas gifts yet.

(8) 你还没把你的作业做完。

You didn't finish your homework yet.

(9) 我不把手机号码告诉你。

I will not give you my cell phone number.

(10) 别把我的礼物打开。

Don't open my gift.

4. Comparison of the adverbs 就 and 才

When used after time words or number-measure phrases, both the adverbs 就 and 才 relate an action to the speaker's expectation of it. 就 is used to indicate that the action took place earlier than expected, or took less amount of time or money than expected. On the other hand, 才 implies the action took place later than expected, or took a larger amount of time or money than expected. While 就 is usually used with 了 at the end of the sentence, 才 doesn't need this modal particle.

(1) 今天是星期六，我睡到九点才起床。

Today is Saturday. I didn't get up until 9:00 am.

(2) 我们一起玩游戏，还在公园里跑步。一直到下午五点半我们才回家。

We played games together and ran in the park. We did not return home until 5:30.

(3) 我们还看了一部名叫《圣诞老人》的电影，一直到十二点才睡觉。

We also watched a movie called Santa Clause and did not go to sleep until 12:00.

(4) 圣诞节早上，我六点半钟就醒了。

I woke up at 6:30 on Christmas morning.

(5) 八点钟上课，我七点半就来了，可是他八点半才到。

We had class at 8 o'clock. I came at 7:30 but he did not come until 8:30.

(6) 今天晚上的作业，他一个钟头就做完了，可是我做了三个钟头才做完。

He took only one hour to finish this evening's homework, but it took me three hours.

(7) 这件衬衫在院售时三四美元就买到了，可是在商场，二三十美元才能买到。

This shirt can be bought at yard sale for three or four dollars; but at the mall, this type costs twenty to thirty dollars.

5. The modal particle 呀 and 啦

Both 呀 and 啦 are often used in a conversation. The modal particle 呀 is often used at the end of a question.

(1) 你最近在忙什么呀?

What have you been busy with recently?

(2) 你不说我怎么知道呀?

How do I know if you don't tell me?

The modal particle 啦 is used at the end of a sentence to express certainty, or in the middle of a sentence to list things:

(3) 当然啦! 父母、兄弟、姐妹、朋友都得送礼物。

Of course! We must give gifts to parents, brothers, sisters, and friends.

(4) 他已经去过中国啦 (了)!

He has been to China already!

(5) 课本啦，作业本啦，字典啦，我都买了。

Textbooks, homework books, and dictionaries, I bought them all.

Exercise 1

Listen to the short dialogs and answer the questions in Chinese characters or pinyin with tone marks.

Dialog 1 Question: 比尔最近在忙什么?	Answer:
Dialog 2 Question: 乐乐今年要给哪些人送圣诞礼物?	Answer:

Dialog 3 Question: 小雨喜欢坐飞机旅行还是开车旅行？	Answer:

Exercise 2 ✍

Follow the example and rewrite the sentences using the 把 construction.

Example: 我做好了今天的作业。→我把今天的作业做好了。

1. 圣诞节前一个星期，她就买好了圣诞礼物。

_____

2. 约翰忘了他女朋友的生日。

_____

3. 请打开窗子。

_____

4. 他没给我他的手机号码。

_____

5. 星期六下午我洗了衣服。

_____

6. 两天以前，我和妈妈就做好了南瓜灯。

_____

Exercise 3 📖 ✍

Read the following sentences and fill in the blanks with 就 or 才.

1. 小红在图书馆一直待到九点多 _____ 回家。

2. 坐地铁去中国城半个小时 _____ 到了。

3. 星期六上午我睡到十点半 _____ 起床。

4. 你们学校下午三点半才放学，今天你怎么这么早 _____ 回来了？

5. 明天 _____ 是星期六了。我要回家看我的爸爸和妈妈。

6. 他还是一个大男孩，今年 _____ 十五岁。

7. 差十分 _____ 十一点了，我们明天再聊吧。我得上床睡觉了。

8. 八点钟就上第一节课了，你为什么八点二十 _____ 来呢？

Exercise 4 📖✍

Translate the following sentences into English paying attention to the underlined parts.

1. 我把饭<u>吃了</u>就跟你谈，可以吗？

_____

飞跃——汉语初级教程学生用书 上册

2. 我很喜欢上网买东西，<u>又方便又便宜</u>。

_____

3. 小英，你在家忙什么呀？——我<u>正忙着</u>洗衣服呢。

_____

4. 玛丽昨天<u>才</u>告诉我，她要回伦敦过圣诞节。

_____

5. 你怎么这快<u>就</u>回来啦？——我<u>把</u>手机忘了。

_____

6. <u>坐汽车旅行又慢又累</u>，很多人不喜欢。

_____

7. 我今天早上五点钟<u>就</u>起床跑步了，你怎么到现在<u>才</u>起床？

_____

8. 小文<u>一边喝着</u>咖啡<u>一边看着</u>电视。

_____

Exercise 5 🗣

Use the 把 construction to describe the following pictures.

五、语言运用 Using the Language

Activity 1

Talk about the following pictures and then write one or two sentences for each picture.

Activity 2

Read David's email and answer the questions.

小张：

　　你好！我在北京学中文已经好几个月了。今天是圣诞节，我祝你圣诞快乐！这是我第一次在中国过圣诞节。现在中国人很喜欢过圣诞节。在一些大商店的门口都有圣诞树，很漂亮。很多人去商店买东西，因为圣诞节期间很多东西大减价。我的中国朋友们还送给了我很好的圣诞礼物。我也给他们送了礼物。

大卫
十二月二十五日于北京

Questions:

1. 大卫现在在什么地方？

2. 中国人对圣诞节怎么样？

3. 在商店门口可以看到什么？

4. 人们在商店做什么？为什么？

5. 大卫和朋友们圣诞节做什么？

Activity 3 👂 🗣

Listen to the following conversation and answer the questions.

1. What will Liu Hong do on Christmas Eve?

2. Where do Americans spend Christmas Eve?

3. Why don't Chinese spend Christmas Eve at home?

Activity 4 👂 📖

Listen to the phone message from Daming to Xiaowen and decide whether the following statements are true or false.

1. 圣诞快到了。	( )
2. 礼物是给小文买的。	( )
3. 大明让小文只去商店买。	( )
4. 小文先用自己的钱。	( )
5. 上网买不花什么时间。	( )
6. 上网买的礼物不知道好不好。	( )

Activity 5 🗣

What do you say?

1. You wonder what has been keeping someone so busy.

2. You want to find out where to buy gifts.

3. You want to explain the benefits of online shopping.

4. You want to explain the reason why you like Christmas.

Activity 6 🗣

Role Play

You learned about a huge Christmas sale at the mall. Call your friend to tell him/her the news and invite him/her to go with you. Make arrangements about when and where you should meet and how you should get there.

Sentences you may need to use:

商场有圣诞节大减价。

我们一起去买东西好吗？

我们……（时间）在……见面。

飞跃——汉语初级教程学生用书　上册

244

附 录
Appendix

生词总表 Glossary

序号	简体（繁體）	拼音	词性	解释	课号
1	好	hǎo	*adj.*	good	1
2	很	hěn	*adv.*	very	1
3	江	Jiāng	*pn.*	a Chinese surname, Jiang	1
4	老师（師）	lǎoshī	*n.*	teacher	1
5	吗（嗎）	ma	*part.*	(question marker)	1
6	们（們）	men	*suff.*	(plural marker for people)	1
7	呢	ne	*part.*	(question marker)	1
8	你	nǐ	*pron.*	you	1
9	你们（們）	nǐmen	*pron.*	you	1
10	您	nín	*pron.*	you (polite form)	1
11	同学（學）	tóngxué	*n.*	schoolmate	1
12	王	Wáng	*pn.*	a Chinese surname, Wang	1
13	我	wǒ	*pron.*	I, me	1
14	先生	xiānsheng	*n.*	Mr., gentleman	1
15	小姐	xiǎojiě	*n.*	Miss; young lady	1
16	谢谢（謝）	xièxie	*v.*	thank, thanks	1
17	也	yě	*adv.*	also	1
18	再见（見）	zàijiàn	*v.*	goodbye	1
19	早	zǎo	*adj.*	early; morning	1
20	不	bù	*adv.*	not	2
21	陈（陳）雨	Chén Yǔ	*pn.*	Chen Yu, a Chinese name	2
22	都	dōu	*adv.*	all	2
23	工作	gōngzuò	*n.*	job, work	2
24	贵（貴）姓	guìxìng	*n.*	What is your (honorable) name	2
25	江小华（華）	Jiāng Xiǎohuá	*pn.*	Jiang Xiaohua, a Chinese name	2
26	叫	jiào	*v.*	be named	2
27	李文	Lǐ Wén	*pn.*	Li Wen, a Chinese name	2

序号	简体（繁體）	拼音	词性	解释	课号
28	玛丽（瑪麗）	Mǎlì	*pn.*	Mary	2
29	忙	máng	*adj.*	busy	2
30	名字	míngzì	*n.*	name	2
31	什么（甚麼）	shénme	*pron.*	what	2
32	是	shì	*v.*	is, are, am	2
33	她	tā	*pron.*	she, her	2
34	太	tài	*adv.*	very, extremely	2
35	太太	tàitai	*n.*	Mrs.	2
36	姓	xìng	*v.*	have … as surname	2
37	学（學）生	xuésheng	*n.*	student	2
38	约（約）翰	Yuēhàn	*pn.*	John	2
39	早上	zǎoshang	*n.*	morning	2
40	北京	Běijīng	*pn.*	Beijing, capital of China	3
41	大卫（衛）	Dàwèi	*pn.*	David	3
42	的	de	*part.*	(structural particle)	3
43	国（國）	guó	*n.*	country	3
44	和	hé	*conj.*	and	3
45	老家	lǎojiā	*n.*	native place; hometown	3
46	林	Lín	*pn.*	Lin, a surname	3
47	伦（倫）敦	Lúndūn	*pn.*	London, capital of the United Kingdom	3
48	美国（國）	Měiguó	*pn.*	the United States of America	3
49	哪	nǎ	*pron.*	which	3
50	哪儿（兒）	nǎr	*pron.*	where; what place	3
51	纽约（紐約）	Niǔyuē	*pn.*	New York	3
52	人	rén	*n.*	person, people	3
53	（出）生	(chū)shēng	*v.*	be born	3
54	台（臺）北	Táiběi	*pn.*	Taipei, capital city of Taiwan Province	3
55	台湾（臺灣）	Táiwān	*pn.*	Taiwan	3
56	小红（紅）	Xiǎohóng	*pn.*	Xiaohong, a Chinese name	3
57	英国（國）	Yīngguó	*pn.*	the United Kingdom	3
58	在	zài	*v.*	be in	3
59	在	zài	*prep.*	at, in	3
60	中国（國）	Zhōngguó	*pn.*	China	3

飞跃——汉语中级教程学生用书　上册

序号	简体（繁體）	拼音	词性	解释	课号
61	爸爸	bàba	n.	father	4
62	大	dà	adj.	big, old	4
63	大学（學）生	dàxuéshēng	n.	college student; university student	4
64	弟弟	dìdi	n.	younger brother	4
65	多	duō	pron.	how much	4
66	个（個）	gè	m.	(measure word for people or certain objects)	4
67	哥哥	gēge	n.	elder brother	4
68	还（還）	hái	adv.	still, yet	4
69	几（幾）	jǐ	pron.	how many	4
70	家	jiā	n.	home, family	4
71	姐姐	jiějie	n.	elder sister	4
72	今年	jīnnián	n.	this year	4
73	口	kǒu	m.	(measure word for individual person when referring to family population)	4
74	了	le	part.	(particle indicating a completed action)	4
75	丽（麗）莎	Lìshā	pn.	Lisa, a female student	4
76	妈妈（媽媽）	māma	n.	mother	4
77	妹妹	mèimei	n.	younger sister	4
78	奶奶	nǎinai	n.	father's mother	4
79	男	nán	adj.	male	4
80	年	nián	n.	year	4
81	年纪（紀）	niánjì	n.	age	4
82	朋友	péngyou	n.	friend	4
83	岁（歲）	suì	m.	year, age	4
84	他	tā	pron.	he, him	4
85	外公	wàigōng	n.	mother's father	4
86	外婆	wàipó	n.	mother's mother	4
87	小	xiǎo	adj.	small, little, young	4
88	小学（學）	xiǎoxué	n.	primary school	4
89	爷爷（爺爺）	yéye	n.	father's father	4
90	银（銀）行	yínháng	n.	bank	4
91	医（醫）生	yīshēng	n.	doctor, physician	4
92	有	yǒu	v.	have; there be	4

序号	简体（繁體）	拼音	词性	解释	课号
93	吧	ba	*part.*	(particle at the end of a suggestion)	5
94	常常	chángcháng	*adv.*	frequently, often	5
95	吃	chī	*v.*	eat	5
96	从（從）	cóng	*prep.*	from	5
97	电（電）影	diànyǐng	*n.*	movie, film	5
98	高兴（興）	gāoxìng	*adj.*	happy, glad	5
99	回家	huí jiā		go home; come back home	5
100	介绍（紹）	jièshào	*v.*	introduce	5
101	旧（舊）金山	Jiùjīnshān	*pn.*	San Francisco	5
102	看	kàn	*v.*	see; look at; visit	5
103	课（課）	kè	*n.*	class, lesson	5
104	来（來）	lái	*v.*	come	5
105	林华（華）	Lín Huā	*pn.*	Lin Hua, a Chinese name	5
106	每	měi	*pron.*	each, every	5
107	那	nà	*pron.*	that	5
108	男孩	nánhái	*n.*	boy	5
109	女孩	nǚhái	*n.*	girl	5
110	跑步	pǎobù	*v.*	run	5
111	去	qù	*v.*	go	5
112	认识（認識）	rènshi	*v.*	know, recognize	5
113	上	shàng	*v.*	go to (class, work); attend (class)	5
114	谁（誰）	shéi	*pron.*	who	5
115	食堂	shítáng	*n.*	dining hall	5
116	室友	shìyǒu	*n.*	roommate	5
117	他们（們）	tāmen	*pron.*	they, them	5
118	天	tiān	*n.*	day	5
119	图书馆（圖書館）	túshūguǎn	*n.*	library	5
120	晚饭（飯）	wǎnfàn	*n.*	dinner; evening meal; supper	5
121	晚上	wǎnshang	*n.*	evening	5
122	位	wèi	*m.*	(measure word for people when referred to by their titles)	5
123	系	xì	*n.*	department	5
124	呀	ya	*part.*	(particle showing a certain mood)	5
125	英文	Yīngwén	*n.*	the English language	5

序号	简体（繁體）	拼音	词性	解释	课号
126	一起	yìqǐ	*adv.*	together	5
127	一下	yíxià	*nc.*	(numeral-classifier for a short duration of an action)	5
128	这（這）	zhè	*pron.*	this	5
129	中文	Zhōngwén	*n.*	the Chinese language	5
130	做	zuò	*v.*	do, make	5
131	作业（業）	zuòyè	*n.*	school assignment; homework	5
132	不过（過）	búguò	*conj.*	but, however	6
133	到	dào	*prep.*	to	6
134	东（東）西	dōngxi	*n.*	thing, stuff	6
135	对（對）不起	duìbùqǐ		sorry; excuse me	6
136	多	duō	*adj.*	many, much	6
137	发（發）	fā	*v.*	give, issue	6
138	放	fàng	*v.*	put, place	6
139	放学（學）	fàngxué	*v.*	dismiss school	6
140	给（給）	gěi	*prep.*	to	6
141	孩子	háizi	*n.*	child	6
142	号（號）	hào	*n.*	date in a month	6
143	今天	jīntiān	*n.*	today	6
144	就	jiù	*adv.*	(adverb used to indicate emphasis)	6
145	可	kě	*conj.*	but	6
146	可以	kěyǐ	*a.v.*	may, might	6
147	里	lǐ	*n.*	inside	6
148	留	liú	*v.*	stay, remain	6
149	买（買）	mǎi	*v.*	buy	6
150	没关系（關係）	méi guānxi		It does not matter/It's OK.	6
151	门（門）口	ménkǒu	*n.*	doorway	6
152	面具	miànjù	*n.*	mask	6
153	明天	míngtiān	*n.*	tomorrow	6
154	南瓜灯（燈）	nánguādēng	*n.*	jack-o-lantern	6
155	能	néng	*a.v.*	can, may; capable of	6
156	日	rì	*n.*	day, date	6
157	日历（曆）	rìlì	*n.*	calendar	6
158	商店	shāngdiàn	*n.*	store, shop	6

附录

序号	简体（繁體）	拼音	词性	解释	课号
159	事	shì	*n.*	matter, thing	6
160	糖	táng	*n.*	sugar, sweets, candy	6
161	完	wán	*v.*	come to an end	6
162	万圣节（萬聖節）	Wànshèngjié	*pn.*	Halloween	6
163	小华（華）	Xiǎohuá	*pn.*	Xiaohua	6
164	下午	xiàwǔ	*n.*	afternoon	6
165	行	xíng	*v.*	OK, alright	6
166	星期	xīngqī	*n.*	week	6
167	要	yào	*a.v.*	want to; need to	6
168	要	yào	*v.*	want, ask	6
169	以后（後）	yǐhòu	*n.*	after	6
170	一块儿（塊兒）	yíkuàir	*adv.*	together	6
171	月	yuè	*n.*	month	6
172	糟糕	zāogāo	*adj.*	too bad; terrible	6
173	找	zhǎo	*v.*	look for; go to (someone)	6
174	半	bàn	*n.*	half	7
175	杯	bēi	*m.*	glass, cup	7
176	本	běn	*m.*	(measure word for books)	7
177	别	bié	*adv.*	don't	7
178	才（纔）	cái	*adv.*	(adverb indicating the lateness of an action)	7
179	差	chà	*v.*	lack; be short of	7
180	迟（遲）到	chídào	*v.*	arrive late	7
181	带（帶）	dài	*v.*	bring	7
182	待	dāi	*v.*	stay	7
183	到	dào	*v.*	go to; arrive	7
184	得	de	*part.*	(verb complement marker)	7
185	得	děi	*a.v.*	must	7
186	第	dì	*pref.*	(prefix indicating ordinal number)	7
187	点（點）	diǎn	*n.*	o'clock	7
188	对（對）	duì	*adj.*	right	7
189	放	fàng	*v.*	show (movie)	7
190	饭馆（飯館）	fànguǎn	*n.*	restaurant	7
191	分	fēn	*n.*	minute	7

序号	简体（繁體）	拼音	词性	解释	课号
192	附近	fùjìn	*n.*	vicinity	7
193	各	gè	*adv.*	each	7
194	跟	gēn	*prep.*	with	7
195	逛街	guàngjiē	*v.*	window-shop; stroll down the street	7
196	几（幾）	jǐ	*num.*	several	7
197	家	jiā	*m.*	(measure word for shop, school, etc.)	7
198	见（見）	jiàn	*v.*	see, meet	7
199	节（節）	jié	*m.*	(measure word for class session)	7
200	咖啡	kāfēi	*n.*	coffee	7
201	咖啡店	kāfēidiàn	*n.*	coffee shop	7
202	开（開）始	kāishǐ	*v.*	begin	7
203	刻	kè	*n.*	quarter (time)	7
204	那	nà	*conj.*	then	7
205	碰见（見）	pèngjiàn	*v.*	run into	7
206	起床	qǐchuáng	*v.*	get up	7
207	然后（後）	ránhòu	*conj.*	then, afterwards	7
208	时（時）候	shíhòu	*n.*	time	7
209	时间（時間）	shíjiān	*n.*	time	7
210	手表（錶）	shǒubiǎo	*n.*	wrist watch	7
211	手机（機）	shǒujī	*n.*	cell phone	7
212	书（書）	shū	*n.*	book	7
213	书（書）店	shūdiàn	*n.*	bookstore	7
214	睡	shuì	*v.*	sleep	7
215	说（說）	shuō	*v.*	speak	7
216	宿舍	sùshè	*n.*	dormitory	7
217	忘	wàng	*v.*	forget	7
218	先	xiān	*adv.*	firstly	7
219	现（現）在	xiànzài	*n.*	now; at present	7
220	洗澡	xǐzǎo	*v.*	bathe, shower	7
221	学（學）校	xuéxiào	*n.*	school	7
222	已经（經）	yǐjīng	*adv.*	already	7
223	一直	yìzhí	*adv.*	straight, continuously	7
224	早餐	zǎocān	*n.*	breakfast	7

序号	简体（繁體）	拼音	词性	解释	课号
225	整	zhěng	*adj.*	exact (time, quantity)	7
226	正好	zhènghǎo	*adv.*	at the right moment	7
227	知道	zhīdào	*v.*	know; be aware of	7
228	中国（國）城	Zhōngguóchéng	*n.*	Chinatown	7
229	帮（幫）	bāng	*v.*	assist, support, help	8
230	帮（幫）忙	bāngmáng	*v.*	help	8
231	办（辦）公室	bàngōngshì	*n.*	office	8
232	比尔（爾）	Bǐ'ěr	*pn.*	Bill	8
233	补习（補習）	bǔxí	*v.*	take a remedial course	8
234	车（車）	chē	*n.*	cart, vehicle	8
235	次	cì	*m.*	(measure word for the happening of actions)	8
236	打	dǎ	*v.*	make (phone call)	8
237	等	děng	*v.*	wait	8
238	电话（電話）	diànhuà	*n.*	telephone; phone call	8
239	点儿（點兒）	diǎnr	*num.*	a little	8
240	短信	duǎnxìn	*n.*	text message	8
241	多少	duōshao	*pron.*	how many; how much	8
242	辅导（輔導）	fǔdǎo	*n./v.*	tutor; to tutor	8
243	复习（復習）	fùxí	*v.*	review	8
244	告诉（訴）	gàosu	*v.*	tell, inform	8
245	给（給）	gěi	*v.*	give	8
246	号码（號碼）	hàomǎ	*n.*	number	8
247	喝	hē	*v.*	drink	8
248	会（會）	huì	*a.v.*	can; be possible to	8
249	鸡（雞）蛋	jīdàn	*n.*	chicken egg	8
250	接	jiē	*v.*	pick up (a person)	8
251	就	jiù	*adv.*	adverb used to indicate emphasis	8
252	开（開）	kāi	*v.*	drive	8
253	块（塊）	kuài	*m.*	piece	8
254	快	kuài	*adj.*	fast, quick, swift	8
255	两	liǎng	*num.*	two	8
256	面（麵）包	miànbāo	*n.*	bread	8
257	牛奶	niúnǎi	*n.*	cow milk	8

序号	简体（繁體）	拼音	词性	解释	课号
258	哦	ò	*intj.*	(interjection expressing understanding)	8
259	说话（說話）	shuōhuà	*v.*	talk	8
260	喂	wèi	*intj.*	hello, hi (in making phone call)	8
261	问题（問題）	wèntí	*n.*	problem	8
262	想	xiǎng	*v.*	think; wish to; want to	8
263	小吃店	xiǎochīdiàn	*n.*	snack restaurant	8
264	小心	xiǎoxīn	*adj.*	careful	8
265	以前	yǐqián	*n.*	before	8
266	在	zài	*adv.*	(adverb used before the verb to indicate an on-going action)	8
267	占线（線）	zhànxiàn	*v.*	(telephone) be busy	8
268	左右	zuǒyòu	*n.*	about; or so	8
269	别的	bié de		other	9
270	比如	bǐrú	*v.*	for example	9
271	衬（襯）衫	chènshān	*n.*	shirt	9
272	穿	chuān	*v.*	wear; put on	9
273	但是	dànshì	*conj.*	but	9
274	打折	dǎzhé	*v.*	make a discount	9
275	等	děng	*part.*	so on and so forth; etc.	9
276	干净（淨）	gānjìng	*adj.*	clean	9
277	逛	guàng	*v.*	walk around in streets, malls, etc.	9
278	贵（貴）	guì	*adj.*	expensive	9
279	还（還）是	háishì	*conj./ adv.*	or/had better	9
280	号（號）	hào	*n.*	size	9
281	好像	hǎoxiàng	*adv.*	as if; seem	9
282	黑	hēi	*adj.*	black	9
283	欢（歡）迎	huānyíng	*v.*	welcome	9
284	灰	huī	*adj.*	gray	9
285	家具	jiājù	*n.*	furniture	9
286	夹（夾）克	jiákè	*n.*	jacket	9
287	件	jiàn	*m.*	(measure word for clothes)	9
288	减价（減價）	jiǎnjià	*v.*	cut prices; sell on discount	9
289	价钱（價錢）	jiàqian	*n.*	price	9

序号	简体（繁體）	拼音	词性	解释	课号
290	加上	jiāshang	v.	add; plus	9
291	块（塊）	kuài	m.	(colloquial word for Chinese yuan and the U.S. dollar)	9
292	裤（褲）子	kùzi	n.	trousers, pants	9
293	蓝（藍）	lán	adj.	blue	9
294	领带（領帶）	lǐngdài	n.	tie	9
295	卖（賣）	mài	v.	sell	9
296	美元	Měiyuán	pn.	US dollar	9
297	便宜	piányi	adj.	cheap, inexpensive	9
298	钱（錢）	qián	n.	money	9
299	球鞋	qiúxié	n.	sneakers	9
300	日用品	rìyòngpǐn	n.	daily use articles	9
301	色	sè	n.	color	9
302	上	shàng	n.	previous, last	9
303	商场（場）	shāngchǎng	n.	market, mall	9
304	上衣	shàngyī	n.	upper outer garment; jacket	9
305	试（試）	shì	v.	test, try	9
306	售货员（貨員）	shòuhuòyuán	n.	shop clerk; salesperson	9
307	双（雙）	shuāng	m.	pair	9
308	虽（雖）然	suīrán	conj.	although	9
309	像…一样（樣）	xiàng...yíyàng		same as...	9
310	鞋	xié	n.	shoe	9
311	些	xiē	m.	some, few, several	9
312	新	xīn	adj.	new	9
313	西装（裝）	xīzhuāng	n.	Western suit	9
314	衣服	yīfu	n.	clothes	9
315	一共	yígòng	adv.	altogether; in sum	9
316	院子	yuànzi	n.	yard	9
317	再	zài	adv.	again	9
318	怎么样（麼樣）	zěnmeyàng	pron.	how	9
319	中	zhōng	adj.	middle	9
320	周（週）末	zhōumò	n.	weekend	9
321	自己	zìjǐ	pron.	self	9
322	半天	bàn tiān	nc.	a long time; quite a while	10

序号	简体（繁體）	拼音	词性	解释	课号
323	本来（來）	běnlái	adv.	originally	10
324	比较（較）	bǐjiào	adv.	comparatively, relatively	10
325	长（長）	cháng	adj.	long	10
326	春天	chūntiān	n.	spring	10
327	出去	chūqù	v.	go out	10
328	到底	dàodǐ	adv.	after all	10
329	低	dī	adj.	low	10
330	冬天	dōngtiān	n.	winter	10
331	度	dù	n.	degree	10
332	公园（園）	gōngyuán	n.	park	10
333	果汁	guǒzhī	n.	fruit juice	10
334	合适（適）	héshì	adj.	suitable, decent	10
335	后（後）天	hòutiān	n.	the day after tomorrow	10
336	华（華）氏	Huáshì	pn.	Fahrenheit	10
337	滑雪	huáxuě	v.	ski	10
338	季节（節）	jìjié	n.	season	10
339	觉（覺）得	juéde	v.	think, feel	10
340	可乐（樂）	kělè	n.	cola	10
341	冷	lěng	adj.	cold	10
342	凉快	liángkuai	adj.	cool	10
343	聊天	liáotiān	v.	chat	10
344	零下	líng xià		below zero	10
345	露营（營）	lùyíng	v.	go camping	10
346	旅游	lǚyóu	v.	travel, tour	10
347	暖和	nuǎnhuo	adj.	warm	10
348	苹（蘋）果	píngguǒ	n.	apple	10
349	晴天	qíngtiān	n.	clear sky; sunny day	10
350	秋天	qiūtiān	n.	autumn	10
351	气温（氣温）	qìwēn	n.	air temperature	10
352	热（熱）	rè	adj.	hot	10
353	热（熱）狗	règǒu	n.	hot dog	10
354	沙拉	shālā	n.	salad	10
355	少	shǎo	adj.	few, little	10

序号	简体（繁體）	拼音	词性	解释	课号
356	摄（攝）氏	Shèshì	*pn.*	Celsius, centigrade	10
357	天气（氣）	tiānqì	*n.*	weather	10
358	王红（紅）	Wáng Hóng	*pn.*	Wang Hong, a Chinese name	10
359	网球	wǎngqiú	*n.*	tennis	10
360	玩儿	wánr	*v.*	play	10
361	下	xià	*v.*	fall (rain, snow, fog)	10
362	想起	xiǎngqǐ		recall	10
363	夏天	xiàtiān	*n.*	summer	10
364	喜欢（歡）	xǐhuan	*v.*	like; be fond of	10
365	雪	xuě	*n.*	snow	10
366	要是	yàoshì	*conj.*	if	10
367	野餐	yěcān	*v.*	go picnic	10
368	一边（邊）……一边（邊）	yìbiān… yìbiān	*conj.*	while; at the same time as	10
369	游戏（戲）	yóuxì	*n.*	game	10
370	预报（預報）	yùbào	*n.*	forecast	10
371	这里（這裡）	zhèli	*pron.*	here	10
372	真	zhēn	*adv.*	really, truly	10
373	最	zuì	*adv.*	the most	10
374	把	bǎ	*prep.*	(preposition introducing the object in the sentence)	11
375	部	bù	*m.*	(measure word for movies, novels)	11
376	不用	búyòng	*adv.*	don't need to	11
377	打开（開）	dǎkāi	*v.*	open	11
378	当（當）然	dāngrán	*adv.*	of course	11
379	方便	fāngbiàn	*adj.*	convenient	11
380	放假	fàngjià	*v.*	have a holiday or vacation	11
381	够（夠）	gòu	*v.*	be enough	11
382	哈	hā	*ono.*	(imitating laughing)	11
383	花	huā	*v.*	spend	11
384	极（極）	jí	*adv.*	extremely	11
385	姐妹	jiěmèi	*n.*	sisters	11
386	就	jiù	*adv.*	(emphasizing the earliness or imminence of an action)	11

序号	简体（繁體）	拼音	词性	解释	课号
387	开（開）心	kāixīn	*adj.*	happy, pleased	11
388	快乐（樂）	kuàilè	*adj.*	happy, merry	11
389	啦	la	*part.*	(end of sentence particle or end of noun particle for a list of things)	11
390	礼（禮）物	lǐwù	*n.*	gift	11
391	明白	míngbai	*v.*	understand; be clear about	11
392	前夜	qiányè	*n.*	eve	11
393	上网（網）	shàngwǎng	*v.*	go online	11
394	圣诞（聖誕）	Shèngdàn	*pn.*	Christmas	11
395	收	shōu	*v.*	receive	11
396	树（樹）	shù	*n.*	tree	11
397	睡觉（覺）	shuìjiào	*v.*	sleep	11
398	送	sòng	*v.*	give, send, accompany	11
399	特别	tèbié	*adv.*	especially	11
400	为（為）什么（麼）	wèi shénme		why	11
401	下	xià	*n.*	under, below	11
402	醒	xǐng	*v.*	wake up	11
403	兄弟	xiōngdì	*n.*	brothers	11
404	样（樣）子	yàngzi	*n.*	look, appearance	11
405	因为（為）	yīnwèi	*conj.*	because	11
406	又……又……	yòu … yòu …		both … and	11
407	有说（說）有笑	yǒu shuō yǒu xiào		talk and laugh	11
408	着（著）	zhe	*part.*	(particle indicating continuation)	11
409	正	zhèng	*adv.*	in the process of (doing something)	11
410	装饰（裝飾）	zhuāngshì	*v.*	decorate	11
411	最近	zuìjìn	*n.*	recently	11

责任编辑：薛彧威
中文编辑：史文华
封面设计：王薇薇

图书在版编目（CIP）数据

飞跃. 汉语初级教程学生用书. 上册 / 林柏松主编，李蓓，于岚编者. --
北京：华语教学出版社，2013
ISBN 978-7-5138-0560-5

Ⅰ. ①飞… Ⅱ. ①林… ②李… ③于… Ⅲ. ①汉语－对外汉语教学－教材
Ⅳ. ①H195.4

中国版本图书馆CIP数据核字(2013)第217751号

飞跃——汉语初级教程学生用书　上册

主编　林柏松　编者　李蓓　于岚
＊
©华语教学出版社有限责任公司
华语教学出版社有限责任公司出版
（中国北京百万庄大街24号　邮政编码100037）
电话: (86)10-68320585, 68997826
传真: (86)10-68997826, 68326333
网址：www.sinolingua.com.cn
电子信箱：hyjx@sinolingua.com.cn
新浪微博地址：http://weibo.com/sinolinguavip
北京京华虎彩印刷有限公司印刷
2014年（16开）第1版
ISBN 978-7-5138-0560-5
定价：119.00元